Daily Life of the Pagan Celts

Daily Life of the Pagan Celts

Joan P. Alcock

Greenwood World Publishing
Oxford / Westport, Connecticut

2009

First published in 2009 by Greenwood World Publishing

1 2 3 4 5 6 7 8 9 10

Greenwood World Publishing
Prama House
267 Banbury Road
Oxford OX2 7HT
An imprint of Greenwood Publishing Group, Inc
www.greenwood.com

Library of Congress Cataloging-in-Publication Data

Alcock, Joan P. (Joan Pilsbury)
Daily life of the pagan Celts / Joan P. Alcock.
        p. cm. – (The Greenwood Press daily life through history series, ISSN 1080-4749)
    Includes bibliographical references and index.
    ISBN 978-1-84645-021-1 (alk. paper)
    1.   Celts. 2.   Celts – Social life and customs. 3.   Civilisation, Celtic.
I. Title.

    D70.A42 2008
    936.4 – dc22

                                                            2008041009

ISBN 978-1-84645-021-1

Designed by Fraser Muggeridge studio
Typeset by TexTech International
Printed and bound by South China Printing Company

For the Librarians of the Institute of Classical Studies Library/Joint Library of the Hellenic and Roman Societies, London, in appreciation of the great help which they have given to me over the past fifty years.

Contents

Preface

A book for school children, published in 1924, which was given to the
author by an aunt, covered the history of Britain from 55 BC to AD 1066.
It provided a reasonable attempt at the history of Britain, at least telling
stories of well-known figures in British history, but dismissed the Celts
in a few sentences. It stated that Roman traders, who came to Britain,
offered beautiful purple cloth, bronze weapons, ivory, vases and other
goods in exchange for those of the Britons. These British goods were
dismissed as tin dug from the mines and skins of wild beasts being caught
in the forests, which covered large parts of the country. The text then
swiftly moved on to the Romans, no doubt with a sense of relief.

To some extent, this ignorance of history of the Celts continued, even
amongst scholars. Yet, attention on the continent had already turned
to Celtic studies, which was probably due to the emerging nationalism
amongst Celtic areas in the nineteenth century. Even so, the Celts were
regarded as a barbaric people, occupying the role of noble savages
amongst archaeologists who were concerned more with the Greek
and Roman civilisations. When attention was paid to the Celts, it gave
a somewhat romanticised view of their life. This has led to some scholars
even denying that the Celts had a civilisation, arguing that this was part
of an attempt by areas with a Celtic heritage struggling to assert their
political and cultural individuality.

It is not the purpose of this book to enter such deep waters. This
book is concerned with providing some introduction to the hierarchical
structure of Celtic society and to the lifestyle of that society. To do this,
a variety of evidence must be considered. The first is the archaeological
evidence. Celtic tribes migrated across Europe from the seventh century
BC and may at first have seemingly left little surviving physical evidence
of their presence. There were admittedly the great hillforts, finds from
graves and artefacts such as weapons, pottery and household objects.
Discoveries at the sites of Hallstatt in Austria and La Tène in Switzerland
resulted in the definitions of cultures, which provided dating evidence for
the Celts. Since then, however, there have been more discoveries, which
have helped to elucidate Celtic practices, especially the evidence, which
has been excavated from graves.

In addition to the archaeological evidence, as a second source, there
was much to be gained from archaeological reconstruction. This does not
include groups of people trying to emulate the life of an Iron Age family.

Instead serious archaeological experiments have been carried out. One such experiment evaluated the storage use and capacity of a number of pits and found them to have provided adequate storage facilities for grain throughout the winter months. Another dealt with the cutting efficiencies of axes. All these provide knowledge of the way of life of the Celts. This is especially true of the site constructed at Little Butser in Hampshire. The site includes a round house and various outbuildings, keeping of animals and growing of corn and vegetables such as those found in Iron Age Britain. Other sites have emulated this, but work at Little Butser provided the impetus for further experimental sites.

A third invaluable source is folklore and legendry evidence. This includes the Welsh and Irish literature including the Welsh epic, *Mabinogion*, and the three cycles of Irish literature. These relate the tales of the Túatha De Danann, the Ulster Cycle that includes the deeds of Cu Chulainn, and the cycle of Finn and Ossian and their companions. Much of the description in these stories is exaggerated, but details of the life lived in Ireland at that time, dealing with Celtic aristocratic and warrior lifestyle, can be extracted. This can be linked to the archaeological evidence, such as that of the Irish hillforts especially the sites of Tara and Emain Macha.

A fourth source is the evidence provided by classical writers. Greek and Roman writers were intrigued by the barbarian nature of the Celts and provided invaluable information about their customs and lifestyle. Travellers, such as Poseidonius, gave first-hand accounts. These sources, especially that of Caesar's *Gallic Wars*, also provide an enormous amount of evidence about the political structure of the Gauls and the relations between the tribes. Much of this literary evidence has to be taken at face value, because this is the only reported evidence that is available. Some of it relating to lifestyle and customs obviously can be checked by referring to the Irish texts and the evidence provided from archaeology.

The fifth source comes from sculptural evidence. The Romans probably trained Celtic sculptors in their craft so that it is impossible to say that the Roman sculptors provided all the reliefs. Roman sculptors, however, may have been instructed to interpret Celtic religious beliefs into visual form. This evidence can be interpreted in several ways as, for example, clothing worn by deities may also be that worn by ordinary people. There are also scenes of daily life, especially on tombstones, that allow interpretation for Celtic lifestyles. These reliefs, and other sculptural remains, may also provide some evidence of the Celtic language but little of this survived into the Roman era. Celtic languages, however, did linger on orally, although there were discontinuities, and were revived in their various forms in the nineteenth century becoming one of the forces of the Celtic revival during that period.

All the above provides a considerable amount of evidence which allows a suggestive interpretation of the lifestyle of the Celtic people. The Celts as a nation stretched from eastern Europe to the western seaboard of Britain. Within that area, there were numerous tribes and presumably different ways of life. Yet, there was seemingly a common practice of coping with ordinary daily living and the hazards which might beset people.

Obviously, any attempt to reconstruct and interpret the daily life of Celtic peoples has its limitations, for it is impossible to deduce exactly what the Celts thought and what were their precise actions. Nevertheless, the aim of this book is to provide some introduction to the history of the Celtic peoples and their lifestyle. It covers the Celtic expansion across Europe, which was due in no small part to the Celts' prowess as a warrior nation. The Celts had a home life based on agriculture and were skilled in arts and crafts. The designs of their jewellery are still admired and used by modern craftsmen at the present time. Their religious beliefs and their burial rites still intrigue their modern descendents. Their superstitious practices and their belief in human sacrifice have led to the media taking an interest as may be witnessed by the success of the cult film, *The Wicker Man* (1973, remade 2006).

In the nineteenth century, there was a revival in interest in Celtic heritage especially in Brittany, Wales and Ireland. This took cultural and political forms and led to a feeling of national Celtic identity across the Atlantic seaboard. Celtic languages were revived and there was a renewal of interest in the Celtic past. This interest has led to a revival of Celtic studies and in more excavations of Celtic sites, which will provide further evidence of this still somewhat elusive people.

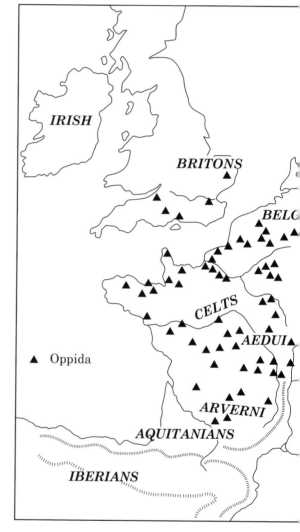

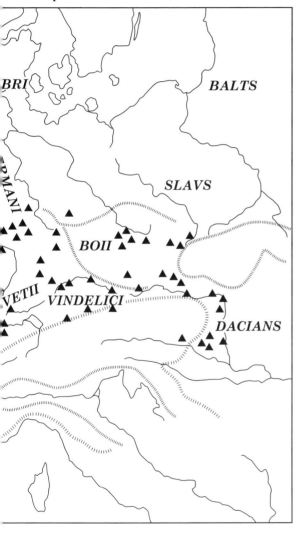

Map of the Celtic Tribes in Britain

Chapter 1
The Expansion of the Celtic World

The Late Bronze Age in central and northern Europe began to change into the Iron Age in about 1200 BC, but it was not until the eighth century BC that iron finally became the dominant metal. The Iron Age Celtic civilisation is defined by two important find sites, Hallstatt and La Tène. It is the artefacts similar to these found elsewhere and relating to these sites which indicate they are of Celtic origin. The Celts did not leave behind great architecture as did the Greeks and Romans. Indeed, little remains in the way of structural remains. Much of the evidence has to be painfully scraped from the earth or deduced from grave finds and personal items. There is an extensive literature in Ireland, and a less extensive one in Wales, carefully handed down by oral tradition, which can shed light on the lifestyle and custom of the Celts. Yet the Celts can be said to have had a civilisation, which at its greatest expanse had spread across Europe and established itself in Asia Minor.

The Celts, however, were not one race but groups of people identified by a common language, which is believed to have been widespread in the sixth century BC, although it may have originated at least two centuries earlier. Celtic dialects probably developed in different areas, but with enough common speech for different groups to be able to understand each other. It was this that bound people together, and it was language, especially in Gaul and Britain, that ensured the evolvement of a Celtic race. Evidence of this language is deduced from inscriptions, mainly the work of classical sculptors, from coins and from place names. Surviving Celtic languages have elements that can be traced back to this original Celtic speech. Two different groups of Celtic speech arose. One group is the Q Celtic or Goidelic, so called because it retained its Indo-European 'qu' (pronounced as 'k' but written 'c'). This form of Celtic has survived in Irish, the Gaelic of Scotland and the Manx of the Isle of Man and may be the result of the relative isolation of those areas. The isolation also from Roman influence may have resulted in these surviving as living languages. The other is the P Celtic or Brythonic (or Brittonnic), which replaced the qu sound with a 'p'. This form of speech, which may have been brought into Britain during the Neolithic period, was the language of Celtic Briton before and during the Roman period and has survived in the Welsh, Cornish and Breton languages.

Celtic speech was alien to the Romans. The Sicilian-Greek historian Diodorus Siculus (active 60–39 BC) said that it was of a figurative nature with much use of alliteration and grandiose phrases. He added that the Celts were boasters and threateners who were given to bombastic self-dramatisation. They spoke in riddles, hinting at things, with a great deal left to be understood. This may have been either because they wished to confuse their enemies or because they were used to describing things in elaborate and repetitive language, a trait noticeable in people who commit things to memory.

The Celts were first mentioned by the Greek historian and geographer Hecataeus of Miletus in the sixth century BC. The Greek historian Herodotus, writing in the fifth century BC, said that they lived beyond the Pillars of Hercules, next to the Cynetes, who lived further west of the peoples of Europe. Herodotus, however, had not taken into account the fact that they had originated in central Europe and had gradually spread across western Europe. The Greek geographer Strabo (64–c.24 BC) recognised Celtic territory more accurately when he said that it reached eastwards as far as the Rhine, southwards to the Pyrenees and northwards as far as the British Channel. Later it was to extend into Britain and Spain.

Classical writers recognised the Celts as a race of barbarians but appeared to be fascinated by and curious about them. The Greeks called them Keltoi meaning fighters, but in the eastern Mediterranean, they were known as Galatians. The Greek historian Ephorus of Cyme (c.400–330 BC) ranked them with the Scythians, the Persians and the Libyans as one of the four great barbaric peoples. The Celts were noted for their bravery. The Greek philosopher Aristotle (384–322 BC) said that there was no word for the man who is excessively fearless. Perhaps such a man might be called mad or bereft of feeling, who feared nothing, neither earthquakes nor waves, as was said of the Celts. Classical writers saw them as a certain physical type probably because they stood out against a darker Mediterranean people. They commented on their tallness, fair hair, blue eyes and long moustaches. The fourth century AD historian Ammianus Marcellinus, who had served on the eastern frontier and in Gaul under the Emperor Julian, said that the Celts were tall of body with rippling muscles and blond hair. Strabo said that he noticed in Rome that very young Celtic boys towered above Romans. The children, he added,

were born with greying hair, but as they grew older, the colour changed
to that of their parents. The Romans feared them but also had a certain
grudging respect for their warrior prowess and never treated a battle with
them lightly, although they eventually mastered Celtic tactics.

Hallstatt and La Tène

The two main periods of the Celtic era have been defined as Hallstatt and
La Tène, after two sites that have revealed evidence of distinctive phases
in Celtic development. In 1846, Johann Georg Ramsauer investigated a
salt mine and over 2,000 graves at Hallstatt in Austria. The excavations
continued until 1863 and revealed a distinctive culture, which was
labelled Celtic or Iron Age A. This was not an imported culture but
had emerged from the Urnfield people of the Bronze Age, who had
developed the technique of ironworking. Material retrieved from graves
and the nearby salt mines had, for the most part, been preserved by
its environment. The finds, which included ironwork, pottery, clothing,
jewellery and other personal objects, allowed a detailed insight into the
culture of these people. The records kept by the excavators included a
remarkable number of watercolour sketches of the graves. The majority
of the graves were dated from the seventh to the fifth century BC.
A similar culture was later identified over an area from Czechoslovakia
to France and Spain. Salt mined at Hallstatt and used as a trading
commodity, as well as trade with Mediterranean countries, may have
played a part in the westward progress of the Iron Age A culture. Further
excavations followed at Hallstatt in 1907, supervised by the Duchess
of Mecklenburg, who not only discovered more graves but also identified
and classified individual finds.

Burials in the Iron Age A period often had funerary four-wheeled carts
and contents, which indicated that trade routes had been established
with Greece and Etruria as early as the third century BC. The richest
graves, found in eastern France and south-west Germany, have been
dated to a period between 600 and 475 BC. Most are situated on the
major trading rivers – the Rhine, the Danube, the Loire and the Seine,
and there was probably a link to these via the Rhone. The Greeks had
established a colony at Massalia in 600 BC, which played a large part
in ensuring that merchants could bring goods from the Mediterranean
regions to central Gaul. Wealthy Gauls imported luxury goods as well

as allowed Greek merchants to gain access to the products and merchandise of Celtic lands.

The Hallstatt people often gathered round chieftains, who lived in fortified settlements especially on higher ground and on hilltops. These were isolated settlements and farmsteads where people tilled their land and farmed their crops. Classical writers referred to these people as barbarians, although their descriptions of the lifestyles indicated that they had a social structure that ensured loyalty to a chieftain and a chieftain's concern for the welfare of his retainers.

A second development in this Iron Age culture was identified from a find site in Switzerland. In 1857, at the site of La Tène on Lake Neuchâtel, certain discoveries were made by Hansli Kopp, a local man who was exploring along the shore of the north-west side of the lake at a time when the water level had been reduced. The finds consisted of a large number of iron weapons, tools, artefacts and wooden piles in the lake. The artefacts may have been cast into the lake as part of ritual; the piles were suggested to have supported a wooden pier or bridge. Archaeologists quickly moved in to examine the site and excavations continued until 1917. Publications of the site and finds began in 1864 and were finally completed in 1923.

The artefacts and weapons recovered were of a different style and form compared with those of the Hallstatt period, but they were similar in style to those that had been discovered in northern France, southern Germany and Austria. The emergence of the La Tène culture, labelled as Iron Age B, may be due to an alteration in trade routes which came from the Adriatic ports of Spina and Adria and also from Etruria. This culture had evolved over the fifth century BC and continued into the early years of the first century AD, and was characterised by a curvilinear form of abstract art. Swords were longer than in the Hallstatt period. A two-wheeled chariot, drawn by two horses hitched to a central pole, probably adapted from that used by the Etruscans, and an efficient fighting machine replaced the four-wheeled cart. Items found in La Tène graves included firedogs, drinking vessels, and wine flagons as well as food including joints of pork, indicating continuance of life in the Otherworld.

The two periods of Iron Age culture were given formal recognition in 1872 when a Swedish archaeologist, Hans Hildebrant, divided the Iron Age into the Hallstatt and La Tène periods, which related to the development of the two Celtic eras. Subdivisions of these periods followed and these were modified in the light of subsequent archaeological discoveries. The enthusiasm to embrace these cultures came from the rulers of certain countries. Napoleon III, Emperor of France (1852–1870), for example, promoted a policy of excavation in France to discover its Celtic roots, with much of the work concentrating on excavating the rich graves, although extensive excavations were carried out on the site of the Celtic chieftain Vercingetorix's fortress at Alesia. Much of the work in other countries concentrated on examining hillforts, especially the defences, and excavations along these lines were particularly prevalent in England in the 1920s and 1930s. It was only in the 1950s that archaeologists began to analyse the lives of the ordinary Celts and their lifestyles.

Celtic expansion in Italy

The main Celtic homeland was in southern Germany, Austria and along the Danube. This area of land did not satisfy the people for long, either because of their warlike nature and love of booty or because expansion in population demanded new areas in which they could settle. The Roman historian Livy (59 BC–AD 17) said that their fierce trait of travelling up and down in war had almost made the world their residence. The expansion of the Celtic people across Europe was, however, mainly the result of their development and refinement of the technique of metalwork. Iron weapons gave the Celts considerable advantage over the use of bronze weapons. These advances were linked to the fact that the Celtic race produced men trained in the use of these weapons and delighting in aggressive warfare, which overwhelmed their opponents. In Ireland the survival of a Celtic literary heritage has supplemented archaeological finds to provide evidence of this warrior Celtic lifestyle. At its greatest expansion, the Celtic world stretched from the British Isles across central Europe to Asia Minor and also menaced the German tribes and the classical world of the Mediterranean. Even if they did not expand into northern Europe, their artefacts found their way into Denmark and north Germany. Isolated Celtic settlements have also been found in Poland, Russia and the Ukraine.

The enthusiasm of the Celts for a warrior life ensured rapid expansion. In 400 BC, they invaded the rich lands of the Po Valley and moved south, establishing a Celtic state known as Gallia Cisalpina. The Greek historian Diodorus Siculus (active 60–9 BC) said that the Celts poured through the Alpine passes in great strength, implying that no one could oppose them. The Celts overran the territory between the Apennines and the Alps, driving out the Tyrrhenians and seizing their lands. They then divided up the land between a number of tribes. The Senones received an area of land between the mountains and the sea, which was scorchingly hot during the summer. They instructed their young men to move against land owned by the Tyrrhenians. The men attacked the territory and sacked the Etruscan town of Clusium in 391 BC.

The Etruscans appealed to their Roman neighbours for help. According to Livy, the Romans, rather than send military help, sent three ambassadors to negotiate with the Celts. The Celts stated that they would not attack provided that Clusium would provide them with land on which they could settle. Taken aback, the ambassadors asked what right the Celts had to make such a condition. The Celts replied that their right was their sword and that all things taken belonged to them. Livy implies that the Celts were particularly interested in the land. But the Celts sought both booty and land, and that they were prepared to fight for these was immediately apparent when they attacked the Etruscans. The Roman ambassadors, against all convention, took part in the fighting, with one of them, Quintus Fabius, even engaging in single combat with a Celt and killing him.

The outraged Celts demanded the surrender of Quintus. The Roman Senate prevaricated at first, offering the Celts money. When this was refused, they decided to hand over Quintus to the Celts. There are two versions as to what followed. According to Livy, Quintus's father, a military tribune with consular power, appealed to the Roman people, who then voted to overturn the Senate's decision. Diodorus records that the Senate appealed to the people so that if the people supported them, they would not be blamed for agreeing to hand over Quintus. They then elected the ambassadors, all from the Fabian family, as consular tribunes for the following year. The Celts were outraged at these actions, and Diodorus, obviously in sympathy with them against this breach of protocol, says that they had every right to be so.

To avenge this insult, the Celts decided to march on Rome. The Romans moved an army northwards but were defeated at the Battle of the Allia in 390 BC. This was the first time the Romans had met the Celts in battle, and Livy implies that they were somewhat overwhelmed by the war cries and tumult of the Celts. The victorious Celts delayed their advance by stripping the dead Romans of their weapons and armour and cutting of their heads following Celtic tradition. This allowed the citizens in Rome to decide their priorities. Some fled the city; others moved their gold, silver and other prized possession up to the Capital. Supplies of corn were also taken up so that they could withstand a siege. Some older men, stating that they would have to die soon, decided to stay in the city. They gathered together their possessions, dressed in their best robes and sat awaiting their fate.

When they reached the city, the Gauls hesitated, as there seemed to be no guards on duty, and they feared a trap. Eventually they swarmed in, and finding no resistance, they wandered the deserted streets. Soon they entered the houses; seeing the old men seated in their rich robes, they thought they were statues, until one Gaul stroked a man's beard. Instantly, the man raised his staff and struck the Gaul. The startled Gauls then lost all their terror of the deserted city and proceeded to sack it with a vengeance, destroying even the ancient records; later, as the Greek writer Plutarch (AD 50–124) records, many of the aristocracy took advantage of this to forge more distinguished records of their ancestors.

Only the Capital held out. Livy records that the Gauls mounted a concerted attack up the slopes of the Capital but were driven back by the fierce resistance of the defenders. According to Diodorus, the Gauls decided to attack at night, but the Capital was saved by the cackling of the sacred geese of Hera, which were kept there. The garrison, warned that the Gauls were climbing up the slopes, instituted a successful counterattack.

The Gauls were little interested in a prolonged siege. What they wanted was booty and they got it when the Romans paid over one thousand pounds of gold to ensure their withdrawal. The Gauls retreated northwards but laid siege to the city of Veascium, an ally of Rome. Here they met their match, for the dictator of the city led a counterattack and seized the Celtic baggage train that contained the gold ransom and much of the booty taken from the city. The Gauls, therefore, moved further north. This Gallic attack on Rome left the Romans with an abiding desire for revenge, which was only finally achieved when Caesar conquered and subdued Gaul.

Celtic heritage, however, left its mark on Italy with the founding of what became Roman cities. In 396 BC, the Insubres had established themselves in the Etruscan city of Melpum or Mediolanum (Milan); the Cenomani settled at Brixia (Brescia) and the Boii centred themselves at the Etruscan town of Felsina (Bologna). The tribe of the Senones settled further south round the region of Montefortino d'Arcevia. Evidence of this advance and settlement comes from finds in graves, the majority being of La Tène style weapons, jewellery and pottery. Often, there is evidence of Etruscan burial practices in cemeteries, indicating that there was either a coexistence of the Etruscans and the Celts or that Etruscan customs had survived.

Further attacks on Rome were, however, repelled. In one of them which took place in 367 BC, Livy records that Manlius, a young Roman, defeated an arrogant Gaul in single combat and took his torc, thus gaining the cognomen of Torquatus. This recorded incident indicates how much respect and fear the Roman had for the Celts. Many Celts, in fact, were later recruited as mercenaries, which may account for evidence of Celtic presence in southern Italy; however, Celtic settlement was confined to northern Italy.

In 334 BC, tired of the Celtic attacks, the Romans concluded a treaty with the Celts in order to free themselves from any Celtic advance so that they could concentrate on subjecting other tribes in Italy, especially the Samnites. This left the Celts free to settle in northern Italy. The Samnites, however, allied with the Celts and, in 297 BC, defeated a Roman army at Camertium. This spurred the Romans to take on the menace of the Celts who were established in northern Italy, but it was not until 282 BC that they defeated the Celtic tribe of the Boii at lake Vadimonis. A settled peace existed for the next fifty years, but it was disturbed by the arrival, in 225 BC, of the Gaesatae, a group moving from central Europe. The Romans were distracted by the invasion of Hannibal, when, in 225 BC, a large group of Celtic Gaesatae crossed the Alps into Gallia Cisalpina and persuaded the Insubres and the Boii to join with them to seize land further south in Italy.

With a force of 50,000 infantry and 20,000 cavalry, the Gauls moved south into Etruria and quickly defeated an opposing Roman force near Faesulae. Another Roman army, however, had moved up swiftly to check the Celtic advance. The Gauls retreated, but a third Roman army was moving to cut off their retreat. The Gauls found themselves trapped between two Roman armies and drew up battle lines facing in two directions. The resulting Battle of Telamon, in 225 BC, was a triumph for the Romans. One Roman consul was captured, and his head was displayed on a spear. The surviving consul, Lucius Aemilius, captured an enormous amount of booty including numerous torcs, which he dedicated on the Capital in Rome. Celtic losses were estimated by the

Romans to be 10,000 Celts taken prisoner, almost all being enslaved, and 40,000 Celts killed.

The battle was the turning point in the Celtic expansion in Italy, although the Boii were still a formidable enemy, stopping the Roman armies between 216 and 201 BC. The Romans, however, began to retake Cisalpine Gaul, and the Celts were gradually displaced from their lands in order to make way for settlers from Rome. Eventually, the Romans were able to establish *colonia* of veterans in Celtic territories, and the establishment of a colony at Narbo (Narbonne) began the process of Romanising Gaul, although it remained for Julius Caesar to complete the conquest of the Celts in Gaul.

Celtic expansion in the eastern Mediterranean

There was another determined Celtic advance towards Greece and the eastern Mediterranean. The Celts had been attracted to Greece because of the wealth of trade that came from that country; advancement into Greece would also seem to provide opportunities both to settle in a rich farming area and for booty. Whatever the case, a large Celtic army moved south. Strabo records that a deputation of the Celts from the Adriatic region met Alexander the Great on the Danube, in 335 BC, with the aim of establishing friendship. It was on this occasion that they gave the famous answer to Alexander, when he asked them what they most feared, expecting that the reply would be himself: they replied that they feared nothing except that the heavens might fall on their heads. It was uncertain whether they really feared this or if they were replying somewhat ironically to the king. They added, diplomatically, that they would value a friendship with such a man as Alexander above everything else. As they were not then a threat to the Greek-speaking world, Alexander agreed to a treaty of friendship with them.

The Greek historian Arrian (AD 90–c.160) recorded that the Celts sent a second deputation, dressed in their full armour, to Alexander after his victory over the Persians in 323 BC, possibly to seek out his intentions, but his death that year led to the fragmentation of his empire and the possibility of a Celtic advance into Greece and Asia Minor.

The Greeks referred to the Celts who were menacing them as Galatians (*Galatae*). The Celts waited for a while before invading Greece in 281 BC, led by a leader called Bolgios. They defeated King Ptolemy

Ceraunus of Macedon and, as was their custom, decapitated him and placed his head on the point of a spear. The Celts then split their forces. One group headed by Leotarios and Leonorios moved southwards in response to an invitation by Nicomedes of Bithynia. Livy recorded that when they came to the Hellespont, they saw Asia separated from them by such a narrow strait that they were inflamed with a desire to cross it. While they were waiting, the two chieftains fell out with each other. Leonorios moved back, but Leotarios used five ships to ferry his followers across the Hellespont.

Leotarios's Celts included the tribes of the Tolistobogii, the Tectosages and the Trocmi. Given that these were tribal movements, the Celts brought their wives and children with them, which was not perhaps what Nicomedes expected. He had invited mercenaries, not groups intending to settle. The Trocmi settled on the coast of the Hellespont, the Tolistobogii received Aeolis and Ionia and the Tectosages some of the interior parts of Asia. The terror these tribes inspired was so great that later, they exacted tribute from everyone including the Kings of Syria.

Nicomedes, however, used the Celts successfully in warfare against his enemies while allowing their families to settle in that area. These Celts, who were to become the Galatians, impressed classical writers with their savagery in battle. They finally gave their name to the territory in Asia Minor called Galatia. This occupation was not by conquest, but agreement. The Celts hired themselves out as mercenaries, raided their neighbours and farmed the land. According to Strabo, these Celts preserved the lifestyle, customs and culture of their warrior past. They retained their Celtic language, which as St. Jerome noted in his commentary on St. Paul's *Letter to the Galatians*, was similar to that of the people of the Treveri with whom he had stayed. St. Jerome was writing in the fourth century AD, so it would appear that over 500 years after their arrival in Asia Minor, the Celts had still retained their style of speech. They even established a thriving slave trade, and Diogenes Laertius, a Greek writer of the third century AD, noted that they had a priesthood of Druids.

Brennus and Acichorius led the second group of Celts. The Greek geographer Pausanias (active c. AD 160) says that both by public meetings and by personal talks with his chief men, Brennus persuaded the members of his group to move south towards Greece, emphasising both the weakness of the Greeks in fighting and the opportunity for plunder. In 280 BC, the Greeks gathered to meet the huge number of Celts, estimated by Pausanias as 150,000 infantry and 61,000 cavalry at the Pass of Thermopylae. A fierce battle took place in which, as recounted by Pausanias, the Celts ignored their wounds, even picking javelins from their bodies and hurling them back into the Greek lines. The Celts were also raked by arrows from Greek ships sailing along the marshy coastline. Eventually, the Celts were forced to retreat. The Greeks buried their dead but were appalled to find that the Celts had left their comrades to be eaten by wild animals or carrion birds. This does seem to be in accordance with the Celtic custom of disposing of dead bodies.

In view of this defeat, Brennus, therefore, detached part of his army and sent them into Aetolia to attack that area. The town of Callium was ferociously attacked and the inhabitants massacred. The Greeks even accused the Celts of eating the flesh of babies and drinking their blood and of raping dead women. This disaster compelled the Aetolians to leave the Greek army, which is what Brennus had planned, as it weakened the opposition. The Aetolians managed, however, to ambush the Celts returning from Callium so that only half of them returned to the camp at Thermopylae.

Meanwhile, Brennus had discovered another route over the mountains revealed by the Heracleots and the Aenianians who were anxious to get the Celts out of their territories as soon as possible. The Celts, therefore, crossed the mountains outflanking the Greek army, by the same path which the Persians had used in 480 BC to attack Leonidas and his Spartan force from the rear. The Celts were said to have been helped in their passage by a mist, which allowed them to surprise and defeat the Phocians who were guarding the pass. If that was the case, it could be that the Celts attributed this to supernatural forces. Such mists are mentioned, for example, at crisis points in the Irish texts. The Athenian fleet removed most of their forces before they could be surrounded.

The Celts then moved swiftly towards Delphi, intending to sack the shrine and its treasures. The Celtic army, however, had been weakened because Acichorius with his Celts had lingered at the town of Heraclea to guard accumulated booty. When he came south, he was ambushed, resulting in the loss of his baggage and supplies. The Celts reached Delphi but did not achieve their object. Herodotus recorded that the god of Delphi told the people that they should not remove any treasures from the shrine because he would protect it. Miraculous intervention played a part. Classical writers said that the gods forced the Celts to retreat by creating thunder, with much of the reverberations shaking the ground, and by lightning, which struck the Celts and their neighbours, setting them on fire. Phantom warrior heroes were conjured up to harass the Celts. Rock falls at night fell on them.

Diodorus wrote that the god of Delphi had also sent 'white maidens' to protect the shrine. Historians have suggested that the 'maidens' could have been snow. Even if the northern Celts were familiar with snow, a blizzard would have disoriented them. Either because of these conditions, intensified by the fact that the Celts were a superstitious people, or because Brennus was wounded and could not urge on his forces, the Celts decided to retreat. Further panic during this retreat was caused, according to the Greek geographer Pausanias, by aid sent by the god Pan so that the Celts, thinking that they were attacking the Greeks, killed each other, leading to 26,000 deaths. A more rational explanation might be that as several Celtic groups speaking different dialects had banded together, they did not understand the commands given, which resulted in the confusion. The Gauls, however, may have plundered Delphi and taken some treasure back to Gaul because according to rumour some of the treasure looted from the shrine of the Tolosates at Tolosa (Toulouse) by the Romans in 106 BC was part of that taken from Delphi.

Brennus died, either as a result of his wounds or by drinking undiluted wine. Diodorus attributed his death to drinking too much wine, even hinting that it was suicide. Pausanias recorded that the Greeks made further furious attacks on the Celts as they retreated and prevented them from getting food and drink, so that not a Gaul got back safely from this advance into Greece. Some Gauls, however, did survive, for they settled around Byzantium, established a settlement at Tylis in Thrace and were active in Greece as mercenaries. They were not finally defeated until about 200 BC.

Celtic expansion into the Iberian Peninsula

A detailed history of the Celts in the Iberian Peninsula is yet to be written. In the 1920s, the theory propounded was that there were two Celtic invasions. One came across the Pyrenees in about 1000 BC; the second in the sixth century BC. A later theory suggested one invasion in the eighth century BC. Neither of these theories is acceptable today. The emphasis, as elsewhere in western Europe, appears to be on cultural drift, with settlers moving into the peninsula in search of land. Herodotus indicated that the Celts had moved into Spain by the fifth century BC, and that they lived beyond the Pillars of Hercules (the Straits of Gibraltar). A third century writer and a famous physician, Eratosthenes of Ceos, says that they were prominent in his time, indicating that the population had increased.

Diodorus wrote that there had been continual war between the Iberians, already established in the peninsula, and the Celts over land, but, obviously, the native Iberians wished to protect their lands against any incomers. He also wrote that the Celtiberians were a fusion of the two peoples and that alliances and unions of the two came only after long and bloody warfare. The evidence does not, however, suggest full-scale warrior invasions, as was the case in Greece and Italy, but favours the theory of groups moving into Spain and of cultural exchanges which enabled them to live in tolerable harmony. Later the two peoples came to some arrangement over land settlement and allowed intermarriage. This, Diodorus said, led to their descendants being called Celtiberians. Thus since it was two powerful races that united and that they had extremely fertile land, which presumably gave them extensive harvests, the Celtiberians prospered greatly.

One tribe, the Vaccaei, agreed that the land and the harvest should be regarded as belonging to the community; each year the land was divided amongst those who worked on it. This might have been an attempt to make every owner work to the best of his ability to avoid being apportioned a poor piece of land the subsequent year. Diodorus also noted that the Celtiberians were noted for their hospitality, because they assumed every stranger to be under divine protection. This would accord with the normal rules of Celtic hospitality.

Evidence of Hallstatt objects has been found as early as the eighth century BC in cremation cemeteries, with urns placed in cists under a tumulus, especially in the Catalonian area. The Celtiberians established an agricultural economy in the lowlands. The main Celtic area seems to have been in north-eastern Iberia, but there is some evidence according to place names that the Celtic language was spoken elsewhere by individual settlement groups. Little evidence of the La Tène culture has been found in Spain. Artefacts, including weapons and gold torcs, which have been found may be evidence of gift exchange, although silver torcs found in the north-west of Spain may indicate that the Celtiberians copied Celtic designs elsewhere. Both Hallstatt and La Tène designs are lacking in later Spanish art forms. The early settlers seem to have established trading relations with the Phoenicians and the Greeks, and a trading post was set up at Emporion on the north-east coast. At first Emporion had connections with Massalia, but it appears to have become independent in the fifth century BC and was issuing its own coins with designs copied from those of Syracuse.

The harsh climate of the north-eastern region with its intensely hot summers meant that flocks had to be taken from the overheated lowlands in the summer to the cooler mountain pastures and returned again in winter. This movement inevitably led to a spread of individual territory and negotiations with neighbouring groups. The Celtiberians did not remain confined to the north-east for long. The Celts spread westwards into the territory of the Iberian tribes of the Vettones. The prolific natural history writer Pliny the Elder (AD 23–79) records that they moved south and then west, into what is now Portugal. He mentioned the Galli settling in the Ebro Valley. Possibly these settlements were the result of excursions by mercenary groups who then brought their families to settle in these regions.

There seem to have been few violent attacks on either side, although the establishment of Numantia by the Arevaci may indicate that some land had been taken by conquest. Many of the Celtiberians could satisfy their warrior traits by offering themselves as mercenaries especially to Carthage. They fought as cavalry but also dismounted to fight as infantry. The Lusitanians were probably the bravest of the Celtiberian tribes; they used a very tough shield and a barbed javelin, which they hurled with great accuracy. One problem, according to Diodorus, was their stamina. They could pursue the enemy quickly over short distances, but could not keep up the pace for a length of time. This tribe, however, could be a menace, because young men, having no land, formed themselves into bands and plundered the countryside. They fled into the mountains to escape capture. Not even the Romans, when they had created Iberia as a province, could put an end to this custom.

Weapons, fine drinking vessels and other items in graves parallel those found in the rest of the Celtic world. Diodorus wrote that they ate well from every kind of meat and that they drank wine mixed with honey, obviously a kind of mead. One curious custom observed by Diodorus, and which seemingly disgusted him, was that although the Celts set great store by cleanliness, nevertheless they used urine to bathe their bodies and clean their teeth with it, thinking that it helped in the healing and the care of their bodies. Urine, however, is now regarded as having some merit in healing as an antiseptic, and it is recommended that wounds should be washed in it if no clean water is available.

Rome took little notice of the Iberian Peninsula until the third century BC, when the invasion of Hannibal, who used Spain as a base from which to lead his armies into Italy, turned their attention to this area of the Mediterranean. The Romans invaded the peninsula in 197 BC, but the Celts had not lost their fighting spirit. Rome often took revenge against any show of revolt, as in 179–178 BC when Tiberius Gracchus destroyed over 300 Celtiberian settlements. Bitter fighting followed after 154 BC when the Celtiberians and Lusitanians had risen again against Rome, resulting in the destruction of the Celtiberian town and fort of Numantia. It was not until the Emperor Augustus had campaigned from 26 to 19 BC that they were finally defeated and a new Roman province was created from their territories.

Expansion of the Celts in Gaul and into Britain

Eastern Gaul was part of the Celtic homeland in both the Hallstatt and the La Tène periods. From there, the Celts had spread northwards into Belgium but more by peaceful contacts through trade and exchange than through war and conquest. Diodorus wrote that Gaul was inhabited by many tribes, the largest being over 200,000 men and the smallest, the Aedui, being about 50,000. When Vercingetorix collected together his vast army to oppose Caesar, he raised over 280,000 from thirty tribes. Usually the tribes were on peaceful terms but constant desire for land and power could lead to outbreaks of warfare, and this, given the high-spirited nature of the Celts, was welcomed.

Tribes in Britain had established contact with Gaul and with the classical Mediterranean in the Bronze Age. Trade in metals, especially tin, was sought. This contact with continental Europe had led to cultural exchanges of goods, which brought about fundamental changes in lifestyle and developments in industry such as metalworking and pottery making. Continental craftsmen designed weapons which were seemingly sought in Britain and improved upon when they had arrived. These included the Hallstatt slashing sword of the seventh century BC and the anthropoid-hilted swords and daggers of the sixth and fifth centuries, which had heads placed on their hilts. Continental curvilinear art forms were also copied on brooches, pins and bracelets. These items, however,

mainly warrior equipment and personal items, may have been part
of gift exchanges rather than goods bought and sold, especially as British
swords and daggers have been found on the continent.

Until about forty years ago, the development of the Iron Age in Britain
was explained by tribal movements from Gaul into Britain. This had
been first suggested in the 1890s, when Sir Arthur Evans had identified
a group of burials in a cemetery at Aylesford (Kent) as being the result
of an invasion by a continental tribe. Further elaborations on this theory
were developed between 1912 and 1920, culminating in an elaborated
exposition by Harold Peake of three distinctive waves of invaders from
1200 to 300 BC followed by one by the Belgae in the first century BC. This
theory remained the popular explanation until the 1960s, when it was
challenged by the theory that Iron Age practices came into Britain
by cultural exchange and a drift of immigrants. Some kind of tribal
movement may possibly have been the case in areas, for example, in
north Yorkshire in the late fifth or early fourth century BC where a group
called the Parisii had a distinctive burial rite with wheeled vehicles. Even
so, this burial tradition, together with that of burials in ditch enclosures,
which lasted until the second century BC, may have been merely an
adoption of a continental practice by tribal elite to enhance their status.

A more definite possibility of a tribal movement was in the case
of Commius, the Gallic king of the tribe of the Atrebates. He had served
Caesar as an envoy on Caesar's first invasion of Britain in 55 BC and
had allied with him in Gaul. Later, however, he joined Vercingetorix in
opposition to Caesar, even leading the force that tried to relieve the siege
of Alesia, and he continued to defy the Romans until AD 50. He then fled
to Britain, taking with him a large part of his tribe and settling in the
Hampshire region. Frontinus, a Roman historian of the first century AD,
recorded that when Commius and his men embarked on ships on the
coast of Gaul, the ships became stuck on an exposed shore when the tide
was ebbing. Commius quickly ordered the sails to be spread, and Caesar,
seeing them billowing in the wind, thought that his pursuit was useless
and turned back. Commius had obviously absorbed some elements
of strategy in his association with the Romans. He was one of the first
chieftains in Britain to use the Latin word *rex* – king – on his coins in the
late first century BC.

Caesar did record that the some of the Gallic tribes of the Belgae had
raided Britain for plunder and then had settled there and began to work
the land. Other settlement came from immigrants who moved into

Britain for a variety of reasons – seeking a new life, fleeing from enemies, curiosity, trading relations and exploration. These settlers had their name preserved later in the Roman town of Venta Belgarum (Winchester), the cantonal capital of the Belgae. Caesar said that he made active preparations to invade Britain because he knew that in their campaigns against him, the Gauls had received constant help from the Britons, which implies strong commitment to a common race, kinship and communication between the two areas. He also noted that, Diviciacus, a king of the Suessiones and one of the most powerful kings in Gaul, had controlled not only a large part of the Belgic country but had had some authority in Britain as well, presumably meaning a part of Britain. On the other hand, the Druids in Briton appear to have been the most influential and powerful in the Celtic world. Caesar says that noviciates went from Gaul to Britain to be trained in Druidic arts.

Much of Scotland remained isolated from Iron Age culture, although some of it was transmitted there through cultural contacts along the Atlantic route. Traces of Hallstatt peoples, probably some warrior groups, are found in the north-east of Scotland dating to about 600 BC. They later developed a distinct grandiose style of architecture, the broch, which provided a formidable defensive structure and was evidence of social status. Possibly from Scotland, elements of Celtic culture moved into Ulster.

The Celts in Ireland

Details about Celtic Ireland come from rather sparse archaeological evidence but mainly from the survival of texts passed on by oral tradition. Classical writers knew little or nothing about the Irish. Strabo, for example, said bluntly that he has nothing definite to tell but that the inhabitants were more savage than the Britons. They were very heavy eaters and were cannibals who when their fathers died, devoured them. They also had intercourse not only with their wives but also with their mothers and sisters. He did admit that in saying these things, he had no trustworthy witnesses to back him up.

Evidence has to be culled from the Irish texts describing a warrior society, written down in the sixth century AD by Irish monks. The *Book of Invasions*, written down in the twelfth century AD, describes the arrival of pre-Celtic and Celtic people in Ireland. The Túatha De Danann

defeated the Fomorians and were themselves defeated by the Milesians.
The Túatha then vanished into the fairy mounds and were reputed
to be the gods of the Irish Celts. The warrior society had its own code
of honour and was ordered into a hierarchical society. The royal sites
were Tara and Emain Macha (Navan), and the ritual sites were those
such as Dun Ailinne. The Irish texts start with the *Book of Invasions*,
which purports to show that groups of people came to Ireland, the main
ones being the Gaels and the Fir Bolg, which seems to imply that they
came from Gaul. Possibly the contacts with Gaul were made in the same
way as in Britain, through trade and similar culture. Druids were part
of Irish society, which suggests contact with Britain. Archaeological
evidence includes swords, similar to those of the later Hallstatt period,
but there are almost no La Tène patterned objects. Some of the jewellery
is similar to that found elsewhere in Gaul. Mention is made of the
wearing of torcs, and one found at Clonmacnois, dated to c.300, may
have been imported from the Rhineland. But the archaeological evidence
is very scanty. It is likely that Celtic Ireland developed very much
in isolation from the neighbouring countries but had a similar society
and culture. As the Romans never invaded Ireland, this Celtic society
remained until the coming of Christianity, which adopted and absorbed
aspects of Celtic society.

Chapter 2
Administration and Society

Most of the evidence for Celtic social structure comes from two different written sources. That relating to Celtic Gaul is mainly provided by Julius Caesar in his account of the Gallic wars with additional information from other classical writers. The other source is the colourful, exaggerated and traditional Irish tales, which had more than a grain of truth, handed down by oral tradition and relating to an archaic society. According to these sources, Celtic society had a distinctive hierarchy. The two principal classes were the Druids, representing the professional groups of lawyers, judges, historians and priests, and the knights, the warrior group. Below these came the craftsmen working in metals and pottery, and at the lowest end of the scale came those who performed the menial tasks. Many of these were slaves working on the land of or servants to the upper groups. The warrior class was divided with kings or chieftains having bands of retainers who served them in return for their keep and for prestige. This is abundantly clear in Ireland where kings led warrior bands on raids and lodged them in great halls. This hierarchical division between the ruling warrior class and the others was made clear after death, when the former were buried in graves containing chariots, jewellery, weapons and other personal objects. The latter were cremated or exposed to be eaten by animals so that their graves are rarely found.

Druids

The Druids were held in high honour. Besides officiating at religious ceremonies and sacrifices, and ruling on religious questions, they acted as judges and historians. They were priests first and foremost and controlled religious rites and sacrifices to the gods. These could include human sacrifices, but Pliny's description of their cutting of mistletoe in oak groves indicated their ritualistic function. Their role as judges ensured control over religious and civilian disputes, both individual and tribal. They determined how much compensation should be paid to victims of crimes or to those whose land was seized unlawfully. Boundary disputes were common, because ownership of land mattered enormously in an era when society was based an individual's status on landholding. Both Caesar and Strabo stated that they also tried cases of murder and decided on the compensation awarded to relatives.

It is not certain how far judgements could be upheld. They may have relied on the personality of the individual Druid. Strabo, when saying that the Druids were judges, added that they were considered to be the most just of men implying that their personal integrity ensured judgements were accepted and implemented. Caesar indicated that there were sanctions that could be applied if judgements were not accepted. Tribes or individuals could be barred from taking part in sacrifices or religious ceremonies. In a society which believed that a sacrifice was essential to prevent a natural disaster or to ensure the growth of a healthy crop, this might be considered an exceptional punishment. If the defaulters sought justice for an offence against them, they would not receive a judgement. Equally effective might be the fact that a person could be ostracised or barred from society. No one would speak to them for fear that they too could be put under a similar punishment. This probably worked extremely well in keeping order.

The Druids had one person, acting as chief Druid, who was their leader. When he died, the Druids chose one of their number to be leader. If one of them was of outstanding merit, he was automatically elected. If several had equal claims, an election took place, although Caesar said that sometimes they fought for the office. Caesar said that in 52 BC, a *vergobret* was elected as chief magistrate and judge of the Aedui tribe from amongst his contemporary Druids.

An example given by Caesar of the extent of their powers related to the Druidic assembly held at Cennabum (Orleans), the main centre of the tribe of the Carnutes. People flocked here to bring disputes for resolution in the assembly. Druidic judgements were binding also on kings and chieftains. The Greek orator and philosopher, Dio Chrysostom (AD 40–c.111), who travelled widely in the ancient world including Galatia and therefore knew of Celtic customs, stated that kings were not allowed to follow any course of action which was not approved by the Druids and even became what he called 'their instruments of judgement'. He added that the Druids were seated on golden thrones, dwelt in great houses and sumptuously feasted. This may be an exaggeration, but it is certain that in Ireland they were often consulted on important occasions such as before a battle was fought.

The Druids were exempt from military service although they might take part in a battle by urging on the action. The Roman historian Tacitus (AD 56–c.117) reported that when the Suetonius Paulinus, the Roman governor of Britain, invaded Anglesey in AD 61 to put down rebellion, his troops were at first overawed by the tribes who were being encouraged by the Druids, and who rained down curses on the Romans. When his men lost their fear of this, they soon defeated their opponents and the sacred groves in which human sacrifices had taken place were destroyed. Diodorus Siculus commented that such was their authority that even when the combatants were lined up ready to commence battle, the Druids could come between them and stop the fighting.

Besides exemption from military service, Druids were also exempt from taxation, a privilege, which had many men applying, or being sent by relatives, to join them, which may have kept up their numbers. Men flocked to them for instruction, which implies an educational role, as well as an effective control mechanism over the young. In the Irish text of the *Cattle Raid of Cooley*, the Druid Cathbad, who was reputed to be the father of King Conchobar, oversaw the education of some young men, especially in religion and certain aspects of augury. Education was conducted by oral methods. The Druids insisted on their pupils memorising the tenets of Druidic law and religion. Caesar said that for this system of education to be effective, it could last up to twenty years. He also remarked that this ensured that nothing was committed to writing and that this was because the Druids wished to keep their doctrine private and thus exert a religious control over the people. The first century AD Roman geographer Pomponius Mela said that they taught in secret using caves and quiet valleys.

They had a reputation as doctors and for their knowledge of medicine, probably herbal medicine. Pliny mentioned that there were physicians in Gaul before the Romans arrived and that Druidic reputation was such that many went to study with them. Added to this were knowledge of astronomy and the teaching of transmigration of souls. The former included, according to Caesar, studying the heavenly bodies, the size of the universe and the physical properties of the natural world. This knowledge was passed on to the young. The latter was promoted as it encouraged men to be brave, even foolhardy in battle, and not spare their own lives.

The practice of divination was also part of the Druids' duties. The Roman statesman Marcus Tullius Cicero (106–43 BC) mentioned the

Druid Divitiacus, whom he had met in Rome when Divitiacus was staying with his younger brother, Quintus Tullius Cicero. He said that this Druid had such knowledge of the natural world that he claimed to predict the future by augury and divination. Divitiacus was also a chieftain of the tribe of the Aedui and had gone to Rome to plead for military help against other tribes and against incursions of the Germans against the Gallic tribes. By doing so, he opened the way for Caesar to intervene in Gallic affairs. It was not unknown, although possibly rare, for one man to hold tribal leadership as well as be a Druid. Divination could be done from the death throes of humans as well as animals, and from the flights of birds. Tacitus bluntly said that they consulted the gods from the palpitating entrails of men. Caesar said that they claimed they could control or overcome supernatural forces by this method. Animals included pigs and cattle, especially bulls. In the story of the *Destruction of Da Derga's Hostel*, King Conaire ordered his Druid, Fer Caille, to sacrifice a pig to discover what might happen to his men. The result is that Fer Caille foretold not only the destruction of the hostel but also the death of the king. Roman augers claimed to tell the future from the flights of birds and the entrails of animals, but it was the practice of human sacrifice which horrified the Romans and resulted in the Romans proscribing them in their territories.

Ascribed magical powers to the Druids included control of the weather so that they could conjure up a dense fog or a heavy snowfall to hide the movements of an army. When the Túatha De Danann invaded Ireland to seize it from the tribe of the Fir Bolg, their Druids caused what was described in the Irish text as a 'great darkness' to hide the invasion. Druids could also change their appearance by shape shifting and could change people into animals and birds if they opposed them.

Druids were not entirely of the male sex. Classical writers commented on Dryades or female Druids. The Greek writer Plutarch (c. AD 50–129) mentioned Camma, a priestess, who was a Druidess in Galatia. Like male Druids, they were appointed as ambassador to other tribes. An essay by Plutarch, *On the Virtues of Women*, mentioned that a Druidess was sent to help negotiate a treaty between Hannibal and the Celtic tribe of the Volcae. He added that Druidesses could take part in the Celtic assembles and helped to calm tempers if matters became too fraught.

Druidesses were reputed to have the same divination power as their male counterparts. Vopiscus, one of the authors of the *Historia Augusta*, a collection of biographies of certain Roman emperors, mentioned that the future emperor Diocletian (AD 240–313), a man of low birth, while a humble soldier in the army, was staying at an inn in Gaul. The innkeeper was a woman, who was also a Druidess. When Diocletian went to settle his bill, she said to him that he was far too greedy and far too economical. He replied that when he became an emperor he would be far more liberal with his money. She said that he would laugh now, but when he had killed the Boar, he would indeed be the emperor. Diocletian killed the Praefectus Arrius (nicknamed the Boar) and became emperor following the assassination of the emperor, Marcus Aurelius Carinus, in AD 285.

In another biography in the *Historia Augusta*, the life of the Emperor Severus Augustus, there is mention of a Druidess foretelling the defeat of the emperor before a battle in AD 235. Her words, 'Go, but do not hope for victory and put not your trust in soldiers', came true. Severus marched north to fight against the Germans but found that the legions were ready to mutiny on account of his discipline. While he was in camp, probably near Mainz, soldiers who would not tolerate his strict regime assassinated him.

In the Irish text of the *Cattle Raid of Cooley*, Queen Medb asks a Druidess named Fidelma whether Medb's armies would defeat those of King Conchobar. She replied that they would not. Fidelma told the queen that she had come from learning her gifts of vision in Albion, which would link in with Caesar's comments that many of the Gauls went to study with the Druids in Britain indicating either that the teaching there was superior or that a more pure form of Druidic lore had survived in what could be consider a more isolated area.

Knights

The other group mentioned by Caesar were the knights or nobles. In Gaul, the usual unit was the tribe, such as the Helvetii, the Veneti and the Aedui. Caesar found that he had to contend with these and noted that they were always intent on extending tribal boundaries either by making political alliances or engaging in open warfare to gain their needs. These tribes were ruled by chieftains, although he noted that the system was being replaced by magistrates (*vergobrets*), who were elected annually similar to the system in Rome, or by a council of elders, chosen or elected to represent different opinions from the tribes.

The equivalent in Ireland was the kings (sometimes queens) who ruled tribes (*túath*). The highest in the hierarchy was a High King, below whom were kings over five provinces or kingdoms. For each of these there was a centre where the king was elected. It was not necessarily a capital, for the kings preferred to tour their territory settling disputes and ensuring that their tribal boundaries were intact. As in the case of Gaul, there were frequent infringements to territorial boundaries, but these seem to have been attempted more by raids than political alliances. The kings were the key personages guaranteeing men in their positions and protecting them on their land. The kings were expected to be generous in their hospitality. The nobles of the Túatha De Danann revolted against their king, Bres mac Elotha, because as the Irish text states, 'their knives were not greased by him and however often they visited him their breath did not smell of ale'. He was also niggardly in providing entertainment and allowing the warriors to prove their prowess in his court.

Archaeological excavations of graves provide evidence of higher-ranking men in society. The Hochdorf tomb excavated in 1978 in the Würtemburg region (Germany), a burial from the Hallstatt culture of about 530 BC, shows how honoured a chieftain could be in death. The burial, beneath a mound 200 feet (60 metres) in diameter and placed within a wooden chamber, of a forty-year-old man, commanding a height of 6 feet 2 inches (1.87 metres), contained an impressive arrangement of grave goods, which included a large couch, a cart, a huge collection of bronze dishes and nine large drinking horns. On a lesser scale, the evidence from the Lexden (Essex) tomb in Britain and a tomb at Goeblingen-Nospelt, Luxembourg, with their rich grave goods – which included bronze vessels and huge amphorae, presumably filled with wine – indicated that a chieftain would indulge himself in the Otherworld.

The evidence for powerful men controlling large groups of men can be seen in the building of oppida. The complexity of their defences and the layout of the interior suggest an organised, directed system, which probably ensured protection for the people of the surrounding area. The oppidum of Danebury (Hampshire) has been suggested to be a distribution point for grain.

Kings or chieftains did not necessarily succeed by right of primogeniture, that is the eldest son succeeding, but by tanistry, that is the eldest eligible male. If his prowess was agreed before the death of the chieftain, he was given the title of Tanist or second. It was vital to have a strong leader rather than a weak one or a regency for a young son. The aim was fitness for the post and a strong leader who could avoid disputes which might weaken the tribe.

Beneath these chieftains and kings came the nobles who could have their own territorial units or were retainers of an overlord. These units could cover a small area. A lake village such as Glastonbury would allow the man in charge to be a minor chieftain. Like the Druids, the knights or nobles were not a closed caste and social mobility was a possibility. The nobles were warrior bands, many being kinsmen of their lord or they might have been adopted under the system of fosterage.

Chieftains could command huge numbers. In 61 BC Orgetorix, a Helvetian chieftain, whom Caesar described as being foremost in wealth and rank, organised a mass movement of his people to obtain more land in Gaul. When this was realised, his fellow nobles put him on trial. He was able to bring 10,000 slaves from his various estates, together with what Caesar describes as his numerous retainers and debtor-bondsmen to support him, thus overawing his persecutors.

It would pay a man to become a client or retainer of a higher lord. He might have to fight for the lord but he had in return status and protection. Caesar emphasised the system of clientship, which could be agreed or terminated on both sides. The overlord did not allow his clients to be oppressed or disfranchised, as this would mean loss of influence for both him and them. In the Irish tales, the bands of warriors seem to have been content with their keep and an opportunity to exhibit their martial prowess. The Egyptian-Greek author Athenaeus (active AD c.200) was scathing of the whole system saying that the Celts have in both war and peace companions (clients), whom they call parasites. Strictly speaking, he was right but it was one way in which a man could ensure protection and make his way towards a higher status. There was perhaps more to it than Athenaeus implied, for he said that the Gauls hold comradeship in the highest esteem and that the most feared and powerful amongst them were those who attracted the most attendants and retainers.

Caesar also implied that a tribe might become a client of another tribe. The Sequani and the Aedui had client tribes, but when Caesar brought the authority of Rome to Gaul, some tribes such as the Remi saw that it would be to their advantage to become client tribes of Rome.

Some popular assemblies were already being established in Gaul. These consisted of freeborn nobles; boys, women and slaves were all barred from attending. Strabo mentioned an intriguing way of preventing heckling which could have stifled free discussion. The heckler could be told to be quiet three times by being approached by a man with a drawn sword. The third time was his last chance. If he persisted, a large piece of his cloak was cut off sufficient to make it clear that it was useless and thus presumably identify him as a troublemaker.

Caratacus and Vercingetorix

Some names of chieftains have survived, mainly because classical writers recorded their resistance to Rome. Caratacus (or Caractacus who has been portrayed in an oratorio by the English composer, Sir Edward Elgar) was a son of Cunobelin, King of the Catuvellauni, and brother to Togodubnus. In AD 43, the brothers opposed the Roman advance into Essex, but when Togodubnus was killed, Caratacus fled to Wales where for over eight years he organised Welsh tribes, first the Silures and then the Ordovici, into resistance against the Romans. According to Tacitus, the innate ferocity of the tribes was heightened by the trust they placed in Caratacus, whom he described as pre-eminent amongst British chieftains and whose tactics were such that he was without rivals. Though inferior in strength of numbers, he was able to make strategic use of the terrain, but eventually in AD 50 he had to meet the Roman forces under the Governor of Britain, Ostorius Scapula.

The site of this battle has been disputed. Tacitus described it as one where the approaches and the escape routes helped Caratacus and impeded the Romans. On one side there was a precipitous slope and on the other a river of uncertain depth. The site has been suggested to be at Llanymynech in central Wales. In this last battle, the Roman troops defeated Caratacus's army, who were described as being without the protection of both breastplates and helmets, and captured his wife, daughters and brothers. Caratacus fled north, seeking protection from Cartimandua, Queen of the Brigantian tribe. Mindful that it was in her interests to keep in with Rome, the queen informed the Roman authority (AD 51) who took him captive to Rome.

The Romans, however, had been impressed by his courage. Tacitus recorded that as his fame had spread far beyond Britain into the adjoining provinces and even as far as Rome, many people wished to see the

man who had defied Rome's power. He was made to take part, together
with his wife, daughters and brothers, in a Roman triumphal procession,
but he never looked like a dejected captive. He gave a defiant speech
saying that had he been as moderate in success as his noble rank and
birth were great, he would have entered Rome as a friend rather than
a captive. If the Romans would spare his life, he would be a memorial
to their clemency. In response to this speech, the Emperor Claudius
pardoned Caratacus and his family. They seemingly lived out the rest
of their lives in Rome, probably being a living example of an emperor's
clemency.

The most vivid example of the control that a chieftain could exert
over tribes is found in the campaigns of the Gallic warrior, Vercingetorix,
whose story can be found in Caesar's Gallic wars and deduced from
excavations carried out in the 1860s on the order of the Emperor
Napoleon III. Napoleon, having written a history of the campaigns
of Julius Caesar in Gaul, established a commission to identify the last
stand of the great Gallic leader. This was identified by excavation
as being at Alesia, and further excavations until the 1950s confirmed this.
Alesia is an impressive plateau 2,625 feet (800 metres) high and covering
222 acres (90 hectares). Springs provided it with water and it seemed
to have been already stocked with grain supplies.

Vercingetorix assumed command over a far greater number of tribes
than did Caratacus. He was the son of Celtillus of the Arvernian tribe.
His father had been killed for attempting to extend his personal power
and the son was equally ambitious. Caesar's campaigns gave him his
chance. In 52 BC, he summoned a council of tribal elders at which
he stated he would campaign for tribal liberties; the council could deliver
him to the Romans or follow him to his death. His eloquence and powers
of leadership succeeded. According to Caesar, Vercingetorix managed
to gather almost 300,000 warriors from almost thirty tribes and,
by his inspiration and clever tactics, succeeded in holding the Roman
legionaries in their forts and camps.

He first invaded Gallia Transalpina hoping to hold the Romans
in the southwest, but in snowy winter weather, Caesar moved swiftly
northwards, forcing a passage through the snowy Cervennes Mountains
to threaten Vercingetorix's own territory. Caesar's soldiers shovelled
away snowdrifts up to 6 feet (1.82 metres) deep to take his opponents
by surprise. The Gallic chieftain withdrew and the war became a series

of sieges, combined with a scorched earth policy, where each side tried to deprive the opposing force of supplies. The people of Avaricum (Bourges) implored Vercingetorix not to destroy their stronghold, which they declared to be almost the finest in Gaul, and somewhat reluctantly he agreed. Avaricum, however, fell to Roman siege tactics and the inhabitants were massacred – Caesar said that only 800 out of 40,000 survived. Caesar failed to take the next stronghold of Gergovia, but when Vercingetorix withdrew into the stronghold of Alesia, Caesar seized his chance for one final attempt to subdue the Gallic tribes.

The siege of Alesia lasted over a month and the nineteenth-century excavations revealed many of Caesar's surrounding camps and a continuous outer rampart 13 miles (22 kilometres) long and an inner wall fronted by ditches with which he encircled the oppidum. Wooden towers enabled the Romans to overlook the Gallic defences. Once the wall was complete the inhabitants began to starve. A huge Gallic relief force, over a quarter of a million strong, failed to break through the encircling line and when Vercingetorix realised this, he surrendered. He galloped into Caesar's camp, hurled his arms and equipment at Caesar's feet and threw up his arms in a gesture of surrender. He made a dignified speech saying that he had not undertaken the war for private ends but in the cause of national liberty, and since he must now accept his fate he placed himself at Caesar's mercy. Caesar, however, was not mindful to offer the same courtesies. Vercingetorix and the enslaved Gauls were taken to Rome and even there he did not receive the same honour as that given to Caratacus, as he was kept in prison for six years.

In 46 BC, Caesar, having decided that Gaul was conquered, held his triumph in Rome. Vercingetorix was included in the procession but was executed soon after. His name, however, lived on as a symbol of Gallic, and later French, resistance to an enemy. The huge statue, erected in 1865 and which crowns the site of Mont Auxois, was a tribute to a charismatic Celtic chieftain who succeeded in uniting the Celtic tribes of Gaul in one last stand against a menacing and powerful enemy. A translation of the French inscription on it added in 1949 and obviously with a reference to the Second World War, records that 'On this plain 2,000 years ago Gaul saved her honour. Pitting at Vercingetorix call her people against Caesar's legions and after her reversal on the battlefield, reconciled with the Victor, united, defended against the invasion of the Germans, opened to the enlightenment of Greece and Rome, she knew centuries of peace.'

Fosterage

In Ireland and Scotland, the custom of fosterage was prevalent. This continued into the medieval period and certainly lasted until the eighteenth century in parts of Europe. The custom entailed the sons of a household, to the age of seventeen, being sent to live with the family of the overlord in order to learn martial arts and other skills which would be of use to them. Girls too could be sent for fostering until the age of fourteen, deemed to be the marriageable age. The children would regard the foster father as their own father and this would enhance the bond of clientship. When they returned to their natural father, there was an implied obligation that the father and his family were bound to the foster parent. Caesar gave hints that the system had been used in Gaul but indicated that the Gauls differed from other areas in that children were not allowed to go up to their fathers in public until they were old enough for military service. A boy should not stand before his father until then. This implies that fosterage had died out in Gaul, but it was certainly in use in Ireland. King Conchobar had a boy-corps 'thrice fifty in number', whom Cu Chulainn defeated quite easily at their games, when he came to join them.

Irish texts indicate that not only was the bond between foster father and foster son close but that the bond between foster brothers was close and lasted when the sons were returned to their natural father. It did not mean, however, that it took precedence over warrior disputes. This was the tragic theme as detailed in part of the *Cattle Raid of Cooley*, when Cu Chulainn fought his foster brother Ferdiad. Although the bond between the two was close, the fight was a matter of honour in which the will of the stronger prevailed. Cu Chulainn only achieved this by his use of the fearsome weapon, the gae bulgae, which when it penetrated the body and its thirty bards opened could not be removed until the flesh had been cut about it.

Fosterage also can be considered part of the hostage system. Taking of hostages was common amongst Celtic tribes. In 54 BC, Caesar ordered the tribe of the Treveri to send 200 hostages to him in order to assure their allegiance. When they arrived, Caesar found that they included the son of Indutiomarus, one of the Treverian leaders, as well as some of his relatives. Caesar also took hostages from some of the 4,000 Gaulish cavalry who arrived to fight with his army. This system ensured some form of loyalty, but these hostages were not given the same education or treatment as that given to the foster children.

Charioteers

Charioteers may be considered to be a separate class. They seemed
to have been especially trained and achieved considerable skill. In Britain,
Caesar said that the Britons detailed servants or others from the poorer
classes as charioteers; Diodorus said freemen were recruited. The use
of the chariot in warfare died out in Gaul and Britain after these areas
had been conquered by the Romans, but in Ireland, chariots continued
to be a vital part of warrior campaigning. Irish charioteers had an
honoured status and were close companions so that there was implicit
trust between charioteer and warrior. Loeg, charioteer of Cu Chulainn,
and Iubar, charioteer of King Conchobar, knew instinctively what their
masters needed and their dress and manners are accordingly detailed
in the Irish texts.

Loeg, whose devotion to Cu Chulainn lasted his lifetime, is described
as a slender, tall, lean and much-freckled man, with curly red hair that
was held by a band of bronze. His cloak opened at the two elbows and
he had a small red-gold whip to urge on the horses. In the tale of the
death of Cu Chulainn, Loeg is mentioned as being the king of charioteers
and the horse, the Gray of Macha, which drew the chariot, as the king
of horses. Sometimes two horses are mentioned, the Gray of Macha and
the Black of Sainglenn. In another tale, Cu Chulainn is described as
sitting with his charioteer Loeg playing a game of chess with the board
between them. As Loeg has his back to the horses it seems that the
horses were so well trained that they could trot on without their
master's control.

Bards, reciters and satirists

Celts with these talents seem to have had a respected status as they could
chant and sing from an extended repertoire to an assembled company.
Diodorus mentioned lyric poets whom the Celts called bards. They were
skilled in their craft of singing a eulogy or a satire to the accompaniment
of a stringed instrument that Diodorus called the lyre, obviously linking
this to the Graeco-Roman stringed instrument. One of the decorations
on pots from Sopron, Hungary, shows a figure holding out a stringed
instrument, while elsewhere two more hold these instruments while
women in balloon-like skirts dance to their tune. Bards extolled the

praises of their lords or of the great heroes, so that one would try to outdo the others. Strabo said that the bards were singers and poets who were held in special honour.

The traveller and historian Poseidonius (c.115–30 BC) mentions entertainment provided by storytellers and bards who provided eulogies in song at Gallic feasts and gives an account of the chieftain, Lovernius, throwing a bag of gold to a Celtic poet or bard who arrived too late for a feast. The bard had gained this by lauding Lovernius as he ran beside his chariot, thus showing that there were rich rewards for those who persisted in entertaining their masters. The Greek historian Appian (AD c.95–c.165) recorded an ambassador of Bituitus, chieftain of the tribe of the Arverni, meeting the Roman commander, Gnaeus Domitius, in 122 BC, and being surrounded by guards and dogs, used as bodyguards. An accompanying musician sang the praises of Bituitus and then of the ambassador himself celebrating his birth, his bravery and his wealth.

The Irish texts often break into poems or songs and continually mention harpists and bards. King Conchobar spent a third of his day consuming food and drink and is sent to sleep by minstrels and musicians. The Irish god, the Dagda, had a harpist whose playing caused people to laugh, cry or go to sleep having marvellous dreams. In the story of the Sick-bed of Cu Chulainn, Druids are ordered to sing and jugglers to perform. Women including his wife Emer also sang songs to him, in order to revive him. The Otherworld is described as being a place where music awaited the heroes. In the story of the *Second Battle of Mag Tured*, the banqueting house of Bres had a harp, which had the power to kill men. The Dagda could play it, and he played the wail strain so that tearful women wept, the smile strain so that the children and women laughed and the sleep strain so that all fell asleep.

In Ireland, a group of men with special status were the satirists. They were usually present at feasts but could appear on a road to taunt a hero making a journey. Their aim was to humiliate a warrior or bring his vaulting ambition down to earth. Cu Chulainn's death is partly brought about by a satirist reviling him for not handing over his weapons. They would also comment on the hospitality of a house, as, for example, in a comment such as 'In this house there is a lean goat and no drink to follow.'

Satirists and other notable persons could put taboos (or *gessa*) on the heroes and other people. In some ways the taboo was a curse, for it seems to have been inevitable that these taboos would be broken and that people could not evade their fate. One main taboo was that the person concerned would not eat their namesake, but Cu Chulainn, whose name meant Hound of Ulster, was enticed by three old women, each blind in the left (or evil) eye, to eat from meat they had cooked on a spit. This was a dog laced with poison and spells. This placed Cu Chulainn in a dilemma. It is a taboo for him to pass a cooking hearth without taking of food but he is forbidden to eat his namesake. Once Cu Chulainn had eaten the meat with his left hand all his strength fell from it.

In the tale of the *Destruction of Da Derga's Hostel*, the power of the taboo was dramatically related in those placed on Conaire, King of Ulster.

Thou shalt not go righthandwise round Tara, or lefthandwise round Mag Breg
The evil beasts of Cerna must not be hunted by thee
And thou shalt not go out every ninth night beyond Tara
Thou shalt not sleep in a house from which firelight is manifest outside after sunset and in which light is manifest from without
And three reds shalt not go before thee to the House of Red
And no rapine shalt be wrought in thy reign
And after sunset a company of one woman or one man shalt not enter a house where thy art
And thou shalt never settle a quarrel between two thanes.

All of these must be avoided and the king had the choice of doing this, but once one is broken, the rest inevitably follow with gathering momentum. The taboo was activated by a weakness on the part of Conaire. Conaire's foster brothers hated him and pillaged the land. They were first spared from death but then banished from Ireland. Later they returned to rob and plunder. Conaire had to go to Munster to settle a quarrel between two more of his foster brothers (or thanes) and to do this he stayed five nights with each of them. Thus the taboos started to be broken and disorder occurred. In the midst of one fight, Conaire accidentally went right-hand-wise round Tara and left-hand-wise round Mag Breg (The Plain of Breg) and in the confusion hunted the evil beasts of Cerna. He and his followers made for shelter to the hostel of Da Derga (Two Reds) and on the way were overtaken by three riders with red hair, wearing red tunics and cloaks, carrying red spears and riding red horses. In vain, Conaire sent his son to call them back, but they replied they were alive but death would witness the cutting of life.

Conaire stayed three nights at the hostel which had seven doorways but only one door that could be moved to block off changes of wind. Thus, the firelight could then be seen from outside and light entered from the outside. During the night, a lone woman of repulsive aspect sought shelter for the night and the laws of hospitality meant that she had to be admitted. Thus, all the taboos had been broken and the destruction of the king and his forces came about when the hostel was attacked by Ingeel, son of the king of the Britons, whose ship brought the brothers back to Ireland. This completed a cycle and marked the closing of a magic ring.

Craftsmen

Craftsmen were held in esteem, for their prowess changed base ores into useable shapes. They had solved the problem of working with high temperatures and their firing techniques improved. From iron ore they provided strong weapons with sharp cutting edges and useful tools – axes, chisels, gouges, augers and saws. The creation of more efficient ploughs meant that crops could produce a greater yield. Nails replaced wooden pegs in the construction of houses. The blacksmith, in particular, was regarded with respect as his craft was enhanced by his representation as the Smith god, which the Romans syncretised with their smith god, Vulcan. Working with bronze and enamel produced intricate jewellery, which the Celts loved. Craftsmen began to specialise in iron, bronze and pottery making. Pottery making developed from hand-thrown pots to smooth pots made on the wheel. Craftsmen could stay in one area but many were itinerant making their way from one settlement to another to sell their wares, thus ensuring their independent nature.

Freemen and slaves

At the lower end of society were the freemen who lived in isolated settlements or who worked on their own land and were protected by their overlord. They would be expected to follow their lord into battle, but their total allegiance was doubtful; when it was necessary to gather their crops, they would leave or be sent away from the battlefield, as Caesar noted when he invaded Britain in 55 BC. Some people would be servants working for their overlord in a personal capacity.

Below these came the unfree members of society. These were slaves who had neither land nor property. Strabo listed slaves as one of the exports of pre-Roman Britain. Diodorus said that the Celts were so fond of wine that they could drink themselves into a stupor. Merchants took advantage of this. They could either charge an incredible price for an amphora of wine or they could barter the wine in return for a servant or a slave. Caesar said that some people neither possessed initiative nor were invited to give their opinion. They were weighed down by debt and heavy taxes or by the injustice of those who were superior to them. Many therefore resigned themselves to become slaves so that they would at least have some protection and presumably some food. Others had been captured in battle and raids thus becoming automatically enslaved. This continued beyond the pagan Celtic era. St. Patrick, born about AD 415, was captured in an Irish raid on the west coast of Britain and taken to Ireland. After six years, he escaped but, somewhere between AD 432 and 455, returned to convert the pagan Irish to Christianity.

Figure 1 Drawing of a slave chain.

Irish society

Ireland had its own strata of society based on the family and the tribe.
As land was held by the tribe who allotted it to kin, and kin could
mean any relation, it was vital to keep track on relations and their
land, a situation that may explain the value laid on ownership of land
in Ireland today. Overall was a High King, chosen from one of the kings
or from the maternal or paternal lines of previous High Kings. Below
him were kings or sometimes queens who ruled their tribe (*túath*) with
the help of an assembly (*óenach*). The king was a dispenser of justice
and a guarantee of its prosperity and order in the land. The tribe was
divided into nobles, freemen and serfs. Also included were divisions
of priests, bards, charioteers and craftsmen. The freemen and the serfs
were beholden to their lord who might or might not allow them to
own land.

The family was divided into kin. The main unit (*gelfine*) included
the man, his wife and any other wives, his children and their wives and
husbands and their children (i.e. grandchildren). A wider unit (*derbfine*)
included the man and his wife's grandparents and the brothers and sisters
of the man and their descendents. A still wider relationship (*iarfine*)
included the grandfather of the man and any other of his descendents
or lateral kin. Lastly came the *indfine* relating to the great-grandfather
and all his descendants.

Women

Classical writers were intrigued by the status of Celtic women, partly
because these women had far more freedom than their Roman counterparts. They could be tough as indicated by the comments of Ammianus
Marcellinus. Many were forced to share their husband's code of honour,
as witnessed by the fate of the woman in one of the Pergamon statues,
where the woman has been killed by her husband before he kills himself
rather than accept capture. Most women, however, were not accepted
as equals, although those in higher ranks could achieve regal and political status. Celtic society was male-orientated. Women were expected
to support their husbands, care for the children and produce food –
household tasks which have continued throughout the centuries. They
would also be expected to help in agricultural tasks such as sowing

seed and reaping corn – help vitally needed at the requisite seasons of the year.

Women were subject to their husband or their brothers or, failing these relatives, other male members of the family. Polygamy was also the custom in some parts of society. Sexual relations were far more open than in Roman society and were tolerated by all Celtic societies, a fact which somewhat shocked Roman writers. They did have one great privilege that could give them some independence. According to Caesar, when women married, the husband received a dowry but had to add a sum equal to this from his own possessions. This had to be kept as a separate account; any interest on it was added to it. When one of the couple died, the other received both portions together with any interest. If this were the case, it would allow a widow to live a comfortable existence, although a well-off woman might be pressurised into marrying another man. There was also a downside to marriage. When a man died in suspicious circumstances the wife and the slaves were interrogated by torture if deemed necessary. If found guilty, all were put to death.

The most powerful women were given a rich burial. The so-called princess's grave at Vix (Cote d'Or, France) of the sixth century BC, excavated in 1953, had a chamber 10 feet (3 metres) square. This thirty-five-year-old woman had been buried with her most prized possessions and the body was placed on a cart, which formed her bier. The contents of the grave included wine-drinking vessels equal in value and esteem to those of a male counterpart, and a huge imported Greek krater, evidence of the high regard in which she was held. An impressive gold torc, probably made in Greece, had been placed round her neck. Other graves of women with elaborate grave goods were found at Waldalgesheim, near Bingen, and Reinheim (Germany). The latter grave produced 200 pieces of jewellery and a bronze wine flagon.

There were queens amongst the Celts. Irish tales recount Medb (Maeve), queen of Connacht, who dominated her hen-pecked husband, Ailill and whose jealousy led to the Cattle Raid of Cooley. She is recorded by an Irish chronicler in the eleventh century as being an historical figure who died about AD 70. A possibly legendary figure called Queen Teuta is recorded by the Greek historian Polybius (c.200–118 BC) on the Illyrian coast in 231 BC. The name comes from the Celtic *teutates* meaning tribe, which is a somewhat vague name.

Boudica and Cartimandua

More definite are the careers of two queens in Britain, which have been recorded by classical writers, but from a Roman point of view. Boudica (anglicised as Boadicea) whose story is detailed by Tacitus has become the archetype of resistance to Rome. Described by Dio Cassius as being tall, grim in appearance with a piercing gaze, a harsh voice and a mass of fair hair, worn to her waist, she was wife to Prasutagus, king of the Iceni, a tribe in East Anglia. Prasutagus thought he had secured the security of his family and his tribe after his death by leaving half his kingdom to his daughters and the other half to the Emperor Nero. It is not clear why he did not make Boudica his heir but his omission was disastrous. The Roman administration, disregarding the daughters' claims as they probably thought that two young girls would not be able to rule the kingdom, moved troops into the territory. According to Tacitus, centurions of a legion plundered the area and the Icenian royal household was treated like slaves. This led to a tribal revolt which was also the result of the ultimate insult, the rape of Boudica's daughters and the flogging of Boudica.

There was an underlying anger in the area because of the Roman confiscation of the estates of the Celtic nobility, linked to the resentment felt elsewhere against the rapacious procurator of Britain Decianus Catus and the imposition of heavy Roman taxes. Boudica led the Iceni, together with the neighbouring tribe of the Trinovantes into a revolt and her decisive command does not seem to have been challenged. Tacitus said that she rode in a chariot with her daughters and that as she approached each tribe she declared that Britons were accustomed to engage in warfare under the leadership of a woman, an extraordinary statement, which implies that other women were leading men into battle or were leaders of a tribe. Women, she said, were not only equal to men but possessed the same valour. Tacitus attempted to demean her by saying that she was an ordinary woman avenging the freedom she had lost, her body worn out by flogging and the violation of her daughters, but this does not allow for the fact that she could summon a huge host to avenge her wrongs and link these to their grievances.

At first, Boudica's military strategy proved faultless, ambushing the Roman Ninth Legion, who had to retire to their base at Lincoln. Leading an increasing number of Britons, she sacked Camulodunum, London and

Verulamium. Her military strategy failed in a final battle against Roman troops under Suetonius Paulinus, which probably took place somewhere north of St Albans, not reckoning against the Roman steadfast wedge-shaped formations. When the Britons fled, the Romans were ruthless in their slaughter not even sparing the women or the baggage animals. Boudica is reputed to have taken poison. Dio Cassius, however, said that she fell ill and died. The British mourned her deeply and gave her a lavish funeral. Her burial place has been hotly disputed even to being placed under one of the platforms of King's Cross Station in London.

The other British queen was Cartimandua, whose story was also told by Tacitus and who described her as flourishing in all the splendour of power and wealth. She was queen of the northern tribe of the Brigantes, a huge tribe with a confederation of districts, as indicated by the number of oppida, which covered an area in the north west of Britain from Lancashire up to the Scottish border. It is not certain how she came to be ruler of this tribe. Tacitus said that she became queen by the 'influence which belongs to high birth', which suggests she was the daughter of the previous ruler, but her rule seems to have been accepted at first. Given the large terrain, by AD 47 she shrewdly realised that her best option was to become a client queen of Rome and by doing this she ensured at least ten years of peace, because the Romans realised that she gave protection to this north western area and saved them from deploying troops in that area. She also proved her loyalty to Rome by betraying Caratacus in AD 51. Tacitus said that from this act came wealth and the self-indulgence of success, but any unrest caused by this act was put down by Roman auxiliaries being sent to her aid.

The self-indulgence probably related to the treatment of her husband. She had married Venutius, whom she thought was loyal to Rome and who either had been her consort or shared her power. He soon, however, became the leader of an anti-Roman faction and either this fact or because Cartimandua was having an affair with Vollocatus, his standard bearer, she determined to discard him and therefore divorced him and promptly married Vollocatus. Not unnaturally, her action outraged Venutius, for it not only was an outrage to his sexual prowess but also to his political standing. Tacitus hinted that this shamed the tribe of the Brigantes, already outraged by her betrayal of Caratacus, and that Venutius roused part of the Brigantes to rebel and also encouraged enemies outside her kingdom to attack. Alarmed at Venutius's action, Cartimandua sought Roman protection and the governor of Britain,

Vettius Bolanus, despatched a force of auxiliary cavalry and infantry. It would seem that resistance was fierce because a legion under Caesius Nasica had to be sent to restore order. These succeeded in rescuing the queen and putting down the unrest and she remained as queen, with Venutius seemingly quiescent but probably simmering with rage, in her tribe, until at least AD 68.

It was left to the next governor Petillius Cerealis who took over in AD 71 to take decisive action. Venutius had rebelled again, and expelling Cartimandua, he took over the leadership of the Brigantes. Cerealis promptly regarded this unrest as an excuse to take decisive action in the Brigantian territory. Venutius fled to the oppidum of Stanwick (Yorkshire), but in AD 72, Petillius Cerealis attacked the Brigantes and overran their tribal area. Tacitus mentions numerous battles, some of them bloody. Cerealis besieged and took Stanwick, slighting the ramparts thus rending the oppidum useless. Later, the town of Aldborough was established by the Romans to provide a focus of civilisation for the Brigantian tribe. It is not certain what happened to Cartimandua. She may have been deposed, been killed or have committed suicide. Her history differs from that of Boudica, indicating that although women could occupy powerful positions and play for high stakes, there was a limit to what a tribe would accept in the way of womanly behaviour.

Chapter 3
Housing and Building Methods

In *De Architectura*, a treatise by the Roman engineer and architect
Vitruvius, written at the end of the first century AD, the author dismisses
all buildings which are not based on stone: 'Some people make roofs out
of leaves, others dig artificial caves beneath mountains, and some, copying
the nests of swallows, shelter in structures made of mud and twigs.' These
comments are obviously a sneer at those he considered to be barbarian
tribes, amongst which he included the Celts. He obviously knew nothing
of Celtic house styles, which could be far more sophisticated than those
which the Romans attributed to those of the barbarians.

The Celts had a variety of forms and dimensions of houses, some
situated as isolated settlements and others grouped together for defensive
purposes. Security was often to be found in large hillforts. Some of these
were used primarily as places of refuge; others were intended less for
defence than to provide permanent sites for houses, industries and other
specialised activities. As such they could be considered to be classified
as towns and might institute some form of political or social control over
a wider area.

Water provided a defence so that crannogs and lake villages were constructed. Excavation of these sites has provided sufficient information,
mainly in the form of postholes, which along with imaginative techniques
and using a basis of ethnographical models, reconstructions of houses
can be attempted. These reconstructions have also allowed examination
to be made of the effects of time and weather on buildings. In northern
areas, lack of timber and unsettled conditions, led to the construction of
stone houses and massive towers or brochs, which were both residential
and defensive. These, though none have been reconstructed, have been
interpreted in drawings to provide suggested living conditions. Attempts
have also been made by interpretation of the Irish texts to provide
information on the communal halls occupied by Irish warriors.

Round houses

Round houses appear to be found only in Britain and evidence for these
goes back to the Late Neolithic period. Their main characteristic is a

circular wall, which supports a conical roof. Some of these have a central post supporting the apex of the roof; others rely on the lateral thrust of the timbers to the circular wall and pairs of rafters can be tied together at the lower ends to prevent any outward slip. Early evidence for these round houses is based on the excavations carried out by Gerhardt Bersu at Little Woodbury (Wiltshire) during 1938–1939. His work was interpreted in a Ministry of Information film produced during the Second World War. Bersu visualised a large house, 50 feet (15.24 metres) in diameter, with two rings of posts supporting the roof that was raised to a peak in the centre by four larger posts. Postholes placed on the southeast suggested a projecting porch. Placed on that side, it could catch the morning sun and avoid the prevailing west wind. Bersu also suggested that the timbers of the house had been continually replaced as they weakened and thus provided shelter for several occupations.

Taking the evidence of this and that of excavations of house sites at Pimperne (Dorset), Balksbury (Hampshire) and those within the hillfort of Maiden Castle (Dorset), three experimental houses were given physical structure on the Butser Ancient Farm Experimental Site (Hampshire) and a large round house at Little Butser open to the public. They were all round houses and they agree with a reference by Pytheas, a fourth-century BC Greek explorer from Massalia, who courageously explored the west coast of Europe as far as the Shetland Isles, but whose account comes to us through Strabo and Diodorus Siculus. One of his comments mentions Celtic houses as being round with thatched roofs.

At Maiden Castle, the houses were small, 19.6 feet (6 metres) in diameter with a central post supporting the apex of the roof. At Balksbury, the house was 29.5 feet (9 metres), with an unsupported roof span. Excavations of the Maiden Castle houses revealed outer postholes set close together, which probably indicated that the walls were of wicker-work covered with clay or daub, somewhat akin to the wattle and daub construction, which became normal practice with timber-framed houses throughout the medieval period. Daub is a mixture of clay, animal hair, grass, straw and other material, which will bind the clay. It is mixed with water and puddled or pressed into the clay. As it dries it cracks, but these cracks can be filled. Such a wall will last for anything up to ten years. In the medieval period, successive coatings of lime wash allowed it to survive for much longer, but the Celts do not seem to have followed this practice. Hazel wood is excellent for interweaving and can easily be obtained from coppicing. Such walls can be extremely strong if well constructed.

It is possible that windows might have been cut into the walls. Pieces of daub with rounded cut-outs were found during excavation of Bronze Age houses at Otománi (Romania) and Fort-Harrouard (Eure-et-Loir, France) which might be window edging. There is no reason why the Celts might not have done this. Roof timbers, made of ash, were probably placed on the walls and the lateral thrust exerted by the weight of the roof was directed round the circular walls. Caution has to be expressed about certain features. Peter Reynolds observed that shallow runs made by mice under the Butser Hill house walls might be interpreted as shallow foundation trenches.

For the reconstructed house at the Little Butser Experimental Site, the main timbers were inter-lashed with supporting beam rings, thus giving additional strength. The roof was given a minimum pitch of 45 degrees. Straw thatching consisting of bundles of straw, tied with concentric rings, was placed over the roof, each bundle overlapping the one before. In all, a ton of straw was needed to cover a roof. This straw came from over 4 acres (1.62 hectares) of land. As the house would be expected to last a long time, such gathering within a season would be acceptable. The restrictions against foreigners in Britain during the Second World War led to Bersu being interned on the Isle of Man. His enthusiasm for archaeology undiminished, Bersu excavated a large round house that he deduced had a roof of branches covered with turf. This type of house is known from other areas as, for example, in Jutland (Denmark). Heat emanating from the hearth combined with external humidity ensures continual growth of the turf. At Nages (France), one site seems to have a roof made of large tree branches over which was laid a thick layer of twigs. This was covered with clay mixed with straw about 4 inches (10 centimetres) thick.

Another experiment based on Bronze Age housing, reconstructed at a site near Truro (Cornwall) suggested that the pitch might be steeper, up to 50 degrees, and that the thatch used could be water reeds. This was also the case with a pottery house-urn, used to collect cremated ashes, dated to c.500 BC, excavated at Königsaue (Germany), which showed a high-pitched roof. Rain would run off this more quickly, thus possibly requiring less maintenance. Given careful maintenance, these houses could have stood for many years. Reconstruction of other houses such

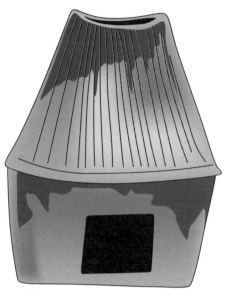

Figure 2 House urn from Königsaue, Germany.

as those at Chassemy (Aisne, France) and Villeneuve-Saint-Germain (Aisne, France) have indicated that these buildings could withstand bad weather conditions. The last was constructed with a far more extensive roof, which was supported by two posts.

The round house built on the site open to the public at Little Butser was 40 feet (15.7 metres) in diameter and 25 feet (7.6 metres) high. A porch was added to it with a double door, but when it was noticed that high winds could sweep in, a smaller door for everyday use was placed to one side. The house has a central hearth but no smoke hole was placed in the roof. The roof covering probably allowed smoke to pass through it. There might have been a problem in that occasional sparks from the fire, sucked up by a conical roof, could have set the roof on fire. Hams hanging from beams could be smoked in the fumes. Basket containers could also have been hung from the beams. The central fire kept the house surprisingly warm in winter and ceramic or iron firedogs, often with animal head terminals, supported spits on which food could be roasted. Cooking pots would be placed in the embers to cook pottage and stews, and cauldrons hung from the beams. At Little Butser, a conical oven has been constructed by the side of the fire. Fuel was put into this and heated. This was removed and food put in to cook, which it did perfectly.

There is an interesting point to be considered which has yet to be answered. The smoke probably drifted into the roof during the day, but on a cold day, when the doors were closed, did the gathering smoke create carbon monoxide within the house and did the smaller door have to be kept open to prevent this? Excavations of other houses have shown that these round houses vary from 15 to 50 feet (5–15 metres). If cooking facilities were not available in these houses, smaller buildings situated round the defensive wall would have provided these.

Fuel would be of wood or peat. The traditional method of cutting peat is to use a tusker, a long bladed spade. This slices out oblongs of peat weighing about 28 pounds (12.7 kilograms). These can be placed one against another, then turned and raised such that the peat is end to end and that the wind can get between the peat oblongs and dry them. Cut in the summer, peat is then ready for winter fuel. It burns cleanly with very little soot and gives out a tremendous heat. Peat is more often to be found in the midland and northern areas of Britain and it is not suggested that this fuel was used at Little Butser.

Benches made of wattle and daub have been found in houses in Hungary and could easily have been replicated elsewhere. Within the larger houses, it would be possible to divide the space with partitions of wood or hide so that family groups could occupy their own areas. The tradition of hospitality, as related in the Irish tales, indicates that travellers would be accommodated and this assumes that sleeping arrangements could be made. Strabo said that the Celts slept on the ground, but other classical references mention the Celts sitting on pelts or hides and eating meals at low tables. He also said that the Celts took their meals on straw couches. These couches could be converted into beds; other sleeping beds could be constructed of leaves and grass or hay covered with skins. Diodorus said that the Celts usually slept on the ground on the skins of wild animals. He then went on to imply that many of the men were homosexual for they slept with a bedfellow on either side. Strangest of all, without any thought for their modesty, they carelessly surrendered their virginity to other men, and far from finding anything shameful about this, they felt insulted if anyone refused the offer. It is certain that the Irish tales assume that close companionship existed between men and that they slept in large halls, but nowhere is there any implication of homosexuality, although this does not mean that it could not exist.

Given a modicum of possessions, a round house could be made very comfortable to keep out the cold and damp. Food debris would be removed and the floors continually swept. There is no need to think of houses that have beaten earthen floors or clay being unhygienic or uncomfortable, for these floors provide sealing layers. Reeds might have been placed over them as was done in the medieval period. It is not known what type of house the Hochdorf prince inhabited, but given the elaborate furniture provided in the tomb, which included the bronze couch on which the dead man was lying, an imported item from Italy, this archaeological evidence indicates a more sophisticated style of living.

Stone and timber houses

Completely different houses have been identified elsewhere, probably because stone was more easily obtained. Dry-stone walling, that is walls made without mortar, were made from stones carefully selected to reduce voids. Some walls, especially those in southern France, had a rubble filled core. At Monte Bibele in the Apennine region of Italy, houses were found which dated to between 490 and 200 BC. Here the Celts had become allied to the Etruscans and as a result their thatched houses were seemingly more sophisticated, being constructed of stone and horizontally superimposed logs and timber reaching two stories and terraced into the mountainside. There seems to be no evidence of upright posts. These buildings were soundly constructed; even so, the houses still had earthen floors with a central hearth. A nearby spring supplied water.

In other parts of continental Europe, stone and timber long houses were built. These were stone houses surrounded by a palisade to confine livestock, but in the winter, the livestock was brought into the house and housed at one end, a practice that continued until at least the eighteenth century. Some of the long houses have smaller rooms or stalls leading off the main living quarters. The open-air museums at Asparn, near Vienna (Austria) and Arnhem (Holland) have reconstructed similar houses from a later date and such buildings give an excellent example of this type of house.

Some buildings were constructed of horizontal beams, that is, walls made entirely of horizontal planks with a complete absence of upright poles. Many form a kind of log cabin where the logs are set directly into the ground or on low sill-beams, which form a plinth. This technique was inherited from the Bronze Age and is mainly found in Germany, as at the Middle Bronze Age village of Buchau (Baden-Württemberg). Here, the rectangular houses were 13–16 feet (4–5 metres) long by 10–13 feet (2–4 metres) wide. Iron Age sites in Alpine regions have shown the same structures. At Hallein (Oberösterreich, Austria), three rectangular houses had low stone walls on which would be set sill-beams and crossbeams. The site of Besançon-St-Paul (France) produced evidence of a two-storey rectangular building, 26–16 feet (8–5 metres) with horizontal beams. The interior had been divided by partitions. These houses were heated by one hearth. A stone house at Les Trémaïe (Les Baux de Provence) showed how simple a house might be. The single room housed a hearth in one corner, a clay bench for sleeping and a storage area for containers.

At Chysauster (Cornwall), occupied until the fourth century AD, houses were placed alongside streets. These oval houses, built of unmortared stone, had a central passage leading to circular or rectilinear rooms with stone flagged floors. Nearby were fougous – the underground storage chambers – and close by the village, a field system indicated that the inhabitants followed agricultural practices.

Brochs and duns

In northern Scotland, Orkney and Shetland, brochs were built and almost 500 are known to exist. These began as dry stonewall houses about 600 BC and their origins are said to be smaller stone-built forts on the Atlantic coast of Ireland. By 100 BC, they had developed into huge, circular defensive towers, large dry-stone structures with walls usually 16.5 feet (5 metres) thicker at the base, surrounded by an outer wall, in which was a fortified gatehouse. The wall surrounded a courtyard in which other buildings were placed. The internal diameter of the towers was wider at the base than at the top to give them greater strength. It is not clear to what height they would have reached, as none have survived complete. Having a single doorway ensured their defence. One or two staircases led to galleries on the upper floors. The interior had living quarters, storerooms and such features as bakery ovens and cupboards built with two shelves.

Most of these features were made of sandstone slabs. At Skara Brae (Orkney), there were two box beds, which could have been filled with heather covered by skins. Tanks contained limpet, cockle and oyster shells, which suggests they had been containers for keeping food. Stone slabs, piled one on another, formed benches. It is not certain whether the brochs housed a single or an extended family. The larger brochs may have been the headquarters of powerful chieftains who exercised control over a wide area and thus over other brochs. These strongly built dwellings, some of the most expressive buildings in northern Europe, must more certainly have been built to exert some form of social control.

The best-preserved broch is on the Isle of Mousa, off the east coast of the Shetland Isles, which still stands to a height of 43 feet (14.1 metres), and has a single door facing the beach. The one, however, which has provided the main evidence for the development of these sites is at Clickhimin (Shetland), which was excavated in the 1960s. The original building within the encircling wall was a round house with a thatched roof, which was occupied during the fourth century to the second century BC. There was a massive blockhouse situated at one point in the surrounding wall, which guarded the only entrance in the wall. This was suggested to be the chieftain's house; in front of it was a parapet walk.

Figure 3 Scottish broch on the Isle of Mousa, of the east coast of Mainland, Shetland Isles.

Half-timbered buildings, two and even three stories in height were placed against the encircling wall. Their ground floors were stables or were used for everyday activities such as grinding corn, curing hides, making pottery and cooking food. Above these were living quarters, reached by wooden ladders. Access to the rampart walk on the walls was gained from here. The floors of these rooms were supported on ledges or project-ing stone courses, a feature that has been noted in other Scottish stone forts, and in Iron Age Alpine forts, especially in the Hallstatt region. Later, the round house was replaced by a huge broch, which was in use until the second century AD.

The main weakness of these structures was that they could be vulnerable to a prolonged attack using firebrands attached to spears. Many of the Scottish brochs show evidence of vitrification caused by burning of the timber floors and the fierce heat of the conflagration. Accidental fire from a central hearth may also have caused problems.

Defence against external enemies could be improved by raising the outer wall, which seems to have happened in some of the Orkney brochs, but many of them fell victim to raiders during the second century AD. Henceforth their stonework was robbed for building other settlements.

This kind of defensive dwelling seems to have been paralleled in Ireland where, according to the Irish texts, tribal chieftains occupied forts with many rooms. These were stone-built structures called duns and their structures appear in the Irish tales. The story of Diamuid told how he fell in love with Grainne, wife of Finn, chieftain of his tribe. The couple planned to escape, but Finn held the keys to the doors. Grainne therefore told her lover that there was a side door, a wicker gate to her chamber, whereby they could escape. This type of door, often covered with hide for greater protection, has been noted in excavations in Europe. Diamuid protested that he was prohibited from going through such a gate by a taboo. So Grainne suggested that he could leap over the walls of the fort by using the shafts of his spears to exert pressure for such a leap. Diamuid therefore went to the top of the fort, using a door to the rampart walk, put the shafts of two spears under him and rose effortlessly with a huge leap over the ramparts, landing onto a grassy field where Grainne was waiting for him. In an earlier tale of the *Exile of the Sons of Usnech*, Naisi, who had carried off Deirdre from the land of Ulster, was alone on the ramparts when he let forth his musical war cry. Deirdre heard this and rushed from her apartments onto the rampart.

Bricriu, when he gave his feast, erected a large house of nine compartments with a high balcony, allowing him to view the interior. The feast was spoilt when Cu Chulainn, when denied the champion's portion, heaved the house up on its side. Bricriu and his wife fell from a first-floor balcony into the middle of the courtyard amongst the dogs.

There are other references in the Irish tales to high buildings, many situated above main gates from which could be observed the approach of enemies. In the tale of the *Burning of Da Derga's Hostel*, a spy, watching from the main gate described what was going on in the various houses in the courtyard. There were seven doorways to the house and seven rooms between the doorways. MacDatho's Hostel was described as having seven doors and fifty beds between these doors. A house with multiple rooms would be fitted out with beds, couches and minor equipment to make them habitable and provide the level of service of hospitality, which was expected in Ireland.

Crannogs and lake villages

These settlements were situated in places, which could more easily be defended. Caesar had noted them in Gaul. He said that when he advanced into the territory of the Morini (a Gallic tribe living on the coast of Belgium and northern France), he found it difficult to defeat them because they took refuge with all their belongings in a region protected by forests and marshes. He was only successful when the marshes dried up.

Crannogs were first constructed in the Bronze Age and almost 400 of these in both the Bronze and the Iron Ages have been found in Scotland; some have also been found dated to a later period in Ireland. The Scottish Trust for Underwater Archaeology has reconstructed one of these on Loch Tay (Perthshire). These structures provided protection against attacks by human enemies and wild animals, for wolves and bears roamed the region during the Iron Age. Piles were thrust into the water and over these an artificial mound of branches, moss and earth was created which could only be approached over a wooden causeway, which could be destroyed if there was an attack on the settlement. The defensive situation would also prevent attacks by bears and wolves on livestock. A house, surrounded by a wooden platform, was built on the mound usually being of 49 feet (15 metres) in diameter. As elsewhere, the walls were made of wattle and daub and the roof would be thatched with reeds. Excavations have also shown that these houses, like the round houses, would be divided into sections, presumably giving some form of privacy to the occupants. A central hearth provided warmth and beams in the roof allowed produce to be smoked.

Crannogs were usually built to house a single house. At Glastonbury (Wiltshire), a lake village was excavated in 1911, where the inhabitants relied on the protection of a swampy area of 2–4 acres (0.8–1.62 hectares). A palisade of piles joined by wattle and daub surrounded foundations of logs reinforced by brushwood, stones and clay. Swiss lake villages also had a floor of clay placed over layers of branches. On the inner side of the palisades were several sections of timber, clay and other material arranged in layers 5 feet (1.5 metres) deep and 10 feet (3 metres) wide, which were suggested to be fighting platforms. The only evidence for the houses were mounds 20–30 feet (6–9 metres) in diameter, which were the remains of round houses with a central hearth. Gradual sinking of the floor resulted in at least ten successive layers being built up, thus resulting in the mound.

Some houses appeared to have stone flags, but every piece of stone had to be brought from at least 2 miles (3.21 kilometres) away. Pathways between the houses were made of rubble and worn sandstone. A landing stage was attached to the village with vertical walls of grooved oak planks driven into the peat. A causeway led to firmer ground, but this might be covered in wetter weather so the inhabitants would need log boats or coracles. One log boat was found, 16 feet (4.8 metres) long, hollowed out to 1 foot (0.34 metres) in depth. It was suggested that the village might have supported a population of between 200 and 300 people. The village lasted from the second century BC to the first century AD, when it was destroyed. Many of the huts were burned as if enemies had at last been able to approach the village, possibly because the marshes had dried up as indicated in Caesar's account of his attack on the Morini.

Hillforts

Hillforts, referred to by the Romans as oppida, were chosen for their location. They vary in size and shape but all are distinguished by their defensive ditches and ramparts, often reaching 33 feet (10 metres) high. Some hillforts may have been used as refuges in times of trouble where people, together with their goods and animals, would gather until danger had passed. Others were large permanent nucleated centres as at Manching (Bavaria, Germany), the capital of the tribe of the Vindelici, which by the first century BC had developed into a Celtic town of 900 acres (380 hectares). It probably had a large permanent population and functioned as an economic production unit. As it was situated on the bank of the Danube, it could collect toll from the boats passing along the river and water supplies would easily be obtained from there. Stout walls surrounded the hillfort. These consisted of a box structure of two stone walls with cross-timbers placed horizontally between them. The centre was filled with rubble and stone. Caesar noted their presence in Gaul and referred to them as *murus gallicus*. The Manching walls were 5 miles (8 kilometres) in length and 16.5 feet (5 metres) high. Within these walls were huts concentrated in the central area, the other spaces being left to the animals. Manching was destroyed in 15 BC probably as a result of the Roman advance to the Danube. Similar walls have been found at Bibracte (Mont Beuvray, France), the capital of the Aedui tribe. This hillfort was abandoned when the Romans founded the nearby settlement of Autun, thus revealing to the Celts an easier and more comfortable way of life.

These large structures imply evidence of defensive planning on the part of an organised political community. They might be defined as civil engineering projects with the intention of providing protection for a settled community. They were probably constructed within a reasonable length of time. A fort of 10 acres (4.04 hectares), which may have housed sixty families, could be constructed within four months provided there was collective organisation with a central authority directing the work and possibly specialists involved for entrances and defensive designs.

Something similar happened in Britain. During the 1920s and 1930s, in Britain, excavations of hillforts concentrated on the defences on the assumption that the prime function of a hillfort lay in the safety it would give to people in surrounding areas who sought refuge in it. This was certainly the case at the recently identified hillfort of Roulton Scar Bank (Yorkshire), where the hillfort, placed on a promontory, backing on to a huge cliff face, was used as a temporary refuge or a giant corral for livestock. At the narrow neck of the promontory there was a 12 feet (3.65 metres) high rampart and timber palisade. Its exposed position made it unlikely that it was a permanent settlement.

It was only in 1934 when Mortimer (later Sir Mortimer) Wheeler excavated one of the largest hillforts in Britain, Maiden Castle (Dorset), that the interior of a hillfort was studied in detail. Wheeler went beyond the triple ramparts, defensive ditches and monumental entrances to concentrate on the interior. The excavation showed that the interior of the site, occupied from the Bronze Age until the first century AD, contained a settlement of round houses with a series of pits used for storage and rubbish disposal. Wheeler was able to refer to Maiden Castle as a hill town. Recent reinterpretation and further excavation of the hillfort has suggested that the size and number of houses might indicate that the site was a central grain store for communities surrounding Maiden Castle. The strong defences of massive ramparts and ditches, reinforced by limestone walls, could not prevent the hillfort being overrun by the Romans during the future Emperor Vespasian's advance towards the southwest in AD 43. The attack may have lasted but a single day, and the inhabitants were later removed to the lowland area becoming citizens of the Roman town of Dorchester.

The claim that a settlement in a hillfort can be a town has been substantiated by excavations at Staré Hradisko (Czechoslovakia) where rectangular stone buildings were arranged along a rectangular grid of streets. A similar pattern was seen at Croft Ambrey and Credenhill (Herefordshire). The large hillfort of Danebury (Hampshire) was occupied from c.650 to 100 BC and ended in disaster when the gate was burned and the hillfort abandoned. The site, which covered 12 acres (4.85 hectares) and probably had a population of between 200 and 400, was excavated in detail over twenty years from 1968. It developed from a simple bank and ditch defence to a more complex earthwork with elaborate entrances. The main gates were probably supported by massive timbers and would have a bridge over the entrance connecting to the ramparts so that the guards could cross it and keep careful watch on anyone approaching.

The interior showed clear evidence of a settlement of two types of houses, one constructed of upright planks and a thatched roof, the other had wattle and daub walls. Some were arranged alongside a road, others placed behind the rampart. The latter have been suggested to be used for storage rather than human occupation. There were a huge number of storage pits, at least 1,600, which raises comparison with the number of those at Maiden Castle. These pits, the equally large number of four- and six-post structures (presumably small, raised granaries) and the storage houses might suggest that the hillfort gathered an intensive production of corn into one place. That corn was gathered from a wide area is revealed by the number of weed seeds found in examples of carbonised grain, which came from a variety of soils. This centralised storage might have been intended as a form of social control by redistribution of a vital commodity.

Irish hillforts

Most Irish hillforts are more simply constructed than those found in Briton. Some called raths or cashels cover a small area. They are enclosed by a small stone or earth rampart and may have been a family farmstead. Others have larger ramparts and deeper ditches and occupy a more commanding position. They may be dramatically placed on a cliff top, such as Dun Aengus on the Isle of Inishmore, Aran, Co. Galway, and which may have had some ceremonial function. These sites were usually in the western areas, which could be significant in Irish tribal or military concerns. Yet others are promontory forts where artificial defences guard the weakest side and other sides descend from a steep plateau as at Lurigethan (Co. Antrim) and Caherconree (Co. Kerry). Within these a large community could be sheltered.

The greatest of these forts, mentioned both in the Irish texts (Co. Meath) and Emain Macha, is Tara which has been identified with the fort of Navan, east of Armagh. Tara, called Ráth na Riogh (Fort of Kings), is placed on a hill rising 300 feet (91.5 metres) above the surrounding countryside commanding an all-round view. It was not intended as a defensive site as the defence consists merely of an outer bank and ditch. Inside are two ringworks, one of which has a mound in the centre on which is a stone structure. This is called the Stone of Destiny and the two names of the site may indicate its special status as the place where the High Kings of Ireland were acclaimed. Inside at one end of the hill are two parallel lines believed to be part of a large banqueting hall 200 yards (183 metres) by 30 yards (27 metres), which was the site of a feast held every three years. In the time of Cormac, the High King of Ireland, there was said to have been 1,000 people feasting, on one occasion, for a week served by 300 men. The site was believed to have been abandoned during the sixth century AD.

Emain Macha – a huge circular hilltop enclosure, covering 18 acres (7.28 hectares) and surrounded by a bank and ditch – was the site of the

Kings of Ulster being both a site of assembly and for making religious proclamations. It probably began in the seventh century BC and excavations have revealed that the site began as a humble farmstead. After 400 BC, a huge timber structure about 450 feet (137 metres) in diameter with timber uprights, set in huge post pits was erected. Inside were four concentric rings of posts. There was a huge post at the centre, which was needed to hold up the roof. This might have been constructed for ritual purposes or was one of the great hostelries mentioned in the Irish tests. Later, about 94 BC, it was replaced by a smaller circular structure, at least 130 feet (39.5 metres) in diameter, covered by a conical thatched roof held up by a central pole 36 feet (11 metres) high. Soon this was burned down, and over the remains was erected a stone mound about 130 feet (39.6 metres) in diameter and 15–17 feet (4.6–5.1 metres) high. The site was occupied until at least the fifth century AD, when like many other sites it was abandoned.

Other royal sites may have been Dun Ailinne (Knockaulin, Co. Kildare), where the Kings of Leinster were proclaimed, and Rathcroghan (Co. Roscommon), the proclamation place of the Kings of Connacht. This site is vast, covering 4 square miles (10.36 square kilometres), but its size may be associated with it also being the place where an annual fair was held. The war goddess the Morrigan was also believed to be associated with the site. Royal sites may have been purely ceremonial places as the Kings and Queens of Ireland moved their courts around the kingdoms staying with their nobles and keeping a firm grip on them.

Some idea of the structures erected on these sites may be deduced from the Irish texts. In the tale of the *Intoxication of the Ulstermen*, two Druids, Crom Deroil and Crom Darail, foster sons of the Druid Cathbad, were on the ramparts of Tara watching and guarding every side of the fort. They saw the approach of a large company of warriors. According to the Irish text, in poetic language they identified the chariots to the fort ramparts, and the shields of the warriors to the columns and frames of the doors of the royal stronghold. All known doors preserved in Irish Iron Age forts have a flat stone or timber beam lintel and the doors were rectangular or oblong in shape, presumably like the oblong La Tène shields. The Druids equated the red spears of the warriors to the antlers and horns of wild beasts, and these would have been suspended above the doors of the forts and along the roof ridge in much the same manner as occurs in modern hunting lodges. The horses of the warriors are then compared to the cattle or flocks of sheep which grazed in the fields round the fort. The attack is a graphic description by someone who knew these forts and houses but who could transpose their features into poetic language.

In a later version of the story, the Ulstermen were taken to a huge, secure, oaken house with a yew door 3 feet (1 metre) thick having iron hooks to secure it. This house was furnished with flock beds and bed coverings. The men were given heated water for washing and provided with plentiful food and drink until they subsided into a drunken sleep. The house was then girded with seven chains of iron and fires were lit below and above it. Needless to say, led by Cu Chulainn, the Ulstermen escape their peril.

Study of descriptions of houses in the other texts allows evidence of these Irish Celtic houses to merge. Given that the tales are the product of the imagination of storytellers, allowance must be made for imagination but equally there may be more than a grain of truth in the descriptions. The houses appeared to be large communal halls with a large numbers of doors, which formed the centre of a royal court, as could have been the case at Tara. These could have been used for feasting, but within them would be compartments given to a variety of uses – grinding corn, smithing and stalling for cattle in the winter months. Sleeping quarters divided into compartments and containing beds would be provided either on the ground floor or an upper floor. The upper floors allowed access to a parapet walk through wicker doors. The appearance of these halls was probably imposing and meant to be so.

The great courts of Ireland in their huge houses and palaces lasted throughout the Celtic period. Later they were abandoned as the missionaries brought the Christian faith to Ireland. In AD 800, the poet Aenghus was to write, 'Tara's mighty burgh perished at the death of princes; with a multitude of venerable champions, the great height of Armagh abides; Rathcroghan has vanished with Ailill, offspring of Victory; fair the sovereignty over princes that there is in the monastery of Clonmacnoise; Aillenn's proud burgh [Emain Macha] has vanished, save that the stones remain; the cemetery of the world is multitudinous Glendalough.' Aenghus lamented the death of Celtic Ireland but rejoiced in the rise of a Christian Ireland led by St. Patrick who founded his Bishopric at Armagh, not far from the principal High Court of the Kings of Ulster.

Chapter 4
Warriors and Warfare

The Celts were a warrior society and their warlike prowess, strength and courage, even foolhardiness, was admired, if not emulated, by other nations. Their social system was such that it was geared to fighting, especially for the aristocracy, in order to accept any challenge and prove heroic status. Strabo said, somewhat contemptuously, that the whole race, which is now called Gallic or Galactic,

'is war-mad, high-spirited and quick to battle, but otherwise straight forward and not of evil character. And so, when they are stirred up they assemble in bands for battle, quite openly and without foresight so that they are easily handled by those who desire to outwit them. For at any time or place and whatever pretext you stir them up, you will have them ready to face danger, even if they have nothing on their side but strength and courage.'

He added that 'their strength depends both on their mighty bodies and on their numbers and because of this frank and straightforward element in their character they assemble in large numbers on slight provocation, being ever ready to sympathise with the anger of a neighbour who thinks he has been wronged'.

The Celts had to keep themselves fit. Strabo noted that they tried not to become pot-bellied and any young man who exceeded the standard length of a girdle was fined. If Strabo's descriptions are accurate, it implies that Celtic wrath was roused on both tribal and personal levels with a delight in conflict for its own sake not just for a reasonable cause, although there could be elaborate codes of honour attached, which ensured that hostilities and aggression could be controlled if convention demanded.

Livy said that the Gauls stood first in their reputation for war. So fierce was their fighting that, he commented poetically, this fierce tribe, travelling up and down in war, had almost made the world its residence. Athenaeus quoting Poseidonius confirmed this love of fighting: 'The Celts sometimes fight after a dinner: they gather their arms to engage in a mock battle – drill, thrust and parry. But sometimes they are wounded and are so irritated that they slay their opponents unless the onlookers hold them back.' This is paralleled by descriptions of the high temperament shown time and again in the Irish texts. Bricrui's feast is a classic example. He was determined to cause trouble and used the awarding of the champion's portion to do this, ordering it to be given to the greatest hero of all. At once Loegaire's charioteer claimed it for his master, but so did the charioteers of Conall and Cu Chulainn. The result was that the three warriors began to fight, putting the house into tumult. It took Sencha the Druid to take the initiative ordering King Conchobar to separate them.

Boys were trained to fight at an early age and the system of fosterage ensured that they learned their warrior trade from one of the finest warriors. Display of personal courage was essential and the taking of arms indicated the acceptance of manhood. The boyhood deeds of Cu Chulainn were probably a typical example of the rivalry, which existed amongst the young men and the urge felt to display martial prowess.

Games and exercises

Warriors kept themselves fit mentally and physically by playing games. In the Irish texts, board games are played, especially *brandub* (black raven) and *buanbach*. *Fidchell*, which is also mentioned in Welsh tales as *gwyddbwyll*, was played on a squared board with wooden pegs representing opposing forces. It could be played for very high stakes as in the Irish tale of *The Wooing of Étáin*, which also had an unexpected agricultural outcome. Étáin was wooed by Eochaid Airem, king of Ireland, and married him, but she had originally been a goddess married to the god Mider. He came seeking her, but she refused to return to him. He therefore approached Eochaid and, producing a silver board, with costly stones set into it and players of gold men, suggested that they played a game. Eochaid said that he would not play except for a stake. Mider said that he would offer fifty high-spirited, dark grey steeds.

Three times Mider lost, probably at his own wish, but instead of accepting the horses Eochaid demanded that Mider perform certain services such as clearing away the rocks from the plains of Meath, removing the rushes round the fort of Tethba and building a causeway across the bog of Lamrach. These tasks were carried out, but it was noted that the oxen, which did this task, wore yokes. Until then the Irish had harnessed oxen by placing a strap across their forehead. In future they would use the method of yoking the oxen.

Because of this denial of the original wager, Mider demanded another game and the stake was that he should hold Étáin in his arms and kiss her. He allowed Eochaid to win the first game but then won the next. Eochaid still prevaricated, but Mider demanded that the wager should be honoured. He took Étáin in his arms and the two were carried through the smoke hole of the house. When Eochaid and his followers rushed out, they saw two swans circling round Tara.

In the Welsh *Mabigonion*, the tale of *The Dream of Rhonabwy* details a game of *gwyddbwyll* played with a silver board and gold men between Owein and Arthur. The games are constantly interrupted by demands by a squire that there are battles being fought and that Owein should come, but each time he replies 'play this game'.

Field sports included a game similar to hockey or the Irish game of hurley. When the young Cu Chulainn made his way to the court of King Conchobar, he enlivened his journey by hitting a silver ball with a bronze curved stick, throwing the stick after it, then a javelin and lastly a spear. Rushing after them, he would catch them in sequence, holding the spear by its tip. When he arrived at the court of King Conchobar, he saw 150 court boys playing a ball game similar to hurley. He dived amongst them and sent a ball into the goal. The boys attacked him but he parried all their attacks. He was then prevented from playing with them, as he had not asked their permission. This did not deter the young hero and so, when they resumed play, in true heroic fashion, he stopped thrice fifty balls from going into the goal and put thrice fifty balls in it, holding all the boys at one end while he alone guarded the goal. At the same time, he so terrified the boys that at least fifty of them pretended to lie dead on the grass so as not to face his onslaught.

The game akin to hockey or hurley may be that displayed on a pottery mould now in the British Museum but found at Kettering (Northamptonshire), where a naked figure holds a curved stick upright in his right hand and a ball in the other. This is replicated by one of the plaques depicting a figure on the ritual crown found at Hockwold-cum-Wilton (Norfolk), who also holds an upright curved stick in the right hand and a ball in the left.

Offensive weapons

The archaeological evidence for arms comes from burials. Swords were the chief weapons. Celtic swords were well forged. Made of iron, they were stronger and more efficient than Bronze Age ones but they could have a flaw. Polybius said contemptuously that at the Battle of Telamon in 225 BC when the Insubres fought against the troops of Gaius Flaminius in Northern Italy, their swords bent after the first stroke and had to be straightened with the foot, thus allowing the Romans to swoop down on them. Hallstatt swords were short, about 16–24 inches (40–60 centimetres) long, with the hilt branching out into antennae.

La Tène swords were longer so that they were a slashing rather than a stabbing sword. These were worn on the right-hand side, often attached by two loops on the scabbard to a waist belt of leather or metal. Some tribes, as seemingly did the Parisii in Yorkshire, wore the sword across the back, but this meant that they took time to draw it. By the second century BC, swords had reached a length of almost 35 inches (90 centimetres), which were more useful for cavalry. The Greek historian, Dionysius of Helicarnassus who lived in Rome from 30 BC, said that warriors threw the whole weight of the body behind the sword as they slashed as if they intended to cut to pieces anyone who opposed them. Diodorus said that the Celtiberians had two-edged swords of excellent iron, capable of cutting anything, and that the men carried a dagger for close fighting. They had a custom of burying swords in the ground to see if there was soft iron in them. If there was, it would rust and the weapon was re-forged. This ensured that the swords were of exceptional quality with a strong cutting edge.

Irish texts mention ivory and gold-hilted swords such as those used by Cu Chulainn and Ferdiad in their fight in the Irish tale of *The Cattle Raid of Cooley*. A wooden or metal scabbard ended in the shape of a ball or a fishtail. One sword found at a burial at Whitcombe (Dorset) had decorative mountings and two iron suspension rings. In addition, men carried a dagger, usually with an anthropoid hilt, that is with a head engraved on the apex of the hilt, probably part of the worship of the cult of the head. The Hochdorf prince wore a decorated dagger encased in gold.

Strabo mentioned a wooden weapon that was thrown by hand with a range greater than that of an arrow. It was mostly used for hunting birds, but it could be used in battle.

Warriors also had a basic equipment of between one and four spears or javelins, using short ones as projectile weapons and longer ones for thrusting. Diodorus noted that some javelins had longer points that the Roman swords. Some leaf-shaped spearheads found in graves were 18 inches (46 centimetres) long, with crimped or cut-out edges. A complete La Tène spear could be up to 8 feet (2.5 metres) long and the Romans had to alter their tactics to prepare for the downward swoop of these spears when they were thrown. Diodorus also mentioned spears about this long, some having straight heads and some twisting round 'its purpose being to thrust and mangle'.

This may be akin to the fearsome weapon mentioned in the Irish texts, the gae bulga, which Cu Chulainn used in his final onslaught against Ferdiad and also in his fight when he killed his own son. It consisted of a spearhead with a large number of barbs below it. When the weapon entered the body, it could not be pulled out without mangling the flesh. In Ferdiad's case, it cut though his shield and iron armour and went through the body until every joint and every limb was filled with its barbs. Diodorus commented that the Celtiberians hurled this weapon to great effect over long distances. Polybius noted that one group of warriors who fought naked apart from wearing a torc were called Gaesatae; these warriors may have used a similar weapon.

Arrowheads have been found in graves. The Hochdorf grave contained a quiver of iron-tipped arrows, but the bow and arrow did not seem to have been used normally in battle. The Gallic chieftain Vercingetorix, however, ordered as many archers who could be found to be sent to him to make good his losses after the siege of Avaricum (Bourges) and triangular tanged arrowheads have been found at the Celtic stronghold of Alesia. Bows and arrows were normally used for hunting and Strabo said that men were killed with arrows in human sacrifice.

A more conventional weapon was the sling stone. These were not used by the Celts in central Europe and their first use seems to be in Brittany during the first century BC. Huge hoards of sling stones have been found at the Iron Age forts of Danebury (Hampshire) and Maiden Castle (Dorset) as if they were stored ready to repel invaders. A pit discovered at Maiden Castle contained 22,260 beach and clay pebbles. The beach pebbles had been carefully selected averaging 2 ounces (57 grams) in weight. Even so, this ammunition failed to stem the Roman attack on the hillfort in AD 43. In Ireland, Connall made a hard ball of brains mixed with lime. Cet stole this and used it as a sling stone to wound Conchobar. Thereafter when boasting, Ulstermen displayed their brain balls. This may be akin to Caesar's report of Vercingetorix's army using incendiary darts and balls of red-hot clay.

The sling was an ancient weapon. Its deadly effect was seen when David felled Goliath, the powerful champion of the Philistines, with a sling stone and then put him to death with Goliath's own sword (1.Samuel 17. 99). Slings that were in use in central Africa for hunting small game in the 1970s were made of leather, the centre part being about 9 inches (23 centimetres) long and about 3 inches (7.5 centimetres) wide, tapering off at both ends. Leather thongs were attached to each end of the centre part. This would be whirled about the head until at the right moment one end would be released to send the stone forward. The same effect could be achieved with a downward swing of the arm. Practice made for accuracy. It was noted in eastern Turkey in the 1970s that young men could throw a pebble to consistently hit a mark over 656 feet (200 metres); carefully chosen stones could be sent much further, even up to 1,312 feet (400 metres). In the classical period, accuracy with this weapon was such that the Romans recruited troops of slingers from the Balearic Islands as part of their auxiliary forces.

Defensive weapons and armour

The main defensive weapon was a shield. They were made in several shapes as indicated by carvings on the Roman arch at Orange (France) and on the Bridgeness distance slab (West Lothian, Scotland). The latter were rectangular with a large central boss. Burials in the Marne region (France) revealed oval as well as rectangular shields. Simple shields could be made of wicker or wood. In a grave at Owslebury (Hampshire), a wooden shield placed across a body was made of three wooden planks with a bronze boss to provide a defensive grip. Some shields found in Ireland were made of alder with a decorated metal rim. Others like the one found in Littleton Bog, Clonoura (Co. Tipperary), were made of sheets of wood covered with leather; these could be bound round the edge with leather or metal strips and have a leather boss. One problem with a wooden shield, as Caesar commented, was that when the Romans threw spears against an invading Celtic attack, their spears stuck into the wooden shields so that the Celts had to stop to pick them out or to discard the shield, thus presenting an easy target. At the Battle of Telamon in 225 BC, Polybius noted that the Celts suffered terrible losses, as the Celtic shields were not large enough to give adequate protection against the Roman javelins. The Celtiberians had light circular wicker shields; the Lusitanians a very tough one.

La Tène warriors favoured a long shield, which covered the head of the warrior. La Tène wooden shields, recovered from Lac de Neuchâtel, were 3.58 feet (1.1 metres) long. Diodorus said, however, that they could be as high as a man. Virgil also said that tall shields protected the Celts' bodies. Some shields were made entirely of metal. These might be oval such as the one recovered from an old river bed at Chertsey (Surrey) dated to the third century BC and have a pronounced central spine down the axis of the shield. Elaborately decorated metal ones recovered from the river Thames at Battersea and the river Witham at Lincoln may have been part of decorated parade offerings for a chieftain, later presented as votive offerings to a river deity. Both shields seem to have been made of thin sheets of bronze bound together with possibly leather or wooden backing. Shields had a pronounced boss on them to protect the hand, which gripped the horizontal bar behind it. Shields could also be used as offensive weapons so that a shield in the left hand and a sword in the right were used for thrusting and parrying. In the fight between Cu Chulainn and Ferdiad at a ford, Cu Chulainn tried to attack Ferdiad over the rim of his shield, but the latter gave the shield such a thrust with his right knee that Cu Chulainn was tossed right across the water.

The Witham Shield appears to have had a design of a spindly boar riveted on to it, which echoed Diodorus's comments that some of the shield had projecting bronze animals of fine workmanship. In the Irish texts, Erc bears a shield with animal designs on it in red gold and Cu Chulainn comes to woo Emer bearing a crimson shield with a silver rim, chased with animal figures. In the tale of the *Fate of the Children of Tuirenn*, Lug took up his black-blue, splendid-coloured, broad-sheltering, chafer-marked shield, and placed it on his back, the usual carrying place. Splendid though such shields were for the Gauls and the Britons, they were no use against a Roman attack. Polybius mentioned that at the Battle of Telamon a body of Gaesatae went into battle naked, possibly thinking that a form of magic would protect them, but as their shield did not cover the whole body the Romans soon dispatched them. This was a ritual concept of war in which they relied on magic protecting them against the enemy. If they were killed, they would go immediately to the Otherworld, a worthy home for a fighting warrior.

Celtic helmets might have two horns like that dated to the first century BC found in 1868 in the river Thames and like those depicted on the Arch at Orange. Diodorus stated that helmets might have long projecting features, and these could be ceremonial, worn to enhance the height and authority of a warrior or to identify a chieftain in a battle. One found at Ciumeşti (Romania) dated to the third century BC had a bird on the crest with wings designed to flap. The Celtiberians wore a bronze helmet decorated with a purple plume. Small bronze figures of boars found on numerous sites may have been placed on the top of helmets as a form of decoration. Some warriors on the Gundestrup cauldron have birds or boars on their helmets. Other helmets are made in the form of a cap made of pieces of bronze riveted together and possibly decorated with enamel or even gold foil, which suggests a ceremonial rather than a practical use. Helmets found in cemeteries in the Marne region in France were of a conical shape coming to an elaborate point. Some had embossed discs with coral settings; others had gold foil on them. These were probably more for decorative than practical use. Equally decorative was the helmet worn by Loeg. His was described as crested, flat-surfaced, and four-cornered, with a variety of every colour and form and reaching past the middle of his shoulders. This was both an adornment to him and an encumbrance. More practical were the Late La Tène helmets found at Alesia and in eastern Gaul, a squat round shape, with a knob on the top, somewhat similar to the German helmets in the First World War.

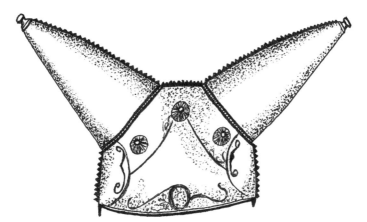

Figure 4 Drawing of a helmet found in the Thames near Waterloo Bridge, London. Courtesy of Linda Ward.

They were possibly derived from Roman helmets as they had cheek pieces and neck guards attached.

Leather also provided some protection. A stone warrior's head found at Entremont (Bouches-du-Rhône, France) wore a closely fitted helmet, seemingly of leather, with a circular brim and flaps on either side to protect the ears. A flap at the back protected the nape of the neck. More impressive were two stone busts found at St Anastasie (Gard, France), dated to the third century BC. These had huge leather helmets descending to the shoulders. A ridge, possibly of metal, came straight down at the back to give protection against a cut from the rear. A similar torso wearing such a helmet was found at Grezan (Gard, France). Both helmets, with their back protection, suggest a resemblance to that worn by Loeg. For

Figure 5 Drawing of a helmet found in a tomb at George-Mellet, Marne, France. Courtesy of Linda Ward.

further protection Diodorus said that the Celtiberians wore greaves made of hair for leg protection, but he does not indicate how these were made.

Several classical writers commented on the Celts going into battle naked. Polybius said that at the Battle of Telamon the naked Gaesatae in the front ranks were 'very terrifying in appearance and gesture, all in the prime of life' and their nakedness was because they felt clothes would hinder them in battle. They were convinced that their torcs and amulets would protect them. The sight of these ornaments, however, made the Roman troops regard such items as booty thus making them all the more eager to fight. Polybius' remarks on naked warriors refer only to the Gaesatae. The Insubres and the Boii, who were at the rear, wore trousers and light cloaks.

Nakedness may have had ritual significance. Romano-Graeco art depicted the Gauls as being naked except for the torc as depicted on the statue of the Dying Gaul in the Museo Capitolino in Rome. A small third century BC bronze figurine found near Rome shows a naked warrior, wearing a horned helmet, about to throw a spear, and having a torc as his sole protection. He also wears a belt, which echoed Diodorus's remark that some of the Celts were so contemptuous of death that they do this going into battle wearing only a girdle. Dionysius of Helicarnassus said that the Celts fought bareheaded, their breasts, sides and thighs all bare. They had no protection from their shields, relying on their long spears and long swords. He commented, 'What injury could their long hair, their fierce looks, the clashing of their arms do us? They are mere symbols of barbaric boastfulness.'

Other classical writers also mentioned the Celts wearing torcs and armlets and although such amulets cannot in any sense of the word be described as defensive armour they had deep religious significance for the Celts as can be noted on the statues of deities wearing them. Wearing torcs probably suggested that Celtic deities protected their worshippers and torcs were obviously considered as defensive magical armour, useless though they were in practice. In 191 BC after the Battle of Bologna, the Romans collected over 1,500 torcs from the defeated Celts.

Not all Celts went into battle naked or so ill prepared. Gauls in the eastern regions adopted breastplates. The Roman poet Statius (AD 45–c.96) said that Vettius Bolanus, governor of Britain AD 69–71, took the breastplate of a British king, which he then wore as a trophy in battle. Diodorus mentioned iron cuirasses as well as chain mail and the wearing of this seems to be confirmed by the appearance of some warriors on the

Pergamum monument wearing chain mail as do stone torsos at the Celtic sanctuary of Roquepertuse (Bouches-du-Rhône, France). Chain mail is a labour intensive product and so fragments of chain mail have been found in Celtic graves as if the warriors had been loath to part with them and deposited at religious sites such as the Roman temple at Woodeaton (England). Other Celts are depicted as wearing leather body protection like the riders on the Gundestrup cauldron and on torsos of statues in Provence. The riders also wear leather breeches. Stone busts at St Anastasie had breast-pieces with three faintly scratched horses on them for decoration or protection, but this was probably of little use against Roman tactics. A bust of a warrior from Grezan wears a breastplate modelled on metal Roman cuirasses.

The Irish texts give descriptions of more elaborate armour but how far they were effective or mere hyperbole is open to dispute. In the tale of the *Fate of the Children of Tuirenn* Lug is described as going into battle wearing a corselet, breast-piece and helmet, his face having the radiance of the sun from the reflection of the helmet. As well as the already mentioned blue-black, splendid-coloured, broad-sheltering, chafer-marked shield, he took his truly handsome, close-edged sword, and his two wide-socketed, thick-handled, hard-venomed spears, which had been smeared with the poison adders' blood. His followers drew broad-edged, gold-crossed swords from blue-bordered scabbards. Finn went into battle even more elaborately dressed. He wore twenty-four shirts of waxed cotton, with over these a plaited three-meshed coat of cold, refined iron mail, a gold embroidered breastplate, a stout corselet with a firm belt decorated with dragons that reached from his thighs to his armpits. The text is careful to say that spears and blades would rebound from this. The weight and splendour of all this protection is obviously to emphasise the strength and valour of the hero.

Chariot warfare

The Romans had met chariots when they were used in great numbers as at the Battle of Sentinum in 295 BC. The tactic that most impressed classical writers in battle was the Celtic dexterity in the use of chariots. Diodorus said that the Celts used two-horsed chariots for journeys and in battle. A charioteer raced the chariot into the battle and manipulated the vehicle, which allowed the warrior to concentrate on battle tactics.

A charioteer in action is depicted on the reverse side of a Roman *denarius* struck at Narbonne about 118 BC. A single warrior armed with a spear and a shield drives the two-horse chariot. As was customary amongst the Celts he rides naked into battle. Behind him is the carnyx, the Celtic war trumpet.

Caesar had never met chariots during his conquest of Gaul, possibly because their use was obsolete there, and therefore was both surprised and impressed when the British chieftain Cassivellaunus used them to oppose him during his invasion of Britain in 54 BC. He noted that they drove all over the battlefield in order to throw the enemy into disorder, before a warrior threw his spear. Sometimes the warrior ran along the chariot pole between the horses, stood on the yoke and then raced back into the chariots before their enemies could react. Charioteers were so expert that they could race the horses as fast as possible, check them and turn the chariot in a moment. Diodorus noted that after throwing the spears the warriors leapt from the chariot to fight with their sword. The charioteers withdrew to a safe distance but were always alert to ensure that if the warriors retreated they could easily mount their chariots to retire from the battle. Caesar's troops countered the Celtic attack by allowing chariots to pass between their ranks, then hurling weapons from both sides as the Celts raced past.

That chariot warfare continued in Britain long after being obsolete in the rest of Europe is indicated by Dio Cassius's account of Suetonius battle with Boudica's army in AD 61. Boudica had led her army into battle in a chariot, riding round to harangue each tribe to urge them to victory and avenge their loss of freedom. In the battle British chariots swooped down on the Romans throwing them into confusion. The Romans used archers to shoot at the charioteers, only to be surrounded by chariots and forced to retreat, before regaining the advantage. Tacitus' description of the Battle of Mons Graupius in Scotland in AD 84 also mentioned charioteers racing wildly between the Romans and the Celtic tribes. They were, however, routed by the Roman cavalry, although there were problems with stray chariots, which had lost their riders running panic-stricken into the Roman ranks. The last mention in classical literature is in the third century AD when Dio Cassius reported that the Pictish tribes of the Meatae and the Caledonians went into battles with chariots drawn by small horses.

In Ireland, chariots were part of a hero's equipment and were the essential attributes of a warrior. In the tale of the *Wooing of Emer*,

Cu Chulainn's chariot is described as being made of fine wood, with wickerwork and a frame of creaking copper, moving on wheels of white bronze. It had a pole of white silver with a mounting of white bronze. The yoke was of gold, the shafts hard and straight as sword blades. As the hero rode to greet Emer, he leapt the hero's salmon feats in the air, which suggests acrobatic turns with an almost nonchalant regard for the rough passage of the vehicle as well as being a display of intimidation. The chariot played a role in the preliminaries and aftermath of heroic endeavour especially if the victor drove away with the vanquished person's head attached to his chariot. More practically chariots were used for raiding enemy encampments or indulging in a frenzied ride after alcoholic excesses. Their use continued long in Ireland after they were discarded elsewhere. One of the most imaginative Irish tales envisages St. Patrick meeting the phantom chariot of Cu Chulainn and his charioteer, which suggests that the chariot was in use in the early Christian era.

Reconstructions of the chariots have been made from archaeological remains found in tombs, ritual deposits and depictions on coins and scratched on stones. One of the earliest finds came from a fifth century BC burial at Le Gorge Meillet found in 1876 (Marne, France), which revealed the remains of a chariot. The wheel ruts would be 4.25 feet (1.5 metres) apart. The warrior laid on the chariot had an iron sword, four spears and a bronze pointed helmet. A meal of pork, eggs and chickens had been placed beside him to feed him on his way to the Otherworld. A bronze wine flagon of Etruscan origin showed that he had plenty of liquor for his journey.

Metalwork found in a ritual deposit at Llyn Cerrig Bach (Anglesey, Wales) was reconstructed to suggest a single-axled vehicle with wooden wheels strengthened by iron tyres and iron hubcaps, drawn by two small horses or ponies with a pole between them. Reconstructions from finds in Yorkshire graves have chariots with a platform and with two hoops on each side; other reconstructions suggest that chariots had straight sides. Possibly some of these sides were of wickerwork so that the chariots could be dismantled easily to be moved to where they were needed. Vehicles were about 1.3 feet (4 metres) long and 6.5 feet (2 metres) wide. One grave found at Wetwang (North Yorkshire) had a dismantled, richly decorated chariot with a platform about 5 square feet (0.46 square metres) and a pole 9 feet (3 metres) long. The wheels were 30 inches (76 centimetres) in diameter. The chariots were open at the front and the back to allow easy access. It is not certain that all chariots were used in warfare; those found in graves could be hearses or the personal vehicles of the grave's occupant. Nevertheless the classical descriptions and the Irish tales are sufficient evidence of chariots being used in warfare.

It should be noted that nowhere in classical literature or in archaeological deposits is there any mention or evidence of there being scythes fixed to the wheels of these chariots. The Persians did this, but the Celts, if they had used this method, discontinued it, although in the Irish Epic of the *Táin Bó Cúalnge*, Cu Chulainn sprang into his scythed war chariot with its iron sickles, its thin blades, its hooks and hard spikes. From a practical point of view scythes would tear off the wheels when they struck a hard object. The only place at present to see such an armed, wheeled chariot is in Thomas Thornycroft's statue (1902) of Boudica and her two daughters portrayed riding furiously towards the Houses of Parliament on the Embankment to the west end of Westminster Bridge in London.

Cavalry and infantry

The Celts were also skilled horsemen. Pausanias reported that when the Galatians invaded Greece in 279 BC, each warrior had two retainers who were also mounted. The warriors went into battle first, but if a warrior was dismounted or his horse fell, his retainer immediately raced up with another horse. If the warrior was killed, his retainer leapt on his horse; if both horseman and horse were killed, the retainer took his place in the battle. If one of the three men was wounded, another one brought him back to the camp. Such skilful organisation meant that warriors were always being replaced. This skill in horsemanship was probably the reason why the chariot was supplanted by the far more effective use of cavalry by the continental Celts. The stirrup had not yet been invented but horsemen could stay firmly in a saddle, which had two tall pommels to hold the buttocks and two front ones angled to grip the rider's legs.

The cavalry were not used as a unit in a tactical attack but were mounted warriors whose skill was useful in battle with either the long slashing sword or the spear. A determined leader would keep horsemen in reserve until the enemy broke and started to run away, then urge on the pursuit to drive the enemy far from the battlefield. There was always the risk that the temptation to loot injured men or the enemy's camp would become so strong that individual horseman would discontinue the pursuit. There were distractions to obtain battle trophies. Diodorus reported that the Celts dismounted to cut off the heads of their enemies, decorated the necks of their horses with them, and then rode off singing a song of victory. At the Battle of Telamon the Roman Consul Gaius fell 'though fighting with desperate courage'; he was decapitated and his head brought on a spear to the Celtic king. It was this indiscipline that made it possible for the Romans to defeat the Celts, but they so admired Celtic horsemanship that they recruited the Celts into the auxiliary of the Roman army, forming them into cohorts and utilising them in a more practical way.

Celtic infantry should more appropriately be described as Celtic tribesmen. There were no standing armies. Each tribe owed a duty of clientage and allegiance to his chief, and those trained as warriors followed their chiefs into battle. Tribes would also join in a confederacy with other tribes. Caesar said that these tribes were then allotted designated places in a camp or on the battlefield. Women, children and scores of camp followers would accompany bands of warriors. These slowed up progress and caused problems on a battlefield, especially when placed at the rear of the fighting. When Boudica's Britons broke before the troops of Suetonius Paulinus in AD 61, their flight was hampered because of the rings of wagons blocking their escape routes. Tacitus reported that given this chance the Roman soldiers did not hesitate to kill the women and the baggage animals gathered by the wagons.

Single combat

Often, fighting allowed a warrior to exhibit his individual prowess and to show who displayed the greater courage. In addition, there were obligations of honour; if a man did not defend his honour, he could be satirised which was akin to being declared a coward. There were social conventions to be observed. Ritual before a battle included a challenge to single combat, which could be the excuse for an immediate response. Diodorus commented that Celtic men reviled each other until one accepted a challenge to battle. The challenger would recount the deeds of his ancestors and proclaim his own valorous qualities, at the same time abusing and reviling his opponent, thus generally attempting to rob him of his fighting spirit.

This was so accepted as part of Celtic honour that it came as a surprise to the Celts when their challenge to Greek and Roman armies for single combat was not accepted, although some Romans did take up the challenge, as did a young Roman soldier, Titus Manlius, in 367 BC. The Roman historian Livy makes much of this event emphasising the battle chant and arrogance of a heavily built Celt against a small Roman armed with a short stabbing sword. The Celt swiped wildly at the Roman, the blade flashing overhead, while the Roman casually thrust his sword upwards though his opponent's loins and belly. In triumph, Manlius took the torc from the Celts, and he and his descendents assumed the cognomen Torquatus. In 348 BC, a tribune, M. Valerius also accepted the challenge of a huge Celtic chieftain to single combat. He was given the cognomen Corvinus because when he attacked his opponent, a crow, perched on his helmet, flew to attack the Gaul's face and eyes, thus almost disabling him. Livy credited this to divine intervention, while the Celts would probably have regarded the incident as sinister, if not a sign that their gods had rejected them, for crows were regarded as omens of death. In the Irish tale of the death of Cu Chulainn, a crow perched on one shoulder of the dying hero. Marcus Claudius Marcellus accepted a challenge of Britomartus, a Gallic King, at the Battle of Clastidium in 222 BC. Marcus won the contest, stripped Britomartus of his gold and silver armour and offered these spoils to Jupiter.

Single combat was common in Ireland and taken up at the slightest pretence. It was preceded by boasting of the deeds of the boaster's ancestors, reviling the deeds of the opponent's ancestors, belittling the courage of the opponent and exaggerating the challenger's own prowess. In this, men were urged on by their followers especially their charioteers. Satirists also joined in the fray, and to satirise a man's honour and warlike capabilities was an immediate invitation to combat. Athenaeus quoting Poseidonius stated that the Celts often engaged in single combat after a feast, the implication being that this was accepted practice, especially if there was a challenge as to who should have the champion's portion. Furious argument often resulted in single combat to the death.

Even close relations were not exempt. Cu Chulainn was challenged by his foster brother Ferdiad and, infuriated by the wonderful feats of arms of the latter, challenged and reviled him. Ferdiad retaliated, but Cu Chulainn retorted that he had not retreated from any one, not even a multitude of enemies, and he would certainly not flee before Ferdiad. Both men were urged on by their charioteers and fought for four days.

On the last day, Ferdiad dressed in his finest garments and carried his massive, fine, warrior shield having fifty bosses with a boar chased on each one and a central boss of gold. The fight lasted long, with even both men's charioteers joining in the fray, but it ended when Cu Chulainn asked his charioteer to throw him his gae bulga. He caught this weapon between his toes and then cast it, so it cut every joint and every limb of his opponent with its barbs. Afterwards, Cu Chulainn lamented and mourned over this foster brother's death in accordance with ritual practice.

Occasionally challenges were not accepted, probably wisely, although the consequences could not be predicted. In the *Story of Mac Datho's Pig*, the warriors of Ulster were boasting about their achievements, and which of them should have the honour of carving the pig for the champion's portion. Eventually the warrior Cet claimed it, but Conall the Victorious approached him and demanded the pig stating that he had never been a day without slaying a Connachtman or a night without plundering, nor had he ever slept without the head of a Connachtman under his knee. Cet agreed that Conall was a better warrior than he but said that if his brother Anluan mac Matach was here he would match Conall contest for contest and that it was a shame that he was not there that night. But Conall said that he was, drawing the head of Anluan from his belt and throwing it at Cet so that blood flowed over him. So Cet had to leave the pig and allow Conall to carve the pig. Some pieces he gave to the men of Ulster, but he sucked up all the rest from the tail so that only the skin and membrane remained. However, this was so regarded as an insult that both Connachtmen and Ulstermen fought each other furiously.

Campaigns

Most Celtic campaigns were probably to extend tribal boundaries, carry out raiding parties on neighbouring tribes to capture their animals and take captive people to work or be sold as slaves. Strabo noted that one of the exports from Celtic Britain were slaves. Caesar said that before his arrival in Gaul, every year Celtic tribes attacked each other or had to defend themselves against a raid. After deciding to do battle, they made frequent vows to dedicate to Mars (presumably their own warrior god) whatever they would capture in warfare and would sacrifice some of the animals they captured. The Celts had no hesitation in hiring themselves out as mercenaries, as one group of Celtiberian cavalry did in joining Hannibal during the Second Punic War, using their long slashing swords to good effect. The Celtiberians were noted for their loyalty as surviving their chieftain in battle was regarded as a treacherous act.

Campaigns would be fought from late spring until early autumn so that fights amongst Celtic groups were usually short, sharp ones.

In Ireland, the Celts spurred themselves into battle at the slightest provocation over land and honour. When Finn's army hurtled into battle, each warrior attacked the enemy furiously, flinging large stones to break heads and helmets. Spears were broken and swords bent, bodies were maimed and lacerated. There was the clang of shields as they were shattered, the crack of corselets as they were broken and the ringing of swords on the crests of the helmets. All this merged with the outcry of the two hosts.

The Celts also relied on a psychological ploy at the beginning of a battle making a massive noise to unnerve the enemy, clashing swords on shields, screaming and singing. Finn's army uttered such mighty shouts that the echo rang in woods, rocks and cliffs, river mouths, the caves of the earth and the cold outer zones of the firmament.

Blowing trumpets and horns increased the noise. Diodorus said that the trumpets were peculiar to the barbarians 'for when they blow on them they produce a harsh sound suitable to the tumult of war'. Remains of trumpets, the carnyx, have been found at Deskford (Scotland) and at Tattershall Ferry (Lincolnshire). Models have been reconstructed from these remains and from images on coins, such as those of Tasciovanus who succeeded his father, Cunobelin, as head of the tribe of the Catuvellauni. The carnyx also appears on the Arch at Orange (France) and on the Gundestrup Cauldron where the warriors are seen blowing them. The carnyx consisted of a long tube at the end of which was an animal's head (probably a boar's head) with an open mouth. In this was a wooden tongue, which seems to have vibrated to produce undulating sounds. According to the images on the Gundestrup Cauldron, the instruments were raised upright as they were blown and these are probably those described by Diodorus as 'producing a harsh sound which suits the noise of the battle'.

Polybius spoke of a dreadful din produced by numerous horn blowers and trumpeters at the Battle of Telamon (225 BC) enhanced by the screaming, shouting and war cries of the Celts, which made it seem that the whole land was alive with the noise. This use of noise to overawe

their opponents certainly made Roman troops hesitate at the beginning
of their attack. Tacitus commented on the noise, increased by the curses
of the Druids, and the confusion it caused the Romans when they
attacked the Druid stronghold on Anglesey. Livy mentioned the yells
and leapings and the dreadful din of arms as the Celts clashed shields
'according to some ancestral custom', all of which was done to terrify the
enemy. He did say that if the Roman soldiers could bear up against the
first onset, into which the Celts rushed with blind enthusiasm, then their
passion exhausted, their limbs would grow lax with sweat and weariness,
their weapons would fall from their hands, their soft bodies and soft
souls would be so overcome with sun, dust and thirst that a man need not
take up arms against them. Livy may not have been entirely accurate,
but he had a point when he commented on the lack of sustained fighting
power. The Celts in battle could easily become discouraged as they were
not disciplined under one man, as the Romans were, but had their own
tribal loyalties, rather than the common good of an army of Celts.

The first Celtic attack mattered. The huge cacophony of sound helped
to urge on the men. It is also possible that their will to fight was fuelled
by copious alcoholic drinking or from even taking drugs. Above all was
the desire for glory. Warriors had no hesitation in rushing into battle
probably urged on by a wish not to be thought cowardly and that if they
died they would be transported to a warrior's finest life in the Otherworld.
Defeated Celts despised themselves. Polybius said that Celts who felt they
were being defeated during the Battle of Telamon were reduced to great
distress and almost lost their reason. Their impotent rage caused them
to throw themselves at the Romans without any regard for their safety,
and those who retreated lost any sense of order and hindered their
comrades thus displaying their cowardliness. Leaders who were defeated
committed suicide for this was a public disgrace. Boudica took poison;
Brennus seemingly took his life after his failed attack on Delphi in 279
BC. Julius Sacrovir, who had accepted Roman rule and was an admired
member of the Gallic aristocracy, followed his Celtic code of honour
when he committed suicide after a failed rebellion against Roman rule
in Augustodunum (Autun, France) in AD 20.

Classical writers noted the bravery of their Celtic foes who withstood
many attacks against overwhelming odds. When Caesar fought against
the Nervians at the Battle of the Sambre during his campaign in Gaul,
he was impressed by the bravery of the tribe. When the first ranks had
fallen the next stood on their prostrate forms. This was repeated, until

the survivors stood on a huge mound of corpses, hurling darts at their
Roman attackers. In the end, almost the whole tribe was annihilated,
so that Caesar stated that only 500 survived out of 60,000 men. Even
allowing for classical hyperbole of numbers, it is clear that the tribe had
conducted themselves according to their own warrior code of honour.

Not all Celts kept to the old traditions. Some tribes adapted and
adopted heavier armour during the third century BC, such as shirts of
iron chain mail and more efficient weapons, becoming resourceful
infantrymen. They were capable of adapting their tactics. When Brennus
invaded Greece, he crossed a river that spread across the plain. His tallest
men he detailed as swimmers. These swam or waded across the river,
while the rest of the army used their shields as rafts for the crossing. Livy
said that the Boii when invading Italy crossed a river on rafts; these might
have been their shields.

Celtic contact with the Romans and the ultimate conquest by Rome
of Celtic lands also made many Celts think about changing their tactics,
but their desire for heroic individual prowess and their traditional ideas
made them, as Polybius said, fail to think rationally, and they lacked the
stamina for a long battle. Some Celtic leaders like Cassivellaunus and
Vercingetorix used tactics which blocked Roman attacks for a while. The
Romans quickly learned to throw their javelins in what Polybius called
'well-aimed volleys', against the massed Celtic ranks, then, protected by
their heavy armour, moved in to corral groups of Celts with their shields,
driving their short stabbing swords into the bare flesh of the Celts and
steadily pushing forward the whole time. The Celts were at a disadvan-
tage as their swords were mainly good for a cut, not a thrust.

Tacitus's description of the last stand of Caratacus against the Romans
in AD 50 indicated Roman tactics. He commented that though at first
the Roman army hesitated, alarmed by the size of Caratacus's army
and by the difficulty of the terrain, they soon formed themselves into
a 'tortoise' covering themselves with their shields to storm the enemy.
'While the light armed auxiliaries attacked with javelins, the heavy
regular troops advanced in close formation. The British, unprotected
by breastplates and helmets, were thrown into disorder. It was a great
victory.' For the Celts it had become either death or fleeing the battlefield.
It was the Roman tactic of a sustained campaign that began to wear
down the Celts.

Once Rome had triumphed, the Romans could channel Celtic love
of warfare to their own purposes. This included persuading the Celts

to join the once hated enemy. Caesar began to recruit Gallic cavalry into his army and, by the early Empire, the Celts were enrolled as cavalry and infantry auxiliary in the Roman army. They kept many of their own customs, but their appetite for warfare directed towards the expansion of the empire and subduing local uprisings was subsumed within Roman military discipline.

Chapter 5
Agriculture and Husbandry

Iron Age society was essentially a rural society. Farming entailed raising crops, tending animals, coppicing woodland and toiling, for toiling it was, at the many mundane tasks, which made up the farming year. Constant application to these tasks was necessary if a family was to survive, especially including provision being made for the winter when food could be scarce. Pastoral farming, tending flocks of sheep and herds of goats and cattle was essential as was the sowing, reaping and storage of crops. Strabo's description in the first century BC of farming in Gaul gives an idea of the effort made to produce food. He says that 'almost all the country produces grain in large quantities and millet and nuts, and all kinds of livestock. None of the country is left untilled except where there are swamps and woods.'

The Celtic year

The Celts had devised a calendar which enabled them to calculate the seasons of the year as well as the elements of time. This has been deduced from fragmentary bronze pieces, dating to the first century BC, found at Coligny (Ain, France). The pieces were reconstructed into sixteen columns, each column divided into four months. The fifth and ninth columns had two lunar months and an extra month in order to adjust the system. This revealed sixty-two consecutive months. Each month was divided into alternate periods of twenty-nine and thirty nights making a year of 354 days. Each month had a dark and a light half indicating the passage of time. A calendar such as this was vitally necessary for an agricultural community that needed to know when was the best time for sowing, growing and reaping or gathering crops. There were also critical periods relating to ritual elements. Pliny, when describing the rituals carried out by the Druids, mentioned that when they cut mistletoe with a golden sickle, the action had to be done precisely on the sixth day of the moon, which, although it had not reached its greatest size, already had considerable influence.

Irish literature provides evidence of the great festivals of the Celtic year. The Celtic year in Ireland had four great festivals and it is probable that similar feast days were held in other parts of the Celtic world. Imbolc (1 February) was dedicated to the god Brigit, later Christianised as St. Bridget. This marked the renewal of spring and the coming of the first ewe's milk. Hence, it was a festival dedicated to fertility. Beltain (1 May), linked to the Celtic god, Belenos, was a cleansing festival when fires were lit or renewed in houses. Fires were also lighted in the fields so that cattle could walk through them and be cleansed. All grass and rush bedding was burned, so that household tasks started afresh. This, although possibly the Celts did not realise it, was the best way to stop infection as pests were burned with the straw.

Lughnasa (1 August) lasting for almost forty days was a welcome festival when food and drink flowed in abundance. It was concerned with the harvesting of the crops and was dedicated to the god Lugh (Ireland) or Lugnos (Gaul). But it was also held to propitiate the gods of the Otherworld to ensure that the harvest would ripen. The last festival of the year and the greatest, although it was the first in the Celtic calendar, was Samain (1 November), which was more a sober and dangerous time. It marked the end of the old year and the beginning of the new and thus allowed the spirits of the dead to become visible to the human world. It was also the time when the male Dagda and the female Morrigan united and thus guaranteed the well-being of a tribe and ensured the fertility of the land.

Land clearance

Land clearance was essential in order to plant crops. This could be done by either cutting down or burning woodland. Experiments in Denmark have shown that iron axes could fell trees of 1 foot (0.3 metres) diameter in thirty minutes. Three men could clear an area of 500 square yards (418 square metres) in four hours using stone or flint axes, but then the stumps of the trees had to be removed from the ground. Modern gardeners can lever the roots of trees out of the soil by using long iron or wooden poles, and this has to be done to prevent continual root shoots recurring. Another method of clearing woodland is by ringing trees and leaving them to wither.

Burning woodland and undergrowth can also clear land. Brushwood burns easily, although fire will spread if it is not controlled. Experiments have shown that crops will grow extremely well in a burned area during the first year, but they will not grow as well in the second year unless the land is fertilised with manure, lime and marl (limed clay). Weeds also grow prolifically in the burned area. These include dandelion and thistle. The first can be used as a vegetable, but all weeds have to be removed before the land is suitable for cultivation. Coppicing also clears woodland, and this is a useful method of obtaining straight poles, which can be used to make wattle fences and walls, as well as providing an excellent fuel. Land clearance was continual and by 100 BC, woodland in many areas had disappeared, exposing heavier soils which could be cultivated, especially once the Celts had invented an iron plough with an iron coulter that dug into the earth and a share that turned over the soil, thus enabling a greater yield to be produced from the land.

Grain

Grain crops were especially important, both as cereals for people and as fodder for animals. This is indicated by the ears of corn, which were stamped on gold coins, in particular those of the tribal chief, King Cunobelin, the only plant apart from the vine to be depicted on a coin. The archaeologist Sir Shepherd Frere suggested that their appearance emphasised the beer-drinking Celts as opposed to the wine-drinking Romans, but the coins also emphasise the importance of grain for Celtic people. Grain crops provided carbohydrates and were an important source of the B group of vitamins. It should be stressed that the Celts had no concept of nutrition and the modern system of vitamins, but they knew what foods were good for them and which to avoid. They also knew instinctively what crops would grow and in what season.

Much of the evidence for grain comes from the identification on archaeological sites of carbonised seeds or plants caused when a building burned down or by over roasting in an oven. The evidence contradicts Caesar's comments in the *Gallic Wars* that most of the Britons in the interior do not grow corn, but live instead on meat and milk. Experiments in growing grain at the Butser Ancient Farm Research Project concluded that the yield from all of the crops grown there was higher than was expected, which suggests that the grain could have supported a larger Celtic population than had previously been considered. All the crops also had a high food value.

The first main cereal crop was einkorn (*Triticum monococcum*), which was known to have grown in the wild before being cultivated. It was a remarkably resistant crop, surviving drought conditions, which could be planted in the spring and left until late summer to be harvested, thus implying that there would be a considerable supply of grain available for the winter. Einkorn also has a high protein level, which would make it a desirable food commodity. This grain was supplanted by emmer (*Triticum dicoccum*), which seemingly gave a greater yield, and spelt (*Triticum spelta*), which because of its hardier qualities had already become an important crop in the Neolithic and Bronze Age periods. Both these wheats had the advantage of being winter-sown crops, which produced grain earlier in the year. This bears out Diodorus's remarks that Britain had two harvests a year, possibly referring to spelt, emmer and hulled barley being winter-sown crops and einkorn and naked barley being spring-grown crops. Most of this grain is bearded and therefore difficult to thresh, but the wheat has twice the protein value of modern wheat. This fact has been appreciated in modern times. Bread made from spelt has considerable value in present health-food promulgation and is now in great demand in Germany and parts of Britain.

Rye was an important crop in the northern regions, because it could be used for human food and as a fodder crop. The Celtic bread made from this was a black bread which both the Greek physician Galen (AD 129–199) and Pliny the Elder said was disagreeable to the stomach. Rye (*Secale cereale*) was, however, a very useful crop as it could survive bad weather. Barley (*Hordeum vulgare*) grew in the wild before it was cultivated. There were two kinds: hulled barley was sown in the winter and naked barley in the spring, which therefore gave two crops throughout the year. It was a practical crop being used as fodder for horses and for human consumption.

The Celts used barley to make a kind of pottage, and also fermented and roasted it before steeping it in water to produce an alcoholic drink, a kind of barley ale. Dioscurides, a first-century AD Greek physician who served with the Roman army, some of which time he obviously spent in Celtic lands, said that it was called *corma*, adding that drinking it caused headaches and bad humours, and that it was harmful to the nerves. The Spanish and British Celts also made an alcoholic drink from wheat. Oats was used as a fodder crop but also was useful to provide pottage which, when scraps of meat or fish were added, provided a nutritious dish. Strabo said that both the Britons in the northern region of the island and the Gauls grew millet, which could be used for pottage.

These grains were reaped with sickles. The sickle had a flint, bronze or iron hook; sometimes these were fixed by a tang or a rivet in a wooden handle. It is not an easy tool to use. Ears of corn grow to different lengths and this could be a problem as the reaper needed to grasp the corn just below the ears to cut off the vital part. Diodorus confirms that the Celts did this when he says that they harvest their grain crops by cutting off only the ears of corn. In doing this, reapers were liable to cut their fingers. Experiments indicate that the best method of cutting is to make an inclined sweep and that an unshafted flint blade performed remarkably well. Possibly, many reapers preferred to use their hands to wrench off the ears and then use the sickle to cut off the stalks, which was used for animal bedding or as floor covering for a house. Iron scythes are also found on some sites, but whether they were used for cutting cereals or grass is unknown.

The Celts may have developed a kind of harvesting machine, which was called a *vallus* by Pliny. This seems to have been a large box with metal teeth mounted at the top of the box at the front. The box was supported on two wheels and moved through a field of corn pushed by steers or oxen. The ears were cut between the sharpened edges of the teeth just below the ears of corn which then fell into a box. Two men worked the machine; one guided the animals, the other walked by the side or in front of the machine either to raise the ears of corn or to knock them into the box. Two reliefs, one from Buzenol, the other from Arlon can be seen in the museum at Arlon.

When the ears had been cut, they had to be threshed. Einkorn, emmer and spelt are difficult to thresh, so it was inevitable that, later, these wheats would be replaced by bread wheat (*Triticum aestivum*) and club wheat (*Triticum compactum*). Most wheats were dried in clay ovens before this took place. They could then be trampled by humans or oxen, which released the grains. If the grain was needed for a future date, storage was necessary and examples of a method of storage have been tested by experimental archaeology. They were based on storage methods carried out in other parts of the world, such as South America and Africa at the present time.

Pit and hut storage

Diodorus said that the Britons stored their ears of corn in covered barns and that each day they took out what was necessary and ground it into corn. Strabo, commenting on Pytheas' remarks about the mysterious island of Thurl lying to the north of Britain, said that the Britons kept their grains in barns and that they threshed these grains in them because they could not do it outside because of the rains and the lack of sun. This would certainly apply to northern Britain. Storage of grain in this manner would be suitable in summer in some areas but winter storage might need more careful consideration in others.

To test a theory about the preservation of grain in winter, an experiment was carried out over two years, 1964–1966, on Broadchalk Down (Wiltshire), based upon excavations carried out by Gerhardt Bersu at the Iron Age site of Little Woodbury (Wiltshire) in 1938–1939. Bersu had discovered numerous pits on the site, which could not always be explained as rubbish pits. These were of three types: globular, cylindrical and bell-shaped. The suggestion was made that some of these might be pits for storing corn during the winter months and this was acted upon.

Several pits were dug in 1964. One 5.5 feet (1.7 metres) deep was lined with a strip of basketwork 15 feet (4.5 metres) long and 5 feet (1.5 metres) wide. Chopped straw was put at the bottom, following a comment by Pliny. This pit was filled by threshed barley and covered with a circular plywood lid, bedded in clay, with rubble placed on the top. When the pit was opened in the following March after a relatively mild winter, the barley was found to have kept remarkable well. The barley in another pit, which had not been so securely sealed, was found to have rotted by the action of bacteria.

The next year, another pit was dug and lined with basketwork and a second one left with its chalk sides. Both were covered with lids made of puddled clay and chalk on which rubble was piled. Dung may also have been used by the Celts, as is the case with some African tribes. It is possible that the lids or plugs may have been made as inconspicuous as possible to keep their presence secret from marauders. The winter was a wet one and some of the water had seeped through the lid but although the top grain had rotted the rest was perfectly sound. In the pit without a basket lining, a crust of germinated grain occurred at the sides and this helped to preserve the grain.

Another pit was opened during the winter, some grain extracted and the pit sealed again. In the spring, when the pit was opened the grain was found to have kept remarkable well. These experiments clearly showed that grain, both for consumption and for seed could be saved throughout the winter in underground storage pits. Two other things noticed were that field mice, if they got into the pits, could be a menace and that the basketwork had to fit closely, otherwise the storage capacity of the pits was reduced.

Similar experiments were made as part of the programme at the Butser Ancient Farm Research Project. The chalk from these pits was spread on the fields as a dressing material. The pits were not lined with wickerwork. Instead, the grain was poured directly into the pits. The results mirrored those at Broadchalk Down. The grain kept perfectly well in spite of the fact that it was not parched beforehand. It was argued that the pits could be used time and time again for the same purpose unless there was excessive rainfall, thus allowing penetration into a pit at its lowest level. When grain was affected by water, it became infected with fungal infestation and so the pit had to be abandoned.

Some pits were also suggested to have been used to produce silage which was a method used in the north of Scotland, the Hebrides and the Orkneys in medieval times. Silage is produced when bacteria (*Streptococcus lactic*), which are present in grass in their natural state, generate lactic acid to act as a preservative agent and thereby 'pickles' the grass. Silage would provide useful supplementary winter fodder for cattle and sheep. If silage is made in a chalk pit, acid reacts with the chalk to produce calcium lactate. Presumably, these pits could only be used once. After that they were used a rubbish pits or for disposal of animal and even human bones. Given the amount of land around a house or a settlement there would be no problem in the number of pits, which could be dug. Water pits, lined with clay, and latrine pits would be necessary, possibly also pits used for dying cloth or tanning if a farm or settlement was to be self-supporting.

The large number of pits dug is revealed at the Iron Age settlement at Gussage All Saints (Dorset), excavated in 1972. There were three stages of occupation. During the first occupation (550–380 BC), 125 pits were discovered, with a combined capacity of 8,087 cubic feet (229 cubic metres). During the second stage (300–100 BC), 69 pits were dug with a total capacity of 7,416 cubic feet (210 cubic metres). In the third stage (100 BC–AD 80), 180 pits were dug with a much larger capacity of 17,657 cubic feet (500 cubic metres), many cutting into the former pits. The whole complex indicated that there was seemingly ample room to dig pits for storage of grain, which on evidence from carbonised seeds seems to have been mostly spelt and oats, and presumably for other uses.

Some of these pits might be for salting meat, although in this case huge quantities of salt would be needed. Peter Reynolds has estimated that if a pit with a capacity of 1.31 cubic feet (1 cubic metre) was dug and filled with 80 percent of meat, then at least 44 pounds (20 kilograms) of salt would have to be added to ensure a successful product. Other products might equally be stored in pits. In Switzerland, until recent times, green vegetables were once stored in this manner. Therefore, Celtic beans, nuts and other foodstuffs might have been similarly stored.

Pits found in Cornwall, such as those which have survived at Sancreed and Caen Euny, are called fogous; in Ireland, they are known as souterrains. Both these types are very dry, having lengthy passages often lined with dry-stone walling and small chambers. These could be used for storage of grain and perhaps for other foodstuffs, especially during the winter months. Pits cannot be dug in a marshy area. They are not found on the east coast of England, but they are found in Gaul and central Europe. In some parts of Gaul, they have flat bottoms and vertical walls.

Some postholes found on the site of Little Woodbury were arranged in groups of four. These indicated small four-post rectangular structures which could have a platform covered with a thatched roof. Archaeological evidence of four-post and six-post structures has been found on other sites. Baskets containing food produce or wood for drying could be placed on the platforms. Produce could also be placed in pottery vessels. At the Early Iron Age site of Saint-Marcel-du Pègue (Drôme), excavations in 1973 revealed structures 13–26 feet (4–8 metres) long set on stone flags, which contained a number of vessels made of cob and containing separately acorns, barley and wheat. Similar structures are still seen in rural areas in Spain and Scandinavia at the present time.

Other suggestions are that the structures were chicken houses, byres, hay stores and even small huts or coverings for wagons. Some sites have two or three of these structures placed near a house; at other sites, such as Danebury (Hampshire), a separate site had been set aside for a large number of these. Single postholes might have been for poles round which a haystack could be built as can be seen in rural areas of Europe today. If the ground sloped, then a platform was necessary to create a level structure, which may present another interpretation for the four-hole posthole structure.

Other crops

Crops were grown in fields or collected from the wild. Many of these are mentioned in the chapter on food (Chapter 6), but it is worth considering the most important crops. One of these was the Celtic bean, a highly nutritious food that, if the shells were eaten, would provide fibre. If humans did not eat them, shells would provide fodder for animals. The bean and other legumes were extremely useful as their root nodules provided nitrogen. The Celts probably followed the practice of crop rotation where grain was followed by legumes, which fertilised the soil for the following year.

Fat hen might be regarded as an essential crop. Its food value is considerable, and it was probably the main green vegetable. The seeds, which are rich in albumen, can be ground into flour. Its leaves are rich in iron, contain minerals, more vitamins than raw cabbage and more calcium and iron than modern spinach to which it has a similar taste. It can, therefore, be used both for human consumption and as a fodder crop; cattle and sheep tolerate it but pigs especially love it. It may be difficult to get the seeds to germinate, so many seeds have to be sown to produce a few plants. Nevertheless, it has a short maturation period, so that spring sowing can produce a large crop, which can be gathered from June to September. The Celts would probably have appreciated both the value of the crop and its abundance, which is indicated by the fact that seeds of this plant have been found in a carbonised state all over northern Europe and in the British Isles.

Flax was also a significant crop. Its leaves could be used as a fodder crop, the stalks when retted provided a base for material and the seeds could be pressed for oil. The stalks have to be placed in oval pits for almost two weeks to allow the vegetable matter to rot. Oval hollows on a large number of sites are suggested to be these pits. The stalks are crushed, soaked again and then combed to produce the thread for the material, which is linen. This material could be dyed with woad, and Caesar mentioned that the Britons used woad to dye their skins. They might have used it for this purpose, but they would certainly have used it for dyeing cloth.

Cultivation

Grain and other crops such as legumes were grown in fields, rectangular in shape, probably about a quarter to a third of an acre, which were surrounded by ditches and fences mainly to keep out wild animals or the household dogs. Rabbits do not seem to have been introduced until the Roman era, but wild deer and straying cattle were always a problem. These fields, which have been identified in the lands bordering the North Sea, would be square or lengthwise according to local tradition. Some fields in northern Germany were huge, covering 10,765–38,751 square feet (1,000–3,600 square metres). Many had banks between them indicating a desire to conserve soil humidity, prevent animals entering them and to stop soil erosion. Two so-called Celtic fields at Little Butser were created, each 9,684 square feet (900 square metres), in order to study soil movement and especially lynchet formation. Lynchets are the small terraces, which are formed between Celtic fields on the slopes of hills due to the method of cultivation and the actions of gravity and climatic conditions. Their appearance is an integral part of any Celtic landscape and a sure indication of cultivation. In Ireland, boundary stones and pillars survive marking field boundaries.

Fields have to be ploughed. The first picture of ploughs appears in the Bronze Age rock carvings on Mont Berg near Nice (France) and at Val Camonica in Italy, but the first archaeological evidence seems to have been the ard, examples of which have been found in Danish bogs. This was a heavy beam, bent at one end, which needed a metal sheath, otherwise the wood would be worn away. Two steers pulled this. These need to be trained as a pair and there can be a problem if one dies because the remaining one may not wish to work with the newcomer. A small bronze fitting of a pair of cattle found at Bulbury (Dorset) and dated to the first century BC seems to represent them ploughing both turning to the left, which is what would have been expected as they worked as a pair. According to the carvings at Val Camonica, one man led the steers while another walked behind holding the beam and making sure that it dug into the ground.

The beam passed between the two steers and it is suggested that both neck yoking and horn yoking were practised. This plough did not turn the sod, and so double or cross ploughing was essential, going first one way across a field and then crossing over it again at right angles. At Val Camonica, the carving appears to show one or two men following the plough and breaking up the soil with a hoe. By 100 BC, however, an iron plough had been developed, and this allowed heavier clay soils to be cultivated. The coulter, a sharp knife-like blade, probably wood covered with an iron sheath, dug into the soil, and the share made a horizontal cut to turn over the sod.

If seeds were planted by being broadcast, that is scattered from a bag by hand, they ran the risk, as the parable in St Matthew's Gospel indicated, of them falling on stony ground. The Celts do not seem to have invented a harrow to rake over the ground. A sowing stick, drawn to create a furrow, in which seeds can be placed, or a dibber making holes for the seeds can be very effective. Once the soil is scuffed over, the seeds stand a good chance of germinating. Rakes, however, have been found in central Europe, which would be another method of covering the seeds.

Livestock

One of the problems in considering Celtic livestock is that many of the animals, such as the *Bos Longifrons*, are now extinct, but it is possible to consider what could have been the breeds. The nearest form of cattle are Welsh, Highland and Dexter cattle, the last being bred about 200 years ago from Kerry cattle, the traditional Irish cow. Its hardiness ensured that it was introduced into Scotland and northern England. These animals can be trained to draw a plough, but they were also regarded as very valuable animals, certainly in Ireland, where Irish values of exchange were based on the value of one milch cow and conflicts were fought over the ownership of cattle. Tacitus comments that the Britons were rich in cattle, which could indicate an abundance of livestock.

In the epic Irish tale of *The Cattle Raid of Cooley*, the ambitious Queen Medb coveted the bull, Donn Cúailnge (The Brown Bull of Cúailnge or Cooley), in order that her possessions should become equal to those of her husband, Ailill, who had a great bull called the White-horned Connacht. The tales exaggerate the prowess of these animals. The Bull of Cúailnge could shelter a hundred Ulster warriors from heat or cold, and fifty boys could play on its back. He would sire fifty calves a day, which would be born the following morning. The epic fight between the two bulls devastated the country and led on to the equally epic combat between Cu Chulainn and his foster brother Ferdiad.

The Donn returned to his native area and bellowed his triumph until his heart broke and he belched out great torrents of blood.

Possibly some of the Celtic fields were used as pasture, and enclosure by means of banks and long ditches meant that the animals could be moved from area to area and moved along paths without impinging on growing crops. Some very large enclosed areas on Salisbury Plain (Wiltshire) with funnelled or winged entrances have been suggested to act as 'ranches' where large herds of cattle could be kept. These were superimposed on smaller Celtic fields and may indicate a shift from agriculture to animal husbandry.

Besides being used for traction, cattle provided meat, milk, hides and leather. Probably young steers were culled for their meat; if they were castrated they could more easily be fattened. Cows would be kept for their milk but would be killed when their milk output declined. Obviously, some of the stock would be selectively slaughtered in winter, but if silage were made in pits, this would provide some fodder, as would other cereals. Vetch can also be a useful winter feed for animals.

Cattle were kept in small sheds in Britain. At Little Butser, these were provided in the form of a small round house. At Black Patch (Somerset), excavations revealed that one building in five was set apart from the rest and surrounded by a fence as if it were kept for livestock. In the Low Countries and northern Europe, cattle seemed to have shared long houses with their owners. These are usually about 33–66 feet (10–20 metres) long and known to archaeologists as byre houses. When excavated, they can be identified as long structures with plank or wattle cross-partitions forming what appear to be a line of stalls, a channel or gutter on the longitudinal axis of the building and an internal cross wall with a flagged or timber floor on one side. Such buildings would provide stabling or cattle stalls for animals; a drainage channel for removal and probable storage of liquid manure, which could be used as a fertiliser; and separate accommodation for the family. Part of the presumed stall area has also been found to be rich in manure. These forms of structure remained in use until the middle of the eighteenth century, often having sophisticated family living quarters, as can been seen in the houses reconstructed in the outdoor Arnhem Museum in Holland.

Horses were kept as carriage animals, for riding and as pack animals. They were small, more like the English Exmoor and Dartmoor ponies, and would be tamed from the wild. The Irish texts give ample evidence of the veneration in which horses were held, the skill of both their riders and the charioteers. Bones found on Iron Age sites indicate that the ponies were 10–14 hands high (110–145 centimetres, 43.3–57 inches). Modern horses stand about 17 hands. Horses may have been used for light traction. In Ireland, horses seem to have been trained to draw a plough. According to a reference in the ninth century AD Ciaran of Munster kept fifty trained horses to till and plough his land.

Sheep were probably like the Manx sheep or the Soay sheep, which are found today on the island of Hirta in the St Kilda group off the north-west coast of Scotland. This type of sheep seems to have survived for over 2,000 years, probably, due to the extreme isolation of the island. There the animals are feral, but on Celtic farms they would need to be domesticated and kept in enclosures. Fences would have to be high as these wiry, strong sheep can leap fences up to 5 feet (1.5 metres) high and can outrun a dog. Sheep provided meat but would be even more appreciated for milk, which could be made into a soft cheese, and wool that had to be plucked not shorn. Plucking took place in early May. For this they would have to be rounded up and brought into a small penned paddock. Goats were kept for meat, tough and strong flavoured as it was, and for milk, especially as they produced more milk than sheep. Surplus milk could easily be converted into soft cheese, and the whey from the milk provided a drink for people or was fed to the pigs. Like sheep, goats could not be allowed on arable land, as they might eat young shoots. They browsed and could strip young trees, although they would be useful in eating weeds and thistles.

Pigs were particularly important, but it is still uncertain how they could be kept under control. There would be no difficulty if there were oak woodlands nearby as acorns provide one of the best diets for pigs. They would be related to the European wild boar and therefore more wild than the present domestic animal. Pigs root with their snouts and can easily dig up areas after harvest. They also manure the ground at the same time so that seed can be sown once they have been removed from the land. Pork was the meat most appreciated at a feast as can be noted by the many references to the thigh being the champions' portion and the fact that thigh bones have been found in the graves of warriors. Small bronze figurines of boars have been found on Celtic sites, some probably being votive offerings. Wild boars were hunted, and their prowess was respected as told in the Welsh tale of the *Mabinogion* detailing the hunt of the great boar Twrch Trwyth. Boar hunts often occur in the Irish texts. A great boar hunt led by Finn and his companions took place before the death of the Irish hero, Finn Mac Cumall. The legendry boar of Formael in the Irish Fenian cycle was described as grey, horrible, without ears, without tail, its teeth standing out long and horrid outside its head and who in one day killed fifty hounds and fifty warriors.

Roe and red deer were also hunted. They might have been kept in paddocks or ranches, as the Celtic field system indicates that there were some large tracks of land surrounded by linear banks and ditches. Deer would be useful for meat and hides as well as the antlers being used for tools.

Chickens would be useful for eggs and meat. They seem to appear for the first time in the Hallstatt period in Bohemia and southern Germany. Caesar mentions their presence in Iron Age Britain, although he says that the Britons have a taboo against eating them, but it would be unlikely that such a good source of food supply would be ignored. Bones found on Iron Age sites indicate that chickens were small. They would be like the Indian Red Jungle fowl, which have particularly fine plumage. Unlike modern breeds of these birds, the Indian Red Jungle fowl can fly and as it likes to roost in trees, it needs to have its wings clipped and be kept in stout pens, probably made of posts linked by wickerwork. Bones found on Celtic sites also attest the presence of ducks. Caesar also says that the Britons did not eat geese, but bones found on Celtic sites seem to indicate that they were kept for meat and eggs. These would be an excellent source of protein and iron, while the goose fat would come in extremely useful for cooking. Geese are also attentive sentries setting up loud cries if anyone approaches them.

An important addition to farming was keeping bees. Most ancient species of bees have been wiped out by disease, but it is suggested that bees in the Iron Age were of a wilder species than the present ones. Cave paintings indicate that wild honey was collected where possible, but to have bees on a farm would ensure a constant supply of honey. Wooden, wicker and even pottery hives would be used, although experiments with pottery hives have indicated that bees in these have not survived the cold of a winter. Honey was the sweetener of the Iron Age, but it could also be used as a preservative, for the brewing of mead and ale and probably as a healing agent. Strabo says that the Britons made a drink from the brewing of grain and honey.

The farm would house a number of dogs and cats. Dogs would be treated as working animals rather than pets. Dog bones have also been found cracked as if they were part of the food chain, but some dogs were kept for hunting. Strabo in the first century BC mentioned that Britain exported 'dogs bred especially for hunting'. This export continued. Nemesianus in the third century AD said that the Britons send us 'swift hunting dogs adapted to our world'. Oppian in the same century said that the wilder tribes of Britain have a sturdy breed of hunting dog, which is called Agassian. The breed is squat, emaciated, shaggy, and dull of eye, not a very prepossessing animal, but endowed with feet armed with powerful claws and a mouth sharp with close-set venomous teeth. Its skill was such that it could track its prey along the ground and also by sniffing the air. Claudian (c. AD 400) said that there was another breed of British dogs, which could break the necks of great bulls. Cats, on the other hand, with their innate refusal to follow any will but their own, were kept as pets or to keep down mice.

Life on the farm

Small farms were probably self-contained units, which would try to supply everything needed on the farm including making pottery for such useful articles as cooking pots and cheese strainers. Animals would be skinned so that their hides could be tanned and made into leather goods. The culling of animals provided a ready supply of meat. Bones would be used for broth or may have been eaten by dogs and pigs. Many bone tools have been found on Iron Age sites – pins, needles, toggles, burins and weaving combs; others were carved into figurines. Surplus tools were available for trading and barter. Numerous Iron Age sites have produced examples of loom weights made of clay or pieced stone indicating that cloth was woven on a farm. Fish might play a secondary role in the food chain unless the farm or settlement was near a river or the sea as indicated by fish bones found on sites on the coast of Gaul.

Excavated sites have also produced evidence of simple smithing techniques for smelting bronze and iron. Bronze was necessary for fittings for horse's harness, carts and even simple jewellery. Iron smelting was needed for tools. Most farms would aim to be as self-sufficient as possible, but people do not live in a vacuum, so the occasional traveller or itinerant craftsman would be welcome as providing an easy method of obtaining goods in return for barter or hospitality offered. Commercial and social interests between neighbouring farms and communities would be necessary for such tasks as rounding up wild ponies or to repel intruders.

Work on an Iron Age farm required considerable effort throughout the farming year, starting as dawn broke and continuing until setting of the sun. This required community effort and organisation to make sure that sufficient food was obtained and available throughout the winter months, which might mean all the difference between life and death. Simulated experiences in Denmark and Britain where groups of people and families have tried to imitate Iron Age lifestyles have shown that it was necessary to have a strong leader who would direct the activities and energies of the personnel into the tasks required for survival and, if need be, ignore the majority wishes. Unless clear direction was given and accepted, the community would disintegrate. There was no time to sit around and argue.

The Irish tales indicate that great feasts were held, but these were supported by large numbers of servants. The vast amount of food and drink mentioned at these feasts creates speculation as to how much was obtained by force, by payment or a kind of tithe from the retainer to the chieftain. It might even be a part of the surplus provided on a farm. For the average Celtic farm, feasts might be held, which celebrated the seasons, ancestor worship, and other activities, but overall hard work was needed for survival, and as Diodorus indicated, such a life could be frugal.

Later, when the Romans advanced through Celtic areas, the Celts adapted their farming techniques to those of the Romans so that more crops could be grown and agricultural existence could become more secure. In southern Gaul under Roman tutelage, for example the tribe of the Saluvii round the Celtic site of Entremont (Bouches-du-Rhône) planted olive groves and began to tend vines. Pieces of amphorae found at the site, which indicate that containers were needed to bottle these products, suggest that wine and olive production had begun there, both to supply the community and probably as the start of a local industry.

The Romans introduced a wider species of plants into Celtic lands, thus enhancing diet. Roman scythes and other tools were a more efficient advance on those that the Celts had used and so helped to produce a greater yield. Better breeding of cattle also helped to increase stock production. Celtic farmers could accept these advances or not as they wished. Agriculture and animal husbandry had made great progress in the temperate climate of Europe and some Celtic farmers did not hesitate to take advantage of Roman farming techniques so that their lifestyle improved considerably. It was the Celts in the wilder area of Europe who clung to their old ways, continuing a lifestyle which had probably changed little over at least 800 years.

Chapter 6
Clothing and Food

In his history of the *Gallic Wars*, Caesar, in a throwaway line about Britain, commented that 'All the Britons cover themselves with woad and as a result, in battle their appearance is very frightening.' The first century geographer Pomponius Mela who gave extensive details of Celtic countries confirmed this, but he gave a clue as to the use of woad stating that it could be for decoration or for some unknown reason. The use of tattooing may have been linked with warrior status as it is today when many military men have tattoos as a form of ritual fellowship. Caesar also added that the Britons 'clothed themselves in skins'. These comments, added to the fact that on some occasions the Celts went naked into battle, and so were regarded as a barbaric people by classical writers, made early archaeologists consider that the Celts had no sense of dress. Subsequent excavations and a study of the Irish texts contradict this attitude. The Celts had a distinctive appearance and a love of dress and often flaunted their wealth with costly jewellery. Status mattered and it could be expressed through passionate adornment in clothing and jewellery. Footwear was another matter as it is rarely mentioned in the Irish texts. From evidence found in graves, both sexes wore shoes usually of leather, although wooden sandals were not unknown. The Hochdorf prince wore leather ankle boots with slightly pointed toes.

In the Early Iron Age, cloth would be woven from wool spun from that plucked from sheep akin to those on St Kilda today. In the Late Iron Age, the use of shears allowed the full fleece to be shorn. Women spun wool by feeding it through their fingers and twisting the thread by means of a clay or stone spindle held just above the ground. Cloth was woven on looms, made out of sticks of pliant wood, possibly hazel, the warp threads being held taut by clay or stone loom weights. These weights are often found on archaeological sites, often lying in groups indicating a collapsed loom. Dyeing was done in metal cauldrons using concoctions of madder, nettles, blackberry, broom and onionskins. Pliny, who praised the skills of the Celtic dyers, said that shellfish supply a purple dye, and purple cloth was prized in clothing worn by the nobility.

Male dress

Classical writers admired the Celts as a handsome race. Ammianus
Marcellinus, writing in the fourth century AD, said that all the Gauls were
of lofty stature, terrible from the sternness in their eyes, very quarrelsome
and of great pride and insolence. Diodorus remarked that 'the Gauls
are tall of body with rippling muscles and white of skin'. He noted that
male clothing was striking with tunics dyed and embroidered in various
colours. These may be what Strabo refers to when he said that people
of high rank wore dyed garments besprinkled with gold. He added
caustically that it was this vanity that made the Celts so unbearable
in victory and so downcast in defeat. An embroidered piece of cloth
was found in an Iron Age excavation at Bruton Fleming (Yorkshire).

The Irish texts revel in their descriptions of clothing. When Cu
Chulainn went to woo Emer, he wore a crimson five-folded tunic, long
sleeved and fastened with an inlaid gold brooch. Over this he wore
a white, hooded shirt interwoven with flaming red gold. In his youth, he
wore a green tunic fastened with a silver brooch, and a golden threaded
shirt. Cu Chulainn's charioteer wore a tunic with sleeves opening at the
elbows. In the *Dream of Rhonabwy*, a tale in the *Mabinogion*, a youth
is described as having a tunic of yellow brocaded silk sewn with green
thread, over which he wore a mantle of the same material with green
fringes. Strabo said that the Belgae wore divided tunics with sleeves
reaching down to their private parts and their buttocks. The Iberians
wore a shorter tunic, often of white with a purple border. Tunics could
be belted. Diodorus referred to the Gauls wearing gold-plated or silver-
plated belts. Male sartorial preening was used both to indicate status
and with a desire to impress the opposite sex.

Tunics could also be made of pigskin, which is supple and long lasting.
These tunics seem to be illustrated on seated torsos found at the sanctuary
of Roquepertuse. One torso has a close-fitting, belted garment decorated
with a lozenge pattern. Another torso of a seated warrior from Entremont
wears a close-fitting jerkin of pigskin, indicated by dots, covering
shoulders and upper arms and coming down to the upper thigh. Loeg,
Cu Chulainn's charioteer, wore a smooth, supple, stitched deerskin tunic,
which, being very light, allowed free movement for his arms.

Cloaks were essential for both warmth and, bearing in mind their
length and fullness, indicating social status. Irish chieftains wore

five-folded, that is very heavy, cloaks; so did Irish heroes such as Cu Chulainn. Diodorus said that the Gallic cloaks were striped with closely woven checks in a variety of colours, fastened with buckles. There was a heavy one for winter and a lighter one for summer. The weave was rough and thin at the ends. The Roman poet Virgil (70–19 BC) confirmed that the cloaks were coloured, commenting in the *Aeneid* that the Celts 'were resplendent in their striped cloaks'. Pliny noted that the Gauls introduced check patterns, while Strabo said that the Gauls wore thick woollen cloaks, which were probably something like a heavy Harris tweed that would keep out the rain. That this type of garment continued to be worn is confirmed by Diocletian's Price Edict of AD 301 when a British cloak (*Birrus Britannicus*) was worth 6,000 denarii, a considerable sum. Irish texts also mention fleecy mantles suggesting sheepskins being flung round the shoulders, a practice which survived in country areas in England well into the nineteenth century.

The Gauls had a Gallic cloak which was adopted in Britain and elsewhere as witnessed by carvings on Roman tombstones. This could be worn indoors or outside by men and women and was obviously an essential garment in the winter months. It was a thick, loose, wrap-over garment, reaching to the ground and with sleeves down to the wrists, and may have been belted or fastened by a brooch. There may also have been an attached hood. Hooded cloaks, as indicted by that worn by the Romano-Celtic Philus on his tombstone at Gloucester, were later adopted by the Romans as being an extremely useful garment, especially in the wetter weather of northern Europe. One practical garment was the hooded short cloak, the cucullus, made of leather or cloth. This is seen on a small bronze figurine of a ploughman found at Piercebridge (Co. Durham) and another at Trier (Germany), which indicates its widespread use in the Celtic world. The cloak was also worn by the triad of Celtic deities who were worshipped under the title of Genii Cucullati, small godlings of fertility and wild places.

There were lighter cloaks reaching to the waist. Polybius mentioned these and the warrior in the Pergamon group wore one. Manannan mac Lir, a distinguished prince of the Túatha De Danna, wore a light green cloak, fastened with a brooch, over a shirt, which matched his white skin. When Elotha, son of the Fermorian king, Delbaeth, went to court Eri, both his cloak and tunic were trimmed with golden thread.

Figure 6 Drawing of a bronze figurine of a ploughman found at Trier wearing a hooded cape (cucullus). Courtesy of Linda Ward.

What marked out the Celts was the wearing of breeches. Diodorus stated that breeches (*bractae*) were close-fitting, and Pliny said that Gallia Narbonensis was originally called Bracata because the men living there wore breeches. This item of clothing can be confirmed by a glance at the mounted warriors on the Gundestrup Cauldron, although, rather puzzlingly, these seem to be a one-piece garment covering both the lower and upper parts of the body, as does the one worn by the horned god on the cauldron. A long sleeved, close-fitted tunic and breeches to the knee were more likely to have been normal wear. Several bodies found in bogs in Denmark were clothed in leggings bound round the legs with woollen strings. Polybius remarked that breeches were made of leather. It was the wearing of breeches that according to the classical writers distinguished a barbarian race. Roman auxiliaries wore breeches, but once the Roman army was established in the northern regions, it was soon realised that this practical garment was essential in the cold weather. Many of the auxiliary cavalry were Gauls and their colleagues copied their use of breeches so that Roman legionaries also adopted a form of breeches. Far too late in the late fourth century AD, the Emperor Honorius forbade them being worn in Rome on the grounds that they were an insult to the city.

There was also a looser garment resembling trousers. They can be seen on a small bronze figurine found at Alesia of a sleeping (or dead) Gaul. Another figurine from Neuvy-en-Sullias (Loiret) is dressed in close-fitting trousers and a tunic worn over them. Both garments have diamond patterns on them. Strabo mentioned baggy trousers worn by tribes living between the Rhine and the Loire, and Polybius said that at the Battle of Telamon (225 BC), the Insubres and the Boii wore trousers. The Roman poet Propertius (c.50 to after 16 BC) commented that the Celtic chieftain Virdomarus, who boasted his descent from the god of the river Rhine, wore striped trousers. A fragment of a monumental bronze statue found at Volubilis (Mauritania, North Africa) has a figure, presumed to be a Celt, wearing trousers with a pronounced check pattern. Over his shoulder was a loose cloak that came to his knees.

Wearing of trousers and breeches was a custom, which came from the European steppe lands, and these were the most practical garments for a horse-riding people or to keep a person warm during cold winters. The custom had probably been adapted from the Scythians. In Ireland, trousers are mentioned as being worn only by servants. Charioteers, however, wore trousers and it is unlikely that these men were classed a servants because of the high regard in which they were held.

Men took an interest in their personal appearance. Ammianus Marcellinus, who had served with the Roman army in Gaul, said that the Gauls were all exceedingly careful of cleanliness and neatness. There was no one in the country, especially Aquitania, where one could find any man or woman who was ragged or dirty. This impression of cleanliness is apparent in the Irish texts. They give the impression that most of the men were clean-shaven, but Diodorus said that the Gauls grew long moustaches that cover the mouth. He adds that when the Gauls drink beverages, the moustaches are so long that 'they act, as it were, as a kind of strainer.' This feature is portrayed on statues such as the Dying Gaul in the Pergamon group. Poseidonius said that the nobles shave their cheeks but let moustaches grow so that they cover the mouth, which may suggest a status characteristic. This may be confirmed by the fact that a wooden comb and large iron razor was found by the prince's head in the Hochdorf tomb suggesting that he liked to be shaved, although he would have been likely to have kept a Celtic fulsome moustache. When the Romans subdued the Celts, men preferred to follow the Roman fashion of being completely clean-shaven and with their hair trimmed. Hats are rarely mentioned, but a conical bark hat had been placed on the head of the Hochdorf prince and the Tollund Man wore a leather cap.

Hair was usually worn long. Livy said that the Celts were tall-bodied and had reddish hair. Irish texts mention flowing locks and golden hair. A group of warriors who came to fight for Medb, queen of Connacht, had flowing hair, fair-yellow, streaming manes. When Eri saw Elotha arriving from the sea, she noted his long golden hair falling onto his shoulders. Cu Chulainn's charioteer had very curly, red hair held with a golden clasp that prevented the hair from falling into his eyes. Cu Chulainn in one tale has his boyish, warrior ardour quenched by being doused three times in a vat of water. When he emerged, he had fifty clear-yellow tresses of hair that were like the yellow wax of bees. In another tale, however, his hair is described as being dark at the roots, brown in the middle and white at the ends. This suggests that he bleached his hair, possibly with limewater. Red, yellow and golden hair, held in place by a clasp or fillet, is often mentioned in the Irish texts. Gallic Celts followed a different fashion training the hair into patterns. Flowing locks, a moustache and bushy eyebrows, however, can be noticed on the statue of the Dying Gaul.

Diodorus said that the Celts were vain about their hair, washing it in limewater and pulling it back from the top of the head to the nape of the neck, 'with the result is that their appearance is like that of Pans or Satyrs'. He added that it made the hair coarse and heavy so that it looked like a horse's mane. Washing in limewater or chalky water not only bleached the hair but when set, could give it a rigid appearance of tightly arranged rows. This can be seen on the head of a seated figure from Bouray (Seine-et-Oise, France) and on the backward swept hairstyle portrayed on Romano-Gallic coins issued during the first century BC. Similarly shaped hair as well as handsome moustaches can be seen on small bronze heads found in the Welwyn (Hertfordshire) chieftain's grave. A stone head found at Mšecké Žehrovice in Bohemia also illustrates these characteristics. Limewater could stiffen the hair. The Irish texts mention that if an apple tree was shaken above Cu Chulainn's head, not a single apple would have reached the ground; all would have been impaled on his fierce bristling locks.

Female dress

Celtic women wore cloaks and tunics. Tunics were long sleeved and reached to the ground; men's tunics reached to the knees. When Eochaid Airem went to woo Étáin, he found her adorned in a long mantle, ornamented with a silver fringe and held by a gold brooch, a hooded tunic of greenish silk embroidered with gold, with bow-pins of silver, and a long purple cloak, hanging in folds, made from a fine fleece, held in place with a golden brooch. The Irish texts mention green, red and purple mantles, colours easily obtained from natural dyes. Fringes were probably sewn on. Fedelm, a prophetess who visited Queen Medb wore a many-spotted green woollen cloak held in place by a silver brooch. Dio Cassius mentioned that Boudica wore a tunic of many colours over which she wore a thick mantle fastened by a brooch.

There were more sober clothes. In the tale of *The Destruction of Da Derga's Hostel*, Cailb, who demanded admittance to the hostel in spite of Conaire's taboo against women entering the hostel after sunset, wore a greyish mantle. Clothing on a woman's body found in a bog at Randers (Denmark) consisted of a brown check-patterned woollen skirt and a scarf in twill weave. Some women probably wore short skirts. Women's clothes from a Bronze Age burial mound at Eglved, Denmark, consisted of a woven three-quarter length, wide-necked, long-sleeved jumper, something like a tee shirt, and a short skirt made of skeins of wool held at the hem and the waist. A similar garment could easily have lingered on into the Iron Age.

Two women's bodies, dating to the Early Iron Age, were found in Huldre Fen, Denmark. Both wore skin capes and one a woven scarf. The one with the fur cape had a skirt gathered slightly at the side. This was woven in a neat squared pattern, made by the alternation of two natural wool colours, a golden brown and a dark brown. The skin capes and the scarf were covering for the upper part of the body. Another from Huldre

Fen consisted of a large length of cloth 5.58 feet (1.74 metres) long and
9 inches (23 centimetres) in circumference. It was open at both ends. This
was a complete dress woven in what is known as circular weave. At the
top was a large fold, which could have been brought over as a hood. A
brooch would have gathered the material at the shoulders. This garment
seems to be portrayed on Dacian women on Trajan's Column. In Gaul,
the practical unisex Gallic cloak was worn, a heavy garment, which hung
in folds and served both as tunic and cloak. One cap has been found. This
had been worn by a woman found in a peat bog at Arden, Denmark.
It was an openwork bonnet, which could be fastened by strings, made
of brownish yellow woollen yarn.

Decorated pots found at Sopron in Hungary, dating to the seventh
century BC, have sketched on them women wearing what seems to be
a bell-shaped garment descending from the shoulder to hemline, ending
in an A-line fashion similar to that designed by Dior in 1947. Dots
on them may indicate balls or precious stones. Other figures seem to be
wearing something akin to a crinoline, but as they are placed beside men
playing a kind of musical instrument, this dress may have been worn for
some form of entertainment.

Women's hair could be woven in plaits. Étáin was described as
combing her hair with a silver comb decorated with gold. Her hair was
divided into two golden-yellow tresses, each one braided into four plaits
with a golden ball at the end of each plait; the colour of the hair was
described as red-gold that had been polished. Descriptions of other
women in the Irish texts mentioned flowing golden hair. Fedelm's hair
was described as being long and golden, with three tresses wound round
her head and another tress falling behind which reached to her calves.
Tacitus said that the women who opposed the Romans on Anglesey had
streaming hair. Dio Cassius said that Boudica had a mass of very fair
hair, which she allowed to fall to her hips. She was also very tall, grim
in appearance and had a piercing gaze and a harsh voice. The last was
probably due to the strain put on it by having to address all her followers.

A relief at Ilkley (Yorkshire) probably depicts the Celtic goddess of the
river Wharfe. Her hair followed Celtic fashion with two long tresses
dangling in front of her, which she could easily have been thrown over
her back as the mood took her. Cailb was described as having hair
reaching to her knees. It would seem that women, conscious of their
crowning glory, did not cut their hair short but either braided it or

allowed it to flow freely and could hold it in place by a ball or some form of jewellery at the ends of the tresses.

Women were not averse to using early forms of cosmetics to enhance their beauty. Most of this information comes from the Irish texts. Eyebrows could be dyed with berry juice, cheeks and lips reddened with a herb called ruan. Some texts are often ecstatic in their descriptions. Thus Étáin, who may have prepared herself for the visit of her wooer, had cheeks as red as foxgloves, eyebrows dark as the back of a stag beetle, a shower of pearls were the teeth, so that it was said, 'Every lovely form must be tested by Étáin, every beauty by the standard of Étáin.' Allowing for all the hyperbole, it is obvious that Celtic women were following an age-old tradition of using all their skills to attract men. Some women were averse to this. Deirdre, the daughter of King Conchobar's chief storyteller, said that she did not redden her fingernails as if making herself superior to other women.

Not all Celtic women were attractive. Ammianus Marcellinus said that 'a whole army troop would not be able to withstand a single Gaul if he called to his assistance his wife, who is usually very strong, with blue eyes, and when swelling her neck veins, gnashing her teeth, and brandishing her sallow, robust arms of enormous size she begins to strike blows mingled with kicks, as if they were so many missiles from a string of catapults'. He added that Celtic women had voices loud and formidable but, to their credit, they kept themselves neat and clean and were always carefully and modestly dressed.

Food

The basic food for the Celts was simple fare, consisting of what could be gathered from the countryside and what could be cultivated, as many were now settled people. Iron Age people would know instinctively what was palatable and what was not. Food would be plentiful in summer, less so in winter, but preservation methods would be known so that food was available. Grain, for example, could be stored in pits during winter months. Without the Celts knowing it, many foods supplied vitamins, calcium and iron necessary to health. This did not mean that the Celts lived a healthier lifestyle. Deprivation of certain essential foods, especially in winter, and in other circumstances, would take their toll.

Nevertheless, the tribal system of society ensured that the majority of its members would not starve.

A substantial dish was pottage (or porridge), made from boiled grain or beans. Lindow Man, so called because the body was found in a peat bog at Lindow Common near Wilmslow (England), had eaten a pottage of wheat, rye, oats and barley, which also contained weed seeds. Tollund Man, found in a Danish bog, had eaten a pottage made from seeds of thirty different plant seeds including barley, linseed, knotgrass and gold of pleasure. Seeds of fat hen are found on Iron Age sites throughout northern Europe. Its leaves can be cooked like spinach and are extremely palatable. Sow-thistle, a herb rich in minerals and vitamin A, was found on Iron Age sites in Denmark. It was known in the classical world as it is mentioned by Pliny, who said that Athena suggested to Theseus that he should eat it before going in search of the Minotaur.

Evidence of foods eaten can be deduced from pollen grains and carbonised seeds. Foods gathered from the wild included charlock, a member of the cabbage family, which is palatable when young. Black bindweed seeds, similar in appearance to buck wheat, were ground into flour to make acceptable bread. Silverweed could be boiled, roasted or ground up to produce meal. Dandelion, sheep's sorrel, wild celery, chickweed and burdock were all palatable. Nettles were very useful, because while the leaves could be eaten, the fibre from the stem could be made into fishing nets or spun into a fine cloth. The water in which nettles were boiled also provided a mild antiseptic. Ransoms, a wild form of onion, provided flavour. Even young beech and hawthorn leaves could be eaten in the spring. Celts near the sea could feast on sea kale and samphire, which grow on rocks by the shore. The latter would have been a useful food source in winter, as it keeps well in salt brine. Sea beet with its characteristic dark green leaves, the ancestor of modern beet, could be identified near the shore.

Peas and beans have been found on most Iron Age sites. The beans are a small variety, which appears to have been cultivated while the peas seem to be a variety gathered from the wild. Peas, beans and lentils, besides being made into pottage, could be baked into cakes and fritters. These legumes can be dried to be stored for the winter and are useful for thickening stews. Root vegetables such as parsnips and carrots, which were gathered from the wild, would be thinner, tougher and more fibrous than present day ones; they would need to be pulverised to make them edible.

Wild seasonal fruits included blackberries, bilberries, strawberries, sweet cherries and crab apples; seeds of wild pear have been found on Iron Age sites in northern Europe. Nuts included hazelnuts, beechnuts and walnuts. Chestnut trees produced a natural harvest that could be eaten raw or boiled to form a pottage or be sweetened with honey. Food would be given flavour by the addition of wild chervil, chives, mint, myrtle and tansy. Oil from seeds, in particular gold of pleasure, was useful for cooking and lighting.

Bread was very important. This could be made from a variety of grain: emmer, einkorn and spelt wheat, barley, oats, rye and millet. Many of these grains were hand-harvested so that they would not be under ripe, which would mean the grain could be overheated and be spoilt. Grain was ground in the Early Iron Age by rolling it with an oval stone on a saddle quern, but by the Late Iron Age the rotary quern was in use. The lower stone was fixed to the ground and the grinder rotated the upper quern by a handle placed in the side or on the top. A stick protruded through a hole in the centre of the upper stone to hold the stone in place, and though this hole, grain was trickled to be ground between the two stones. At least two grindings were needed. Grinding grain would be a task for women or slaves, and the method produces about 80 percent stone-ground flour. This might have some grit in it so it was sieved through wicker baskets or cloth but the ground-down teeth noticed in some skeletal remains reveal that the method was not always successful.

Sourdough bread made from half-baked bread can be soaked in water with some added fruit juice, or with a little dough kept from one batch added to the next to keep the yeast alive. Fermented wine or beer was added to dough to produce leavened bread. Pliny commented that when the corn of Gaul or Spain was steeped to make beer, the foam that formed on the surface was the process for leavening, 'in consequence of which those races have a lighter form of bread than others'. Carbonised remains of a flat bannock shape were found on the Iron Age site of Glastonbury in England, seemingly baked on a hot flat stone. Experiments showed that dough would bake as the stone cooled and the resulting bannock was pulled off easily leaving only a thin crust on the stone. In the Ulster Cycle tale of *Bricriu's Feast*, Bricriu included five score cakes of wheat cooked in honey. Modern experiments have shown that when dough, placed in a pan filled with honey, was baked in an oven, the dough absorbed the honey, thus making a delicious sweet bread, somewhat akin to a rum baba. Honey formed an important part of the diet as it was the only sweetener.

Even if grain was not ground, wheat sprouts could be of use. Whole wheat grains could be soaked in water for several days and rinsed and dried at the end of each day. When kept after that in a warm place, the wheat sprouts have a liquorish taste, which would give variety to food. Bread need not be made from grains. Silverweed, as indicated, has roots, which can be ground into flour suitable for bread making. Black bindweed can be dried and ground into flour. Beans and seeds of fat hen and the common orache can be used, as can acorns, which are also useful as food for pigs. Strabo said that people in northern Spain ate acorn bread for almost two-thirds of the year because it could be stored for a long time.

Athenaeus quoting Poseidonius said that the food of the Celts consisted of a few loaves of bread, but large quantities of meat were eaten boiled or simmered in cauldrons and pans or roasted over coals on spits. Hunting was a way of life so that deer, hare, wild boar, birds and other game were available. Caesar said that the Britons had a taboo against eating hare, geese and fowl, but the presence of cracked bones on some Iron Age sites seems to suggest otherwise. Eggs would be a welcome addition to a diet. Pork was the most popular meat, but mutton, kid and beef were also eaten. Poseidonius said that the Celts, having checked that their chieftain had been served, 'partake of this in a leonine but cleanly fashion, raising up whole limbs in both hands and biting off the meat, while any part which is hard to tear off they cut through with a small dagger which hangs attached to their sword-sheath in its own scabbard'.

In Celtic society, the bravest warrior received what was known as the champion's portion. Athenaeus knew of this tradition: 'When the hindquarters (of a pig) was served up, the bravest took the thigh piece and if another man claimed it they stood up and fought in single combat to the death.' Thighbones, found in Celtic graves, indicate that the honour of a joint was given to a dead warrior to take with him to the Otherworld.

Meat was spit-roasted over an open fire on a bar set between two upright iron poles. It could be boiled or stewed in a cauldron, an easy method to prepare a meal if vegetables were added or even the addition of a herb pudding wrapped in a cloth. The cauldron would be suspended from the roof or from a tripod joined at the apex. In the Irish *Story of Mac Datho's Pig*, Mac Datho, a landowner in Leinster, held one of the five hostels of Ireland, in which there were seven fireplaces, all having a boiling cauldron. In each of these, a salted pig and an ox would be boiled daily. Anyone who passed by thrust a flesh fork into the cauldron and could have whatever he brought up with one thrust, whether it was a large portion or nothing.

Another method of cooking meat was by pot-boiling, in use both in the Bronze Age and the Iron Age. An archaeological experiment at Ballyvourney (Co. Cork) in 1954 revealed how it was done. Hundred gallons (454.6 litres) of water, placed in a stone-lined pit (*fulachta fiadh*) was heated to boiling point by dropping hot stones into the water. A 5 pounds (2.25 kilograms) leg of mutton was added wrapped round with straw to keep it clean. This cooked perfectly in about 3 hours 40 minutes. The technique can also be used to heat water or milk in cooking pots. These methods have also been demonstrated at an annual festival held at the reconstructed Iron Age site of Biskupin in Poland.

Athenaeus commented that the Gauls living besides rivers or on the Atlantic coast ate baked fish flavoured with salt, vinegar and cumin, which indicates another method of cookery. Fragments of baked clay found on Iron Age sites are probably the remains of river clay wrapped round fish or meat and allowed to dry before these parcels were put into shallow pits filled with hot firewood to bake the food. Fish would include eels caught with a trident or in a net.

Dairy produce was essential and the Celts took full advantage of this. In doing so, they consumed fat and protein in a balanced form, as well as having a useful form of calcium. Evidence of milk products has been found on the insides of pottery pieces. Milk from cows, goats and sheep was drunk or used to make butter or cheese. Columella said that for nomadic tribes that have no corn, sheep provided their diet, hence the Gaetae (a tribe living north of the lower course of the Danube) are called 'milk drinkers'. In this, Columella was doing the Celts an injustice as they did grow corn, but classical writers believed that the drinking of milk and eating of butter was the mark of barbarian tribes. Strabo commented that the Belgae had large quantities of food including milk and that the inhabitants of the Cassiderides – thought to be the Scilly Isles and Cornwall – live off their herds. Milk would be available all year round, but richer and sweeter in the spring.

Pliny stated that the barbarians have lived on milk for centuries but that they do not know the blessings of cheese. Strabo said that the British Celts have plenty of milk but do not make cheese because their customs are simpler and more barbaric than those of the Gauls. It seems, however, unlikely that such a useful food as cheese was not eaten, especially as cheese was known to be consumed in Celtic Ireland. An Irish poem written in the twelfth century AD but believed to be part of an earlier tradition describes a fort in culinary terms as being surrounded by a sea of new milk, and having thick breastworks of custard, fresh butter for a drawbridge, walls of curd cheese and pillars of ripe cheese. Soft cheeses could be easily made and would provide a useful addition to the diet. Storage of cheese was a problem but hard cheeses could have been placed in man-made underground structures known as fogous in Cornwall and souterrains elsewhere. Tacitus, when speaking of the Germans, said that they hollow out caves underground where they can escape the winter's cold and store their produce.

Pliny said that the barbarians considered butter their choicest food; eating differing quantities distinguished the wealthy from the lower orders. Cow's milk was commonly used, but sheep's milk gave the richer butter. Strabo said that the Celtiberians in Spain ate butter instead of olive oil with their bread even though they had access to olive oil. Milk supplies would decrease in winter but storage problem seems to have been overcome in some areas. Wooden casks containing a fatty substance called 'bog butter', some casks containing as much as 40 pounds (18.2 kilograms), have been found in Irish and Scottish peat bogs. Although this is suggested to be adipocere, a waxy material formed from animal fat, some is conceivably butter, pale yellow in colour and having a grainy consistency. It must have been put into a bog to preserve it during summer months and removed when required in autumn or winter.

The main drink of the Celts was beer, probably barley ale, which was drunk in great quantities, for beer drinking was a communal activity. There were two kinds of beer: a wheaten beer (*cuirm* or *corma*), prepared with honey, and a plain beer. Strabo said that Gauls concocted a drink called *zythos* from barley and that they washed honeycombs and used the washings as a drink, though it is not clear if the two are connected. The honey beer would be stronger and sweeter and probably more expensive. The other beer was probably barley ale, a more inferior product, although some of the Celts added cumin to it. Pliny went further saying that the Gauls have many types of beer made in several ways and with various names. Types of beer can be made from meadowsweet, nettles, dandelions, fruits and even twigs of spruce and yarrow. The most usual way of preparing beer was by converting a product into malt, which was then dried until it was hard. Then it was ground and mixed with water to form a mash. The mixture was allowed to ferment, which was then boiled and strained to obtain the liquid. The Celts even had a god called Mars Braciaca as indicated on an inscription carved on an altar found in Derbyshire, meaning god of malt.

Literary evidence is again confirmed by archaeological finds. The grave of the Hochdorf aristocrat included a cauldron, which could contain up to 110 gallons (500 litres) of wine, honey mead or beer. Inside it, in confirmation, were found the dregs of mead flavoured with thyme, mountain jasmine, knapweed and meadowsweet, ample sustenance for the Otherworld. Close by were several golden drinking horns, which tend to confirm the Irish tales of warriors drinking from such horns, filling them from a central cauldron. The site also revealed two trenches containing a large amount of pure hulled barley, which was probably deliberately germinated as if there was a brewing establishment nearby.

Wealthy Celts had developed a taste for wine before the Roman conquest of Gaul and Britain. According to Athenaeus, wealthy Celts drank wine imported from Italy and the statement is confirmed by finds in Celtic burial tombs. Large groups of amphora indicate that wine would both be available for the journey to the Otherworld and be served in it. A Celtic burial mound of a chieftain at Lexden (Essex), dating to the first century BC, contained seventeen amphorae, some that once contained wine imported from Pompeii. One amphora had a capacity of 158 gallons (720 litres). The Hallstatt noblewoman's grave at Vix contained imported wine-drinking vessels. These included Attic cups, an Etruscan flagon and a huge bronze krater, 5.33 feet (1.64 metres) high, with a capacity of 242 gallons (1,100 litres) decorated with gorgon heads, Greek warriors and chariots. This was so large that it must have been brought from Greece in pieces and assembled on the site. Other items of wine-drinking gear, mainly of Etruscan origin, have been found in other graves in France.

According to tradition, the Gauls were introduced to wine about 400 BC. Arrius of Clusium wished to avenge the seduction of his wife by Lucumo, a young prince. He therefore went to Gaul with skins of wine, olive oil and baskets of figs, all luxurious products, which the Gauls did not know. The Gauls came to appreciate wine much more than beer which then seemed to them as barley rotted in water. As such they were induced to cross the Alps into Italy and attack Lucumo's men. They did not stop at Clusium but went on to besiege Rome. Wine, however, was their undoing, for sated with wine, they left their camp unguarded, which enabled the Roman commander Camillus to slaughter the unsuspecting Gauls.

The Greeks, however, had introduced the southern Gauls to olive oil and wine as early as the seventh century BC with the trade being centred on Massalia, where finds of amphorae give a date of at least 650 BC for an import trade. By the fifth century BC the Gauls were growing vines and an early wine industry had been established, which later the Romans would develop so that southern Gaulish wines would be exported throughout the empire. Tons of broken amphorae found on two sites, Toulouse (*Tolosa*) and Châlon-sur-Saône (*Callonum*), seem to indicate that these were major centres.

Athenaeus said that the Celts drank from a common cup, which was passed round a group. The men drank a little at a time, but this was done frequently. The result was often drunkenness leading to uproar and fighting. Some tribes were aware of this failing. The Gallic tribe of the Nervii banned drinking wine because they believed, probably rightly, that by imbibing, their warriors would prefer soft living to hard fighting.

On the whole, the Celts seem to have had a reasonably adequate diet. Much would depend on the weather, avoidance of crop disease and the ability of families to obtain food and store it in sufficient quantities to escape famine periods. Caesar mentioned that crop shortages in Gaul caused unrest. Celtic areas conquered by Rome were introduced to more efficient agricultural practices, better food production and the introduction of new products. Food once obtained purely from the wild could be cultivated in gardens. A change of lifestyle certainly happened in southern Britain in the first century AD where, as Tacitus said, young noblemen were urged to follow Roman ways of living so as to be an example to others, but before that, much of Celtic Gaul had realised the benefit of copying Roman agricultural techniques and adopting more sophisticated culinary tastes.

Feasting

Meat, grains and milk were the basic foods, but there were occasions when more was required. The Celts loved feasting and probably took advantage of the four great festivals to indulge themselves. At feasts, plenty of meat, beer and wine were necessary. The story of Lludd and Llefelys in the Welsh tale, *Mabinogion*, mentions a year's provision of food and drink for a feast, although this was taken by a supernatural being who packed it into a huge basket to carry it away. The Irish tales provide the best evidence available for descriptions of Celtic feasting. The amount of food gathered for a feast could be prodigious. In *Bricriu's Feast*, Bricriu's preparations for the feast for the men of Ulster and their king, Conchobar mac Nessa took a year, including building a house at Dun Rudraige in which to serve it. The food included not only the honey cakes previously mentioned, but also seven-year-old boars fed on fresh milk and fine meal in springtime, curds and sweet milk in summer, nuts and wheat in autumn, and beef and broth in winter.

There was, however, a social purpose to the feasting. Feasts were highly structured, social gatherings where hierarchy of status and its public affirmation could be tested. There was a pattern in the seating. Warriors sat in a circle, with the host sitting beside the most important man, a king, a noble or a famous warrior. Others sat round the circle in accordance with their importance. Behind each man might be his shield man, and his spearman, whose duty was to guard their lord, would be on the opposite side. Servers carried round drinks in terracotta or silver jars.

Strangers were invited to feasts, but the rules of hospitality demanded their hosts waited until after the meal to ask them who they were and what they wanted. This tradition was often abused by Celtic enemies, when, for example, Mithridates, king of Pontus, in the third century BC, invited sixty chieftains in Galatia to a feast and then slaughtered them. Even so, this tradition of hospitality was basic to the Celts and one that seems to have continued throughout the following centuries.

According to Poseidonius, quoted by Athenaeus, and the Irish tales, one of the main purposes of a feast was to allow Celtic warriors to boast about and to exhibit their prowess. Other classical writers also confirm this custom. The fight over the champion's portion is one of the themes in the story of *Bricriu's Feast*, for his devious purpose was to set the men of Ulster at odds. The resulting fight and difficulties connected with the contest extended beyond Bricriu's house until eventually Cu Chulainn was accepted as champion. Although King Conchobar knew what Bricriu intended, the Ulstermen had to accept the invitation to his hospitality or run the risk of being thought cowards. Archaeological evidence confirms the literary tradition of the champion's portion. Bones of a pig's thigh have been found in graves in Britain and Gaul indicating graves of Celtic warriors.

A second outcome in a feast was the tradition of single combat. Many Irish heroes were challenged during the course of a feast, not only over the claim to the thigh portion, but because they might be branded and satirised as a coward in verse by a bard or a satirist. The third outcome could be the pledging of gifts. A man could pledge his life for gold, silver and some jars of wine. He took the pledges and then handed them to his kinsmen and friends to accept the gifts. For this he had to be sacrificed and pay the price. He lay down on his shield and resigned himself to having his throat cut with a sword in order that the gifts would be valid.

During the feasts, nothing was lacking, to ensure that the heroes got drunk and merry. The Irish tale of *The Intoxication of the Ulstermen* describes how, on the feast of Samain, king Conchobar gave a feast at the stronghold of Emain Macha. This included a hundred casks of every kind of ale, which led to the indulgers leading a furious ride through Ireland levelling every hill, clearing every forest, cutting the roots of great trees and drying up every river. There are few wilder descriptions in literature of this drunken chariot ride, but allowing for the hyperbole, both this and the other tales indicate that when food and drink were available, the Celts indulged themselves to excess. This also was part of the jockeying for position in the social structure where a feast had been the occasion for young warriors to attest their prowess.

Chieftains were expected to entertain their followers to great feasts. Poseidonius commented on the feasting habits of the Avernian leader, Lovernius, father of Bituis, who was dethroned by the Romans. He held a great feast lasting many days for his followers, set in a large square enclosure, 1.5 miles (2.41 kilometres) each way. Within this, he prepared so great a quantity of food that for many days all who wished could enter. Attendants would serve food and expensive drink continually from vast vats. A bard who arrived late was required to run behind the chieftain's chariot but was thrown a bag of gold for his attempts to keep up. In return, the chieftain was rewarded with a song extolling that even the tracks of the chariot gave gold and largess to mankind. This was obviously part of Lovernius' attempt to indicate his power and an example of conspicuous consumption on the grandest scale. In Galicia, which was also settled by the Celts, Ariamnes gave a feast, which was said to have lasted a year, held in temporary halls throughout the country to which even travellers were invited.

Entertainment was important. Satirists were allowed great licence by being able to insult or make fun of the warriors' foibles. It was one way of inciting men into single combat or to perform other deeds. Bards were hired to entertain the guests but mainly to extol the feats of the heroes. Boasting was inevitably part of the entertainment, hence the fights which broke out during the feasting as in the tale of *Mac Datho's Pig*.

Beer drinking was part of this social activity and so it was drunk in great quantities, although, as mentioned, Diodorus commented that they also drank water with which they had cleansed honeycombs. He said that the Gauls who normally drank beer become addicted to wine when it was imported into the country, but drank it unmixed and without moderation, as he said, 'by reason of their craving, when they are drunken they fall into a stupor or a state of madness. Consequently, many of the Italian traders, induced by the love of money which characterises them, believe that the love of wine of these Gauls is their own salvation. They receive in return for one jar of wine a slave, a servant in exchange for a drink.' Poseidonius also said that wine was unadulterated although sometimes a little water could be added.

In fairness, Ammianus Marcellinus reported that Cicero said in an aside, when defending Fonteius in 121 BC, that the Gauls did mix wine with water, which they had once thought was poison. He added that the Gauls were 'a race fond of wine, and disposed to numerous drinks resembling wine'. Some Gauls, when drunk, rushed around in 'aimless revels'. The archaeological evidence of the Hochdorf and Vix graves, together with that from other sites in Gaul and Britain confirm the Celtic liking for great quantities of drink. At the Sheepen site adjoining the pre-Roman site of Camulodunum (Colchester, England), pieces of amphorae revealed that wine was imported from at least nineteen different sources, including Italy, the Iberian Peninsular, southern Gaul and Rhodes. No matter how much beer was drunk, the Celts obviously appreciated wine in large quantities.

Other feasts were connected to the Celtic head cult. As the Celts worshipped the head as a living force, it is not surprising that they kept the heads of their most distinguished enemies in chests and showed them to strangers. These were probably the ones which the Greek geographer and historian Strabo (c.64 BC–AD 24) said were embalmed in cedar oil and exhibited to guests at feasts. These customs, and that of human sacrifice, was one reason why the Romans proscribed human sacrifice when they overcame a Celtic region and put down the Druidic priesthood, which had encouraged it. In so doing, they may have also curtailed, at least in some areas, the Celtic tradition of their own forms of feasting. It would be replaced, however, with Roman forms of dining, which also included patrons and wealthy citizens providing feasts for their clients and supporters.

1. Aerial view of Hod Hill hill fort, Dorset, indicating the Roman fort constructed within the hill fort after the Celts had been evicted.

2. Aerial view of Maiden Castle hill fort, Dorset showing the formidable defences.

3. Statue of Vercingetorix, Alesia.

4. Statue of Boadicea (Boudica) on the Embankment at Westminster Bridge, London, accompanied by two females, possibly her daughters. The chariot has scythes on the wheels.

5. Reconstructed round house, Little Butser, Hampshire.

6. Reconstructed turf hut. This would have been similar to a Celtic hut.

7. A spear and a reconstructed wooden shield.

8. Anthropoid hilts of Iron Age swords from the Marne region.

9. Reconstructed model of a chariot.

10. Statue called the Dying Gaul. A Roman marble copy of a third century BC Hellenistic bronze original.

11. Detail of head of Dying Gaul showing the torc.

12. Statue of Gaul stabbing himself after killing
his wife. Roman copy from the Pergamon statues.

13. Statue of a captured Gaul.

14. Rotary quern.

15. Relief showing a reaping machine.

16. Model of woman wearing a torc, bracelets and a brooch.

17. Gold plate from Mold, Wales at The British Museum.

18. Village sign at Snettisham, Norfolk, showing a torc. Over 200 torcs were found in the area between 1948 and 1992.

19. Gundestrup Cauldron.

20. Relief of Genii Cucullati, Housesteads.

21. Relief of Mother Goddesses in hierarchical pose.

22. Relief of Mother Goddesses in relaxed pose.

23. Relief of Esus.

24. Seated figure of Cernunnos on Gundestrup cauldron holding a serpent and a torc, and surrounded by animals.

25. So-called Temple of Janus, Autun (France).
This is a surviving cella of a Romano-Celtic temple.

26. Model of Celtic temple.

27. Reconstructed door frame from the shrine at Requepertuse (Bouches-du-Rhône, France), showing the niches in the pillars ready to display decapitated heads and the bird placed above, ready to fly, which will carry the souls of the departed to the underworld.

28. The 'Tarasque de Noves'.

29. Chariot Burial.

30. Celtic tomb burial at Welwyn Garden City.

31. Reconstructed head of Lindow Man.

32. Head of Tollund Man.

Chapter 7
Arts, Crafts and Technology

Polybius, when speaking of the Celts in the Po valley region, said that they lived simple lives and had no knowledge of any art or science. Obviously, he was looking at them through classical eyes and was considering their lack of figurative art, which was such a feature of the classical world. He was also aware of the Roman intention to conquer Gaul and bring what was considered to be a barbarian nation under Roman rule. It was therefore almost his duty to speak of a seeming lack of art in disparaging terms. Often the misinterpretation of Celtic design, especially the sinuous curving of a stylised human form was regarded as crudity of expression and thus a barbarian trait.

The term Celtic art, for the purposes of this book, covers the period between the seventh century BC and the second century AD in Britain and on the continent. In Ireland, the term can be used until at least the eighth century AD. It is still used today for examples of jewellery based on Celtic curvilinear designs and intertwining motifs. Celtic art concentrates on abstract patterning and subtlety of form. Craftsmen seem to have had an instinctive knowledge, especially in engraving, of utilising high relief with deeply engorged area so that light flickered over the patterning giving it depth and movement. This was particularly evident in bronze mounts and brooches.

Celtic art cannot be entirely divorced from the human form. Human figures, especially warriors, had been portrayed on scabbards found at Hallstatt. Celtic contact with the Roman world, however, meant that for the first time Celtic deities were portrayed in human form, many based on a classical equivalent. Metal workers incorporated human bodies and faces, possibly distorted, into their work. It would be impossible for the Celtic civilisation not to incorporate ideas and designs – which would enhance their work, influenced, as they were from the early fourth century BC – by Greek, Etruscan and Roman imports into central and northern Europe.

Hallstatt and La Tène

The Hallstatt style can be identified by simple geometrical designs –
hatched parallel lines, chevrons and circles. The emphasis is on pattern.
When people and animals are represented as incised on the pottery found
at Sopron (Hungary) dated to the seventh century BC, they are crudely
sketched in outline. Six lines may give the back, legs and head of a deer.
Later developments, however, do make more attempts to provide more
recognisable human forms, especially of those of warriors. Faces begin
to appear peering out of foliage and natural vegetation.

Imports from Etruria, Greece and later from Rome began to inspire
more interesting developments in style, which became more common
in the La Tène period. These can be deduced from the contents of graves,
especially those of the Celtic nobility. Patterns were not copied but
reinterpreted in a Celtic form. Certain designs were popular – the
palmette, the lotus and vegetal fronds such as acanthus. Geometric styles
were not discarded but made more interesting utilising depth to produce
light and shade. Curvilinear forms were especially successful, as were
animal patterns. Such objects as wine jugs, imported from Etruria,
inspired artists to produce similar objects but with handles, incorporating a human face at the base and an animal head at the top. Trade
ensured that these ideas quickly spread across Europe, but it depended
on individual craftsmen as to whether their wares were crude imitations
or more inspired works of art.

Metalworkers

Metalworkers and smiths were revered and held in great honour
by the Celts, probably because the making of metal objects from such
apparently useless material as iron ore represented an extraordinary
technological advance. They may have learnt their craft from the Near
East where iron ore was abundant especially in the Anatolian mountains.
Smiths guarded their secrets carefully, and they had their own god,
a smith god, who became identified with the Greek Hephaistos and the
Roman Vulcan. Representations of this god are particularly common
in northern Britain.

The name of the god was known in Irish and Welsh literature.
In Ireland he was called Goibhniu, and in Wales, Gofannon. Goibhniu

was the smith of the Túatha De Danann and also brewer of the ale that kept the Túatha perpetually young. In the story of the *Second Battle of Mag Tured*, the Fermorians marvelled at how sharp the weapons of the Túatha De Danann were. This was because every evening Goibhniu made javelins, swords and spears. Luchta, a wright, made shafts by three chippings and forging the rings which held the shafts. Credhne the brazier or metalworker made the rivets by three turns to hold the rings in place. Mention is also made of Colum Culleinech, who was a smith of three new unspecified processes. Another craftsman was Diancecht, who was also a physician but devised a silver arm to replace one which Nuada, king of the Túatha De Danann, had lost in battle.

Excavation of ironworking sites has indicated how the process of smelting was achieved. One smelting site was found at Corby (Northamptonshire) in 2006. This had housed five furnaces in use between 100 BC and AD 50. Three were sunken shaft furnaces, a furnace where the lower part of the structure was put in a pit dug into the ground. A clay shaft structure was constructed within the pit, with a bell-bottomed chamber leading up into a tall cylindrical chimney rising above it. The outer edge of the pit was then backfilled with clay, possibly to provide additional stability to the shaft. The furnace was filled with iron ore and charcoal, which, if it was well packed, would provide a temperature of 1,200 centigrade. This would be enough to smelt the iron ore. Once this was done, the chamber would be cracked open and the pure iron allowed to run off. The waste slag also needed to be cleared out. After this procedure, rather than waste the use of the furnace, the hole was sealed ready to smelt the next batch of iron ore. No evidence for the preparation of charcoal was found on the site although there were several ore-roasting pits. The amount of roasted ore suggested that essential preparation was needed before the ore was put into the furnaces.

The advanced use of iron had resulted in the production of stronger weapons and tools and smiths' skill in craftsmanship gave them a respected status in society. Iron ore was smelted to obtain the metal, but metal was not cast. Rather, it was forged so that it was continually heated and hammered into shape. Swords could be made of stripes of alloy hammered together. Shield mounts in particular show skill and display subtlety. Many of the motifs had been taken from classical or oriental sources; others were purely of abstract design incorporating a love of ambiguity. Some were purely Celtic in design such as the *triskele* (based on a debased triangular form). The Waldalgesheim form, so called from objects found in a grave in Germany, was largely made up of designs taken from vegetation and the use of the foliated scroll. A late first-century BC bronze shield boss found in the Thames at Wandsworth had a sinuous tendril-like pattern, which evolves into the heads of two monstrous birds.

Household objects included tankards like that found at Trawsfynydd (Wales). This is made of wooden staves and a wooden base, bound together by bronze wire. The bronze handle is formed of elaborate scrolls of the *triskele* pattern and four elaborate knobs to hold it to the cup. Equally attractive are the bindings on wooden buckets. The Aylesford (Kent) bucket had its wooden staves bound by a bronze band. This is decorated in repoussé work consisting of flower patterns and two spirited horses tossing their heads back over their shoulders as they prance around. There are also two bronze-helmeted heads with closed eyes and having an enigmatic expression forming handle escutcheons. Iron firedogs like those from Capel Garmon (Wales) and the chieftains' burials in Essex and Hertfordshire were used to hold food over or near the fire. Their upright posts usually resemble ox heads at the top.

Bronze mirrors are particularly interesting for their engraved backs. The front was highly polished to give a somewhat opaque view of its owner. Some were of iron, but it was the bronze ones that were often elaborately decorated on the back, sometimes with inset enamel that allowed a craftsman to show his talent. It is no wonder that women requested that these objects should be buried with them, presumably to enable them to enhance their appearance in the Otherworld.

The back of the Desborough (Northamptonshire) mirror, dated to the first century AD, has outlined areas filled with short lines known as basketry. This design is rare in continental Europe but frequently found in the British Isles. The curvilinear outlines of circles and triangles are so meticulously drawn that they must have been done with a compass or an equally accurate tool. The whole pattern on the back of the mirror appears to be in continuous flowing motion. This kind of decoration is also found in openwork *phalerae* (armour decoration), especially in the Marne region in France and on the decorated horse harness plaques found in the Champagne region. The late first-century BC Holcombe (Devon) mirror also had a design which suggested that it was produced with the aid of compasses. The design gives the impression of being symmetrical, but closer inspection reveals subtle differences. The handle has a surprise, for when it is held upright, the part against the mirror represents a grinning cat's face.

A mirror from Aston (Hertfordshire) is simpler in design with three huge scrolls forming three circles with incised decoration. When the mirror is placed with the handle at the top, a monstrous face appears with globular eyes and a huge nose or snout, thus adhering to the Celtic belief in shape changing, where humans and animal dissolve into different forms. The handles of both the Desborough and the Aston mirrors are plain, consisting of links forming circles, but even these can suggest a human figure when held upright. It is probable that the owner did not hold the mirror upright when it was enhancing her face but looked into it as it was held downwards by a slave. The problem about this was that it would be the slave who had the chance to appreciate the design. Mirrors, however, might have been kept on the walls of buildings with the handle at the top, thus allowing their subtle shapes to be appreciated.

There is often exuberance in Celtic art, which can be linked to the boastful attitude exhibited by the Celts at social gatherings and in battle. They may have been for ceremonial use or have been used in warfare to identify the chieftain. These elaborate helmets, found especially in the

Figure 7 Drawing of helmet found at Amfreville (Eure, France). Courtesy of Linda Ward.

Marne region of France, take the form of huge pointed helmets or have long antennae rising from a bronze cap. A bronze and iron low cap-like ceremonial helmet found at Amfreville (Eure) was decorated with gold leaf. The decoration incorporated naturalistic tendrils in a scroll like a *triskele* pattern and a wave-like pattern, which may have been derived from Greek art. Seemingly more practical was a helmet dredged from the Thames near Waterloo Bridge, which was made of bronze with an enamel inlay with huge knobbed horns. Yet, even with this there was a problem as it is made of thin metal, which would not have given much protection, and as its horns stuck out sideways, any hit on them could have given their wearer concussion. This helmet, too, was therefore for ceremonial purposes.

The Celtic war trumpet, the carnyx, has already been mentioned as being struck on a gold coin. The remains of the head of a carnyx was found in 1816 at Deskford (Scotland), and when its purpose was finally recognised, it was reconstructed by the National Museum of Scotland. It is a masterpiece of Celtic art with a head shaped like a wild boar with an upturned snout and decoration, which mirrors folds of skin. This head lacks the erect crest, ears and enamelled eyes, which it once had. For the reconstruction, these were added together with a wooden tongue and a long cylindrical tube.

Many of the designs on Celtic metalwork seem to have had a double function. At first sight they display an abstract pattern. On closer examination, a face may emerge. This is particularly apparent in handle escutcheons, such as a late fifth-century BC bronze flagon from Kleinaspergle (Germany) and a gold torc found in mid-fourth century BC at Reinheim (Germany). These also indicate the Celtic belief in shape changing. Some designs are more definite. A pair of fourth-century BC flagons from Basse-Yutz (Moselle, France), elegantly designed with concave-sided profiles, have handles designed as small dogs, and with a chain joining them to the lids, crowned with similar animal heads. A tiny duck rests on the spout. The handle escutcheon of a flagon found in the princess's grave at Waldalgesheim has a bearded human head from which springs a leaf-like feature. This feature appears on other bronze articles and sculptures and may indicate a symbol of divinity.

Human faces on other bronze objects are either obvious or hidden in the design. An early third-century BC chariot mount found near Paris suddenly reveals itself from what appears to be raised spiral decoration as having a face with bulbous eyes. An escutcheon of a third-century BC

bronze cauldron from Brå (Jutland, Denmark) becomes a fearsome
owl mask. The cauldron 6.3 feet (2 metres) in diameter and holding
131 gallons (600 litres) also had an ox head escutcheon whose design
may have been derived from the Near East. The cauldron was found
divided into pieces in a bog, obviously an offering to a deity. A fragment
of another cauldron found at Rynkeby (Funen, Denmark) displays
ox heads and a female face with long hair; round the neck is a torc
indicating authority and divinity.

The most remarkable survival from the northern Celtic world is
undoubtedly the Gundestrup Cauldron, 14 inches (32.5 centimetres)
high, 27 inches (69 centimetres) in diameter and with a capacity
of 30 gallons (136 litres), found in 1891 in a Danish bog. This had
also been carefully divided into pieces before being placed as a religious
offering in the Danish bog. It was probably brought into Denmark from
Dacia in the first or second century BC. Although possibly not made by
Celtic craftsmen, its iconography depicted on the plates was pertinent to
Celtic religious beliefs. Deities, foot soldiers and cavalrymen decorate
plates, and round the outside are plates displaying presumed heads
of deities with long arms holding up figures as if to sacrifice them.
A bearded god holding a wheel possibly represents the god, Taranis.
Animals depicted on it include both mythical and real – griffins,
elephants and leopards.

Jewellery

The Celts loved jewellery and wore bracelets and armlets. Some
bracelets, however, found in Switzerland, were of glass. In Britain, jet
bracelets were common, made from deposits obtained in Yorkshire
or Dorset. Gold and bronze were preferred, probably because they were
more practical and valuable. Many were of twisted wire or plain with an
appliqué pattern. Fortunately, gold seems to have been easily obtainable.
It could have been panned from rivers in Ireland, and gold mines existed
in Europe. Diodorus mentioned that the Celts accumulate large quantities of gold for their personal adornment, wearing bracelets on wrists
and arms, huge rings on their fingers and golden torcs round their necks.
Classical writers mentioned the torcs; Virgil said that the Celts' milk-
white necks had gold collars round them. Knobbed anklets have also
been found.

The Celts wore corselets of gold, and Strabo, commenting on their traits of childish boastfulness, said that they had a passion for gold and a love of decoration. This would include brooches (*fibulae*) of gold, silver, bronze and iron, which were necessary to hold cloaks in place. Many have a curving shape being both functional and decorative. Most brooches had a spring and a catch plate like a modern safety pin so that they would fasten securely. Some were decorated with coral or enamel, and the decoration may have been with the intention of providing protection to the wearer, as that found at Clogher (Co. Tyrone), with three enamel studs indicating the symbolic triad. Others were more elaborate. Cu Chulainn wore a salmon-brooch of inlaid gold. Sometimes anklets were worn, a fashion not unlike silver chains fastened round women's ankles today.

Belts were of bronze or gold. These were often used to hold a sword. Elotha was girded with a golden hilted sword, inlaid with silver and studs of gold. The Hochdorf prince wore a gold belt plate and a decorated dagger encased in gold. Men had to be careful not to pull their belts too tight. Strabo remarked that a fine was levied on any man who became pot-bellied and exceeded the standard measure of the belt so that it could not be fastened or that it overhung the belt. Women in the Münsingen-Rain cemetery in Switzerland who were buried in the third century BC had worn an elaborate bronze chain belt. Their bracelets, on the other hand, were of glass.

Poseidonius stated that added to the Celtic temperament of high-spiritedness must be added boastfulness and a love of decoration, for they wore bracelets on their wrists and arms and gold torcs round their necks. Wearing a torc is mentioned frequently by classical writers and capturing one in battle became a prized possession, as did that taken by Titus Manlius. His family passed it down through the generations. In addition, the family adopted the cognomen Torquatus, which was handed down as an honoured surname.

Torcs could be made of gold, silver, iron and bronze. They seem to have been worn first in the fifth century BC and T.G.E. Powell suggests that they were adopted from Persian examples. They were at first hollow tubes, which could be prised apart to fit round the neck. Later, the rods were twisted, but remained pliant so that they could be pulled apart. The ends finished in elaborate terminals. Some torcs had a moveable piece set into them. Those from central Europe seem to have been more elaborate. One from Erstfeld (Switzerland), dated to the late fifth century BC, is of

openwork with intertwined animals bodies and men's heads. Most of
the torcs dating to the mid-fifth and late fourth centuries BC were found
in the graves of women, but these may have been placed there after
death. One, with elaborate decoration, including palmettes, was found
at Waldalgesheim (Germany) in a fourth-century woman's grave. The
'princess's grave' at Reinheim near Saarbrücken (Germany) contained
gold bracelets, brooches and a torc with elaborate decoration on the
terminals. The Vix princess had a gold torc weighing 1 pound (454 grams).
Its elegant shape combined with filigree work has been suggested to be
Greek in origin, but whether imported or made by an itinerant Greek
craftsman is impossible to say.

Usually men wore torcs. A gold torc was found round the neck of the
body of a prince found in the Hochdorf tomb. One found at Trichtingen,
Wurttemberg (Germany), dating to the second century BC, was of silver
coating an iron core. The terminals end in benign looking bull's heads,
both wearing a torc as if for added divine protection. As its weight is over
13 pounds (5.9 kilograms) it must have been intended as a votive object
rather than as a neck decoration. A first-century BC gold torc found in the
Broighter hoard (Co. Derry, Ireland) is of a hollow tubular design with
intricate spiral decoration and was possibly a votive object rather than
intended to be worn. The stone statue of an armed Gaulish warrior from
Vachères (France) shows him dressed in a heavy mail shirt. Significantly,
he wears a torc, which seems to be of tubular design. This may indicate
his rank or be his method of protection. Elotha had five circlets of gold
round his neck, which emphasised his high status. Two torcs found
at Clonmacnois (Co. Offaly, Ireland) date from c.300 BC. One had ends
decorated with S's in gold relief. Other decoration was suggested to be
derived from the Hercules knot, a motif favoured by goldsmiths in the
fourth and third centuries BC because of its magical properties.

The torc probably had more significance than being such an ornament.
It was placed round the necks of statues and reliefs of deities, as on the
bronze figure of the god found at Bouray (Seine et Ouse, France) and the
horned god, Cernunnos, on the Gundestrup Cauldron. The god not only
wears a torc but also holds up another in his right hand as if emphasising
its ritual significance. When worn, it had both ritual and social
significance. The bronze figurine of a naked fighting Gaul, found near
Rome, and the stone statue of the Dying Gaul both wear a torc round
the neck, which suggests that the torc was also regarded as some form
of protective amulet against an enemy.

The elaborate decoration of these pieces can be seen in the Snettisham (Norfolk) and the Ipswich (Suffolk) torcs. The Snettisham finds, made during 1948–1950 and 1964–1968 and in 1990, consisted of a large number of whole torcs and fragments of others. Most came from separate pits and they may have been buried hastily to prevent them from being stolen; if so, the owner never came back for them. A more probable explanation, relating to the sheer numbers found, could have been ritual deposition. The finest was a heavy torc, weighing over 2 pounds (867 grams) with eight strands of gold twisted together, being soldered into ornamental terminals. A coin, wedged into one torc terminal, gave a date of 50 BC. Five torcs found at Ipswich in 1968 were interlinked together; a sixth was found in 1970. The finder washed them in the kitchen sink before realising their significance and taking them to the Ipswich Museum. Dated to the first century BC, they were made from multifaceted gold bars with the ends bent back to form loops. Over fifty torcs have been found in Norfolk, probably worn by nobles in the Iceni tribe, indicating the wealthy status of the area.

Ireland has produced finds of gold gorgets. One from Glenisheen (Co. Clare), dated to c.700 BC, has chased decoration, with two plaques placed at the ends. It obviously rested below the neck of the wearer but was not in the class of a torc. Similar to these are the lunulae, shaped like a crescent moon, which also rested below the neck. The Celts also wore necklaces. Cassius Dio reported that Boudica wore round her neck a large golden necklace. She might have worn this as a symbol of her chieftainship or for protection when leading her tribe into battle.

A unique find was made in 2000 in Hampshire. This consisted of four gold brooches, two necklaces, a chain to link two of the brooches (the other was not found) and two gold bracelets. These were dated to the late first century BC. The necklaces were made of fine gold wires skilfully woven together, creating a very flexible chain, a technique more common in the classical world and usually found in the Mediterranean regions. The craftsman who made them was obviously from this area. Their terminals could also be pinned together. The two necklaces were of different sizes and were obviously meant as a set for a man and a woman. The necklaces would have been placed round the necks while the brooches would fasten cloaks held together by chains. There are two possibilities as to their presence in Britain. A Mediterranean craftsman may have come into Britain to make them, or more likely, they were given as presents to some chieftain or important Celt. The curious thing is that the discovery of these objects was away from any cremation or inhumation burial, so they may have been hidden for safekeeping or possibly part of a ritual practice. It is easy to mention any isolated burial as ritual, but the purpose of the hiding of this presumably valuable jewellery does present a problem.

Coins

Designs on coins were one of the ways in which Celtic rulers could express their power. The use of coins, which probably began as a result of trade with the Greek world, made use of Greek coins, for the Celts first relied on barter and a tradition of hospitality. The first coins to be struck in the Danube Basin in the late fourth century BC were based on a silver tetradrachms of Philip of Macedon. This depicted the king riding in a chariot, a design that would have appealed to the Celts. This design was reinterpreted, sometimes with the head alone, sometimes with the chariot disintegrated into a stylised pattern of disjointed wheels and parts of a horse. Other coins found in Bohemia copied a gold stater of Philip V of Macedon. Caesar said that the Britons used bronze or gold coins, and iron ingots of fixed weights. Native coinage in Ireland, however, did not begin until the Christian era.

Coins were cast from metal into moulds of burnt clay, which provided fixed weights. They were then placed between two metal stamps to produce a design. Designs could be provided from animals (bulls, boars, wolves, bears or goats), birds and mythical beasts, such as a man-headed horse and a goat-headed snake. Religious icons such as torcs, wheels, trumpets and cauldrons also appear. The head could be displayed as a Celtic mask or an attempt made to reproduce the features of a ruler. Later, the abbreviated name of a ruler could be added, accompanied by the word REX, copying Roman practice. Cunobelin, ruler of the British tribe of the Catuvellauni, was issuing his own coinage some years before the Roman conquest. Coins could be made of gold, silver and bronze; in Britain they were sometimes struck in potin, a mixture of copper and tin. Tribes issued their own coins, which have provided archaeologists with their names, those of their rulers and allowed assessments to be made of regional distribution. Sometimes, they give a picture of Celtic life like those on a British gold coin of Tasciovanus which shows a man on horseback waving a carnyx or Celtic war trumpet in the air.

Sculpture

Stonemasons were influenced by classical sculpture. This is first evident
in Gaul, as some Gauls, anxious to adopt Roman culture, demanded
a more artistic representation of the human figure. From here, the
presentation spread across the Celtic world and eventually to Britain.
Encouragement of art depends on patrons who are willing to buy works
of art and support artists. Roman authorities insisted on more obvious
representations not only of deities but also to portray themselves on
tombstones, and sculptors were willing to oblige even if their artistic
standards could not match those of purely classical sculptors. Celtic
gods could be easily represented once they had been syncretised with
their classical counterparts, so that Apollo represented any Celtic male
healing god and a bearded Jupiter became a bearded Taranis. Gods that
previously had only been identified with a function soon found a Roman
counterpart, as did the Celtic smith god with Vulcan and the huge variety
of water deities. Even a river god could be portrayed as indicated by
a bearded head found in the Thames in London. Its pose related to that
of the Roman god of the Tiber, so presumably this is the god of the river
Thames.

Deities that had no classical equivalent were given a plastic identity.
Thus, Epona could be shown standing by a horse or riding side-saddle
on one; Cernunnos adopted bull's horns or deer's antlers. The triad of the
three Mother Goddesses and the Genii Cucullati were easily displayed,
sometimes in an elaborate sculpture and sometimes sketched in outline,
a reference that the Celts would understand and which reverted back
to their love of linear pattern.

Bronze figurines were easily cast, either following the conventional
shapes of classical form or following the Celtic tradition of stylised
representations. Small bronze figurines of boars often bristle with fury
in their representation and those of horses can be indicated by a series
of lines. A small bronze female figure found at Neuvy-en-Sullias (Loiret,
France) in a hoard of bronzes and possibly depicting an athlete is naked
as classical tradition demanded but is a delineated rather than a detailed
figure. Hair, face and ribs are merely sketched in, but with her legs apart
and her arms extended, she epitomises the essence of dance. The mark
stamped on it, *S(c)uto*, indicated the pride of her creator.

Some stone sculptures display the enigmatic concept of the Celts.
A fifth–fourth-century BC stone pillar, 4.67 feet (1.5 metres) high, found

at Pfalzfield (Germany), displays the long Celtic heads with leaf-shaped, long, upright crowns surmounted by further leaf forms. A Janus (two-faced) head on a pillar 7.5 feet (2.3 metres) high, from Holzgerlingen (Germany), surmounted by leaf crowns and with hands clasped over its stomach displays a grim visage with a wedge-shaped nose and slit mouth. Celtic deities were forbidding and vengeful. Rarely is there any indication of a benign being. A slit mouth and closed eyes usually indicated a dead person as seen in heads at Entremont.

The Janus form, which may have been adapted from the Romans, appears at the Celtic sanctuary of Roquepertuse. Two heads with lentoid-shaped eyes are placed back to back. Slid between them are the remains of a beak of what must have been a gigantic bird. This must also relate to the huge bird that sits on top of a doorjamb below which are pillars with niches to receive decapitated heads. The Janus head has a subtle carving which is not immediately apparent and which can take a sinister significance, a form of shape shifting. It is a shorthand form of Celtic expression, which emphasised the mysterious powers of the deities. One Janus head has compressed lips expressing subjection to the inexorable power of death and the other has opened lips rejecting this and expressing belief in life in the Celtic Otherworld.

Another form of purely Celtic expression comes in the snarling, anthropophagous beast of the Tarasque (Monster) of Noves (Bouches-du-Rhone). This monster sits upright on hind legs. From its jaws hangs a human limb, an arm or a leg. Its paws rest on two heads, almost oriental in appearance, with flowing beards and eyes closed. It is a kind of Cerberus who devours men leaving only their heads behind. This powerful statue represents the concept of the ravaging and devouring power of death and human sacrifice and was intended to inculcate both awe and terror into those who saw it.

Animal deities often are depicted merging with human ones as many deftly accomplished statues of Cernunnos reveal. At Reims (France), a sculpture of a cross-legged Cernunnos, bearded, horned and wearing a torc to express his divinity and power, bears in his lap a bag, possibly filled with money. Below are a ram and a bull, and he is flanked on one side by Apollo and on the other side by Mercury. The fact that he is seated and dominates the scene indicates that the sculptor intended to emphasise Cernunnos' authority over the other gods.

A more enigmatic figure from Euffigneix (Haute-Marne, France) of 11.75 inches (30 centimetres) shows the torso of a human figure.

Carved onto him is the figure of a boar, with carefully detailed bristles along its back. The sculptor has shown that the god has emerged from the animal but the animal still clings to him emphasising his divine form.

Other crafts

The Celts had learnt to make glass by the fifth century BC and used it in the production of jewellery. Glass beads were a popular form of ornament, as were glass bracelets; blue, white and yellow were popular colours. Glass animals were also made, and a small glass dog dating from the second century BC was found at Wallerheim (Germany). Glass eyes added interest to statues and gave them a more lifelike appearance. One blue-and-white glass eye remains in the bronze figure of a cross-legged male, with hooves for feet and a torc round the neck, found at Bouray (France).

Glass was used in enamelling techniques in jewellery and metal vessels, where it was fused onto copper alloys. A third-century BC sword found at Kirkburn (Yorkshire) is made of iron, with a hilt decorated with iron and bronze studs covered with enamel patterning. The pommel, rather surprisingly, is of horn, with iron binding strips, and the total number of components in the analysis of the find made at the British Museum in London was discovered to be seventy. Enamel could come in a variety of colours, but the favourite was red. Red glass inlay is on the boss of the shield found in the Thames at Battersea (London). Enamel was used on the previously mentioned helmet found at Amfreville. Enamel was often used in brooches as in a brooch found in the Polden Hills (Somerset) where the scroll-like patterns were filled with enamel. Coral was also used for beads and decoration.

Pottery developed considerably during the Celtic period from hand-thrown pots to those made on the wheel in the La Tène period. This type of pottery was widespread on the continent but was not common in Britain until the Late Iron Age. Firing techniques also improved so that oxygen could be used to enable pots to be fired in different colours. Pottery was stamped with animal designs or geometrical ones; cross-hatching was also common. Designs could also be made by painting pots with different colours before firing. Graphite could be added to give a metallic colour.

Celtic woodworkers were extremely skilled. Carpenters made planks by splitting trees with wooden wedges and the improved iron axes made short work of cutting down trees in the huge forests which covered Europe. Houses were constructed of mortises and tenons. Elaborate gateways guarded hillforts and classical writers mention Celtic bridges. Smaller items such as bowls were made on the wheel. Buckets, such as that found at Aylesford were made of strips of wood held together by metal bands often elaborately decorated.

Transport progressed from hollowing out canoes to building ships, especially by Celtic tribes who lived on the coast. A huge dugout canoe dating to the third century BC was found at Hasholme (Yorkshire). Caesar said that the Veneti had the largest fleet of ships in which they traded with Britain and that they excelled all other tribes in experience of navigation. He also said that the Gallic ships were rigged differently to the Roman ones and were made with flatter bottoms so that they could sail in shallower waters. High bows and sterns allowed them to sail in heavy seas and violent gales; the hulls were made of oak to enable them to stand the shock of the waves. The cross timbers which were made of beams a foot wide were fastened with iron bolts as thick as a man's thumb. Anchors were secured with iron chains, not ropes. The boats, which carried wine barrels along the Rhine and the Moselle, were sturdy vessels with an elaborately carved prow.

Wheelwrights produced wheels for chariots and other carts. The Celts had developed several forms of wheeled transport and wheelwrights could produce the rim of a wheel from a single piece of wood. Besides the war chariot, which could have wicker or wooden sides, there was also a two-wheeled passenger carriage. The *carruca* was a four-wheeled waggon which could convey heavy goods. Other four-wheeled carts and carriages were used for passengers and goods. The Cisalpine Gauls used a *plaustrum*, a heavy waggon with iron tyres on the wheels and drawn by oxen. The iron tyre would be heated by a blacksmith and then placed round the outer rim. This gripped the wheel and enabled a wheel to be constructed without the use of pegs and nails.

The Veneti used raw hides or thin leather to make the sails of their ships, which indicates the skill of leatherworkers. Leather and cured hides were also used to cover curraghs, small, round, wicker-made boats, rowed with ores, similar probably to the type used at the present time. Leather seems also have been used to produce armour, judging by statues from southern Gaul which appear to show some form of leather jerkin. Leather sandals, shoes, belts and hats have been found throughout Europe.

Spinning and weaving techniques were common to all households as the numerous finds of bone and antler needles and stones and clay loom weights prove. Clothing has already been discussed, but it is clear that the Celts could produce warm and fashionable garments. The British woollen cloak could be sold for a high price in the Roman markets and the so-called Gallic cloaks, which acted both as cloak and tunic, were especially useful in keeping out the cold.

Chapter 8
Religion, Superstition and Cults

Religious belief

In considering Celtic religion, there are problems. Many inscriptions record the name of a Celtic god; sculpture, reliefs and bronze figurines portray them, but these were made by inscribers and artists working under Roman supervision. The Romans believed that the gods could be portrayed in human form, whereas the Celts thought more in abstract forms, and to a great extent believed that their deities acted through natural phenomena.

Were the Celts a religious people? That depends on what is meant by religion. Julius Caesar said that the Gauls were devoted to ritual observances, but this does not mean that they had fixed ceremonies and services; however, if the Irish evidence is examined, the four important occasions of the years were commemorated. These festivals would have needed some supervision either by a chieftain or a priest.

Possibly the Celts had priesthoods, of which the most important one was the Druids, and priesthoods would perform certain rites. The individual Celt, however, would probably be more concerned with placating or encouraging specific forms of nature – forces that would affect his life, his family and his livelihood. He could identify a personal god with familiar things – stones, trees and water – and this could connect with more nebulous phenomena – thunder and lightning. Everything would have a deity, hence the huge number of individual names which were revealed by Roman inscriptions. The Romans would understand this as they also associated natural phenomena and places with deities, sometimes alluding to the all-embracing *Genius loci*.

In an effort to prevent disaster and to obtain the good will of the deity, an individual Celt would follow certain practices and observances. These could include offering food and presents, the erecting of something that represented that deity – a stone or a piece of wood. The relationship could be purely mercenary, demanding good health or abundant crops in return for an offering to the god, which probably reveals more magical than religious belief. Yet this was an entirely practical way of trying to understand, pacify and regulate malignant and beneficent forces that could not otherwise be explained.

The Celts first worshipped the actual object as a divinity with power in itself. Later this idea changed. Sir James Frazer in *The Golden Bough* (1890) underlined this point, stressing that when consideration of a tree is not related to the spirit of the tree but as a home that the spirit can quit at will, then religious thought is making progress. Animism passes to polytheism. In other words, a Celt, instead of considering a tree as a living conscious being, saw it as an object in which resides a supernatural being. This being, therefore, passes from one tree to another and in a certain measure is the master of the trees, thus it ceases to be a tree spirit and becomes a woodland deity.

This can be seen in relation to Celtic tree gods in Gaul. At first, the cult, as indicated on inscriptions, which were dedicated in the Roman era, is related to the individual tree – *Deus Fagus* found in the Pyrenees, *Deus Robor* in Angouleme. Each tree, not the species of tree, is divine. Later, the deity is incorporated in six trees, as recorded in the inscription *Sex Arboribus*. *Dea Nemetona*, the deity of the grove was found at Altripp (Germany). These give the god an existence away from one single tree. The deity has ceased to be confined within its tree or within a small space but has now emerged a deity in its own right, free to move about. Thus, the god is now a god of trees rather than confined to a single tree. Later, the deity would be portrayed in sculpture as standing under or against a tree in human form, but this was the result of Roman influence, for the Celts would not have portrayed the deity in this way.

Yet, if the Celts had considered deities as being able to grant a favour, then they had already visualised mentally these deities to be in the likeness of men, rather than abstract beings. This also would have applied to animal deities and would lead to a development from an animal to an animal god. A bear, for example, becomes *Deo Artio*, the bear goddess recorded at Berne (Switzerland). A small bronze figurine found here shows a female offering a bear a bowl of fruits; she is the protector of bears and also is a goddess of plenty as she nourishes them. *Dea Arduinna* is both a boar goddess and linked to the region of the Ardennes (France). Reliefs of Cernunnos, found in Gaul, show a deity sitting cross-legged, with antlers of a stag on his head, giving him both human and animal powers. When a relief at Donon (France) shows a man with a stag behind him, the transformation from stag god to god of stags is complete, but the portrayal of this transformation can only be revealed once the Romans have portrayed the divinity in sculptural form.

Some Celtic tribes believed that they were descended from a particular animal. This is totemism – the animal god regarded as the ancestor of the tribe or as the parent of a social group. The taboo against eating horseflesh was because the horse was believed to be an early ancestor. Caesar remarked that the Britons did not eat hare, fowl or goose. Archaeological evidence has disproved this, but the custom may have survived in some areas as respect for ancestors.

Once the deity of an object becomes established, it is then necessary to give it personality and form. Sculptors, probably trained by the Romans, were able to do this, providing attributes to distinguish the deity, just as in medieval times attributes were used to distinguish Christian saints. Interpretation on the relief would vary with the skill of the individual artist, but the attributes would leave no room for doubt.

There is still uncertainty about whether the Celts did have images in human form before the Romans. Caesar says that the Celts had images of Mercury, but it is not clear whether he refers to the Roman images of Mercury or to earlier Celtic ones. Tacitus remarks that the Germans 'do not, however, deem it incompatible with the divine majesty to confine the gods within walls or mould them into any likeness of human form'. This could also apply to the Celts. Until the coming of the Romans, the Celts probably preferred symbols to imagery so that a thunderbolt could portray a sky god, a wheel portrayed a sun god and an axe portrayed a warrior god.

Religious festivals

The four great festivals, which divided the Celtic year in Ireland and probably in other parts of the Celtic world, have already been mentioned (Chapter 5). These, which were connected with the seasons of the year and with farming activities, would probably have been celebrated with feasting, games and contests, and some kind of religious ceremony, possibly even with human sacrifice. The rituals associated with them would have been strictly observed. Other festivals might be held where there were markets, but these can only be a matter of speculation. Pliny's descriptions of the Druids gathering mistletoe suggest that this was some form of ceremony. Tacitus' description of the suppression of the Druids on Anglesey hints that religious ceremonies took place there.

A ceremony may be indicated on the Gundestrup Cauldron. It had been divided before being carefully laid out in the bog; since then the plates have been restored. Several relate to Celtic religion such as that depicting the horned god Cernunnos sitting cross-legged before a procession of animals and holding a torc in the right hand, a symbol of power, and a serpent in his left hand, a symbol of the Otherworld. Beside him is his counterpart, the stag. The plate showing a procession of warriors and another with a huge figure (probably a god) plunging a smaller figure headfirst into a cauldron also suggest that some kind of ceremony is taking place. These scenes and the fact that the cauldron was ritually deposited in the bog obviously indicate a religious origin, possibly connected with willing success to warriors going into battle.

It is likely that at these festivals sacrifices were made, either human or animal. Caesar comments on these and evidence seems to come from human remains found in bogs. Tollund Man and Lindow Man who had eaten what seemed to have been a ritual meal before being buried suggests that they were sacrificed, possibly, at religious festivals.

Cult of the human head

The Celts practised headhunting and from this developed a cult of the human head, which appears to have been common in all parts of the Celtic world. Gaulish money and metal artefacts show warriors holding severed heads aloft. Diodorus Siculus and Strabo both refer to this, remarking that the heads of the most distinguished captives were embalmed in cedar oil and shown off as prized possessions. Even if offered a large sum of money, their proud owners refused to sell them. Diodorus said that the Celts cut off the heads of their enemies and attached them to the necks of their horses. A striking example of this is seen in the legend of the Irish hero Cu Chulainn who returned from his first fight with his chariot graced with the bleeding heads of his enemies. Trajan's Column in Rome also shows scenes of warriors riding with the heads of their enemies. The Dacians seem to have followed this custom as the Column shows heads impaled on stakes on the wall of fortresses. There is a parallel in Britain where skulls found in ditches during excavations at the hillforts of Stanwick (Yorkshire) and

Bredon Hill (Worcestershire) may have once been placed impaled on the ramparts.

The custom seems to have been long practised. Livy said that in 216 BC in a battle between the Romans and the Boii, the Roman consul Postumus was killed. His head was cut off and mounted with gold to serve as a cup to offer to a deity in a temple. This seems to have been a common custom. Heads were impaled on stakes or on the ridges of houses of Celtic chieftains. He also remarked that at the Battle of Sentinum (295 BC), the Gauls marched with the heads of their enemies on lances or attached to their horses' manes. Eventually, as Strabo remarks, the Romans put an end to this practice, but by then the head had taken on a religious meaning as well as being incorporated into art.

This practice of decapitation was not only to show prowess in battle. The Celts believed that the head could be divine and symbolic of Otherworld powers. It contained the soul and decapitation could have prevented the dead warrior from returning to life or even barred him from reaching the Otherworld. The head itself began to be regarded with awe and develop a power of its own. In Ireland, Sualtach's head continued to shout at Emain Macha, after it had been struck off, to rouse men to battle. In the *Mabinogion*, Bran's severed head entertained his companions for several years. The head thus became a symbol of divinity, having a living, independent force.

This is made explicit at the shrines of Entremont and Roquepertuse, both dating probably to the third century BC. The Romans destroyed both about 123 BC, but excavations have revealed their purpose. At both these places, blocks of stone have heads carved on them alongside niches in which severed heads could be put. At Entremont, a stone pillar 8.4 feet (2.57 metres) has heads incised on it. These are simply drawn with a U-shape indicating eyes and nose. There is no mouth as these heads represent the speechless dead. At Chorey, statues are shown with no heads; they were not human statues, for each has a flat surface at the neck where a human head could be placed. The Entremont evidence has been extensively examined and the French archaeologist, Benoit, insisted that the finds reveal a cult of the head. The head is the spirit of the dead enemy, or perhaps a friend if decapitation had been his fate, and might even be a sign of victory over death.

One carved head at Entremont had a hand placed on it, which has been identified with the mystic union of the dead with the Roman god

Hermes who led heroes to the Otherworld. A statue of a cross-legged figure places his right hand on a head. Cutting off a lock of hair dedicated the man to Hades, a ritual gesture of protection and possession. At Roquepertuse, stones of three pillars form an entrance to the shrine and have skull-niches ready for the heads of enemies. Above is perched a stone bird, poised ready to fly, indicative of the bird who carries or accompanies heroes on the journey to the Otherworld. A stone with four heads from Entremont, two males below, two females above, is probably a monument to the dead. The male heads have the hair combed back in straight lines indicating they have been washed in limewater.

Throughout Europe there are examples of a single head being the object of veneration, many carved in stone, others created in pottery or another material. The head with powerfully staring eyes from Towcester (Northamptonshire), and those found along Hadrian's Wall bear witness to their image. A sculpture of a sphinx holding a human head between its paws, found at Colchester (Essex) may indicate syncretism of classical and Celtic beliefs. Both the Sphinx and head have equal emphasis. The sphinx is not the usual representative of ravishing death. Death has the ascendancy, but the head represents man accepting his fate with resignation. Males skulls found in storage pits at Danebury may have had a function of protecting the grain.

This ritual of the cult of the head can be intensified. The janiform heads found at Boa Island and Kinaboy in Ireland remove the image from the real world and enhance its supernatural powers. Triplication further increases the potency of the deity. Images can take the form of three separate heads, as at Corleck (Ireland), or a triple-faced head, as found on several examples near Reims, where the eyes serve three images.

The cult of the head was linked with the Celtic respect and love of horses. A decorated bronze bucket from Aylesford depicts a head placed between two stylised horses, and the head and horse are also alternated on the Marlborough (Wiltshire) vat. These may represent the ride of the dead, similar to the symbolism of the frieze of horses in the Roquepertuse temple and the frieze in the temple at Nages (Gard, France) where horses and heads alternate.

The cult of the head was also linked to water. Wells have been found containing skulls, not cast in to dispose of them but having a ritual purpose. The shrine of Coventina's well at Carrawbrough (Northumberland) contained a human skull and several small bronze heads. At Haywood (Wiltshire), a well contained human skulls as did the underground pool in the river Axe at Wookey Hole (Somerset). Most of these skulls belonged to people who had died or been killed when they were between the ages of twenty-five and thirty, when they were most active. The association between heads and wells lingered into the Christian era when wells are associated with murdered saints, who, like St. Melor in Cornwall, had his decapitated head cast into a well. The head of the decapitated St. Lludd (Brecknockshire, Wales) rolled down a hill until it hit a rock from which a spring gushed.

Water cults

Veneration of water has always been a characteristic of primitive people who endowed water with the power of the deity. Indeed, it could be argued that this superstitious power still has a hold today as witnessed by the numbers of coins thrown into fountains. At Gatwick Airport, pools of water near the entrance to the airport gateways contain masses of coins thrown in by travellers to ensure good luck before they board their flights. In a more primitive age, rivers especially attracted personification probably because of their power for good or ill, but any stretch of water could be considered to be the home of the deity. These were not considered to be major gods but part of a vast number of minor godlings, often nameless or ill-defined, who had to be placated and pacified. If a spring flowed freely, the deity was pleased; if it dried up, reparation had to be made for some known or imagined misdemeanour.

That this worship continued beyond the Celtic era is evidenced by the instructions of the Christian Church. Clause 23 of the Second Council of Arles in AD 453 ordered Bishops to take steps to oppose the worship of trees, springs and stones, and as late as the seventh century AD the Councils of Rouen and Toledo continued to urge prohibition of the worship of natural phenomena. The Christian Church probably found it better to ally with these deities rather than oppose them so that often a Celtic deity was metamorphosed into a Christian saint, who, for example, presided over a holy well.

Many of these wells are connected with healing. St Triduana's well, at Restalrig, near Edinburgh, is dedicated to the saint who tore out her eyes rather than suffer the attentions of Nechtan, king of the Picts.

This well became renowned for curing eye diseases. At St Teilo's well (Pembrokeshire), people were said to have been cured when they drank out of a human skull, a clear link with the cult of the head.

Most of the names of water deities are known through the *interpretatio Romana*, which is the name given to a formless, abstract Celtic deity by the Romans, who visualised it in human form. They also Latinised the Celtic name of the deity. One such is Coventina who presided over a well at Procolitis on Hadrian's Wall. One relief depicted her floating on a water lily; another showed three nymphs, each holding a beaker of water in one hand and a bowl in the other from which water is flowing. Coventina may be compared with Sequana, whose temple was discovered at the source of the river Seine. Votive objects cast into the water include those representing deformed limbs, obviously by people hoping for a cure. Other water deities included Verbia, goddess of the river Wharfe at Ilkley (Yorkshire), Icovellauna at Sablon in the Moselle Region and Ancamna at Trier. The Celtic goddess Sulis was connected with sun worship, but her primary function, associated with the hot springs at Bath, was as a goddess of healing. This linked her to the Roman goddess Minerva, allowing the Romans to erect a huge temple and baths dedicated to Sul-Minerva.

Male water deities can be deduced from Mars Condatis, whose name implies waters meet or confluence of streams, worshipped on at least four sites in County Durham; Nodens whose huge temple, overlooking the river Severn, at Lydney (Gloucestershire) was devoted to healing; and Nemausus who presided over healing springs at Nimes (France). Celtic water deities are frequently found associated with Apollo in Germany and Gaul. Several have Celtic consorts as at Hochscheid on the Moselle where Celtic Sirona is linked to Roman Apollo. Statues of water deities – such as that found at Chesters (Northumberland), where the god reclines on a mask of a water deity with flowing hair and beard – are often based on those portraying Roman water deities, like that representing the Tiber at Rome.

Probably every river, spring and lake had a deity presiding over it, the respective deity's name now unknown. The powerful attraction of water meant that objects were deposited in it to placate the deity. Large hoards of metalwork found at Llyn Cerrig Bach (Anglesey) as well as objects deposited in the Thames at London Bridge and at the source of the Seine build up a picture of the power exerted by these deities. Amongst the objects deposited were heads (now found as skulls), weapons and bronze and wooden figurines of gods, anything to placate the deity, avert the power of evil and encourage healing.

Warrior gods

As a warrior race, it was inevitable that Celtic deities included gods of war. Not surprisingly, many became linked in the *interpretatio Romana* with Mars, hence Mars Belatucadrus, Mars Toutatis, Mars Camulos and Mars Cocidius. Cocidius, whose inscriptions are mainly found in the western area of Hadrian's Wall, is also linked to Silvanus, Toutates and even with Jupiter Optimus Maximus. The root of his name 'cocco' indicates 'the red one', a link with blood. The worship of Belatucadrus was again centred round Hadrian's Wall. The name incorporates a Celtic compound meaning 'handsome in the slaughter' or 'mighty to kill'. Reliefs show these deities wearing armour, often a crude version of Roman military dress, and carrying a shield and sword or spear.

Irish warrior goddesses include the Morrigan and the Macha, both having complex characteristics and functions that inspired terror amongst warriors by their shape-changing nature. Yet, the shape-changing nature of Celtic warrior gods also had a beneficent aspect, as indicated by Cocidius being linked with the Roman woodland deity, Silvanus. The Celtic name of Mars Olludius at Custom Scrubbs (Gloucestershire) refers to 'great tree', a connection with the early Italic Mars who was a fertility deity associated with prosperity of the crops. Mars Lenus at Trier is linked to a local Celtic healing deity.

In Britain, worship of the goddess Brigantia reveals the complex nature of Celtic religion. One inscription at Castlesteads refers to her as *Dea Nympha Brigantia* – an association with a water cult. On an altar at Corbridge (Northumberland), she is linked with Salus, an association with a Roman goddess of healing. A relief at Birrens (Dumfriesshire) links her to Dea Caelestiae, the Semitic Tanit, an association with the celestial sphere. She wears a helmet and carries a spear, thus associating her with the warrior aspect of Minerva. On two inscriptions found in Yorkshire, she is linked to the abstract concept of the goddess Victoria. The Romans interpreted her as a warrior goddess associated with victory, possibly for propaganda purposes. Some of her altars are dated to the third century AD when probably the Emperor Severus encouraged this *interpretatio Romana* to promote his Romanisation drive in Britain. Thus, the local Celtic divinity became an agent of Roman propaganda and was used as a focus of loyalty for the province.

Devine couples, triplism and the Matres

Many Celtic deities are local to their areas, their names appearing once. One such deity is Antenociticus (also known as Anociticus), whose cult was centred at Benwell on Hadrian's Wall where a temple was dedicated to him. Arecurius at Corbridge and Viridius at Ancaster (Lincolnshire) are also specifically local deities. Some had a wider appeal. Epona, whose cult appears to have been widespread across Europe, was a goddess associated with the breeding and welfare of horses. On reliefs and small statuettes she is depicted riding side-saddle. The Celts relied on their horses for prowess in warfare, hence the popularity of the cult with a warrior race.

Divine couples are frequently found. These are male and female deities sharing and participating in similar functions. Sucellus and Nantosuelta occur in Gaul. Sucellus holds in one hand a hammer and in the other a pot; the hammer links him with the Roman god Vulcan, the pot with a local wine trade. His consort is depicted in Alsace carrying a pole with a representation of a house on the top, thus identifying her as a deity with domestic and protective functions. The Roman Mercury, found with the Celtic Rosmerta, is more complex. The goddess often adopts Mercury's attributes of caduceus and purse, thus linking the two deities as protectors of travellers and merchants. She is also shown with a basket of fruit, a symbol of fertility.

Deities and religious objects were often represented in threes. Bull figurines with three horns and three-headed or three faced images are common and deities are represented in threes like the Genii Cucullati and the Matres. The figure three and the triad were especially important. The number three may be symbolic as perhaps indicating youth, maturity and old age or it may intensify the nature of the divinity or the object.

The cult of the Mother Goddess or Matres was widespread throughout the Celtic world. Inscriptions refer to this cult as *Deae Matres* in Gaul and Britain and *Matronae* in Cisalpine Gaul and the Rhineland. They could be worshipped singly or as a triad. There are no literary references to the cult but it can be deduced from statues, reliefs and inscriptions. The cult is of ancient origin. Wooden statues, showing the deities naked with enlarged pudenda emphasising their fertility aspect, and dated to the first century BC, have been found at the Celtic healing sanctuary of the Source des Rochers de Chamalières (Puy-de Dôme, France). Figurines of these deities are found in tombs, thus linking them with the cult of the dead and presumably as protectors against evil, a feature that can be traced back to the Neolithic period.

The Matres were enthusiastically worshipped by both soldiers and civilians, perhaps more so by the poorer classes who would invoke their protection against the ills of daily toil and every possible emergency. The Matres could hold in their laps fruit and bread, symbols of fertility and representative of the age-old, worldwide cult of the Terra Mater, mother of all mankind. They are associated with Fortuna, goddess of good and ill fortune but whose main role was concerned with prosperity.

Reliefs usually display them seated and facing forwards in a stiff hierarchical pose, as does one at Cirencester (Gloucestershire), where they rigidly gaze ahead, holding respectively fruit, bread and fish, representative of different aspects of fertility. In the Rhineland, they wear huge circular headdresses, a convention local to the region. Their connection as protectors in childbirth is indicated by the fact that some figures suckle children. Mother goddesses at Autun (Soane-et-Loire, France) have a child, a patera and a cornucopia. At Bonn (Germany), one of the Matres has long hair rather than the huge headdresses worn by the figures on either side of her, thus seeming to illustrate youth amongst old age. Far more relaxed is a sculpture at Cirencester where the three deities encourage the children to play between them.

Inscriptions indicate a Celtic-wide worship. A dedication at Winchester (Hampshire) refers to the Matres of Italy, Germany and Gaul, and another at York to the Matres of Africa, Italy and Gaul. On the other hand, the Matres may be specifically localised, for example the Matres Glanicae at Glanum (Bouches-du-Rhône, France). The Matres Treverae were worshipped in the Trier region by the tribes of the Treveri. The epithet Suleviae found in Britain, Gaul, Hungary and Rome indicates a widespread nature of the cult. At Bath, the epithet became a personal divinity on an altar dedicated to the Suleviae by Sulinus, a sculptor. The worship of the Matres could be public as was that associated with thermal springs at Aix-les-Bains and Gréoulx (France) and also by military dedications, especially on Hadrian's Wall. Their worship could be private as witnessed by the numerous small figurines, silver plaques and other objects. These often took the form of a single figure holding an object, such as the figure at Ashcroft, Cirencester, which held three apples, or that at Naix (France) who held a dog, a symbol of healing, and fruit, a symbol of fertility.

The cult of the Matres could become more specific. Sculptures and inscriptions dedicated by women, sailors and merchants have revealed a worship of the goddess Nehalennia at Domburg at the mouth of the Rhine and at Colijnsplaat on the east Scheldt estuary. The goddess's constant companion was a dog, which is often associated both with healing cults and as a symbol of death, the latter being a constant companion of seamen. Pipeclay figurines made in the Rhineland of a single Mater nursing two infants display a maternal nature and fertility role as the Deae Nutricies. This fertility role is emphasised in the area round Cirencester where reliefs have been found depicting a Mother Goddess accompanied by three Genii Cucullati, who are also associated with fertility and death.

The term Matres is not known in Ireland, but the Irish texts refer to the three Machas who were associated with war and fertility, while the Morrigan often took the form of three warrior goddesses whose shape-changing nature could alter the course of a battle by confusing the warriors. As such, represented by the Morrigan in the form of a crow, sitting on the shoulder of Cu Chulainn, they were present at his death when he was slain by Lugaid.

Great gods

Three of the greatest Celtic gods were Esus, Taranis and Teutates (or Toutates), their names being recorded in Romano-Celtic inscriptions and also by two commentaries, both making use of the *interpretatio Romana*, in the *Pharsalia* of Lucan preserved at Berne. The first commentary links Esus with Mars, Taranis with Dis Pater and Teutates with Mercury. The second equates Teutates with Mars, Esus with Mercury and Taranis with Jupiter. These interpretations give the impression that the functions of the deities are interchangeable.

Teutates appears to have been a deity as protector of tribes. The First Berne Commentary records that victims were sacrificed to him by being thrust head down into a vat of water. The ritual is seemingly portrayed on the Gundestrup Cauldron. Teutates is often associated with Mars, which emphasises a warrior aspect, and this would associate with protector of the tribe in a time of war. Teutates is also syncretised with Mercury, which ensures a protector of merchants and traders. Esus may have had similar functions or be a warrior god as he, too, is identified with Mars. The deity is carved on two reliefs, one at Paris and another at Trier, where he is attacking a tree with birds in the foliage. The symbolic meaning is not clear, but birds in Celtic mythology are often alluded to as messengers or conveyers of heroes to the Otherworld symbolising both death and rebirth.

Taranis has perhaps more straightforward functions. His association with Dis Patter and Jupiter imply a connection with both the Otherworld and as a sky god. On several altars, he is syncretised with Jupiter Optimus Maximus, and thus regarded as the greatest of the gods. His most important attribute is the wheel, which both represents thunder and is symbolic of the sun. This might be that portrayed on a plaque on the Gundestrup Cauldron. The Celts might wear an amulet in the form of a wheel as a protection against evil forces; a wheel was also carved on funeral monuments and a bronze wheel was even placed on a priest's sceptre found at Willingham Fen (Cambridgeshire).

Even more complicated is the symbolism of the so-called giant columns, which are common in eastern Gaul and the Rhineland; almost 150 have been identified. These huge columns sometimes have at the top a carving of a horseman rearing above a giant figure, which is apparently struggling out of the earth. On others, the hands of the giant support the horses' hooves as if both have equal strength. Sometimes the horseman is replaced by a standing figure, which places one foot on the head of the giant. French archaeologists have given this column the names of *la colonne du dieu, le cavalier au géant* and *le cavalier à l'anguipéde*. Some of the figures wear Roman military uniform, thus equating them with Jupiter and the personification of the Roman Emperor. This seems to suggest that columns could be erected at public expense.

The whole conception is a Romano-Celtic complex. The columns, usually with a Corinthian capital, are symbolic of the Roman Empire and the 'cavalier' is representative of the Emperor, Jupiter and Taranis. Those of a Roman disposition would visualise the concept as the Celts conquered by the might of Rome; others would recognise the Celtic Taranis, especially as the figure sometimes holds a wheel. The giant, emerging from the earth, sometimes has his legs transformed into serpents, thus intensifying the symbolism of the power of evil and also the chthonic (or underground) element; the 'cavalier' represents the power of good against evil and light against darkness. Valerius Flaccus, a Roman who wrote a poem, the *Argonautica*, in the early AD 70s, included a reference to the Gallic tribe of the Coralli worshipping Jupiter and associating him with wheels and columns. Some of these columns were erected at healing shrines, giving them a connection with water cults, so the serpents may be also representative of water serpents in which case the horse is symbolic of the earth.

Shrines and temples

Worship of Celtic deities was often personal. This could take place in groves, by the side of springs and rivers or in the home. Lucan, in his *Pharsalia*, written about AD 65, mentions a grove in Gaul, with trees smeared with human blood, where idols of dreadful aspect grinned in the darkness, presumably referring to the cult of the head. Pliny speaks of groves where priests cut mistletoe with a golden sickle. Shrines could be constructed by springs. Coventina's well on Hadrian's Wall consisted of low walls placed round a pool. Most deities were connected with natural phenomena; there was no need for elaborate ritual.

There were also sites set aside which could be consecrated to a deity or be a place in which offerings were deposited. These take the form of rectangular or square banked enclosures given the German name *Viereckschanze* meaning a quadrangular earthwork. Most of these sites have been found in southern Germany and Czechoslovakia. These could have been meeting places for ceremonies, like the sites of Tara and Emain Macha where the Irish High Kings were crowned, or for religious festivals of some kind. Many of these sites contained ritual pits or shafts. At Holzhausen in Bohemia, one shaft contained a post surrounded by organic material identified by chemical analysis as flesh and blood. Diodorus Siculus makes references to these where he says that there is a peculiar and striking practice amongst the Celts in connection with the sacred precincts to the gods. In the temples and precincts, they would deposit large amounts of gold as a dedication to the gods. No one ever touched these for fear of the gods, although, he adds, the Celts were a covetous people.

Not all offerings needed to be on a large scale. They might consist of miniature objects, such as shields and spears like those found at Worth (Kent), axes at Richborough (Kent), and votive objects as those dedicated to Mars found at Woodeaton (Oxfordshire). This tradition of miniaturisation was not confined to the Celts but was a common practice throughout antiquity. The Celts held them in special reverence, for miniature weapons, agricultural implements and talismans – swastikas, crosses and wheels – frequently made in bronze or gold, have been found on numerous religious sites.

Often, objects were broken before being dedicated to the deity, either so that humans could not use them again or to make sure that their power was transferred to the deity. Devotees who wished to recover from illness gave objects of their diseased parts. Excavation of the shrine of Sequana at the source of the Seine revealed wooden replicas of deformed limbs and body parts indicating arthritis, hernias, goitres and broken limbs. Sequana herself is revealed in bronze as a goddess standing in a duck-prowed boat with arms outstretched to welcome worshippers to her shrine.

The cult of healing was common throughout the Celtic world. Nemausis welcomed worshippers to the shrine in Nimes; Glamis to his shrine at Glanum. It was, therefore, inevitable that Celtic and Roman deities should become syncretised, their functions being merged as one. Apollo was frequently syncretised with Celtic water and healing deities. In some cases, what had been a humble shrine was rebuilt as a temple in the Roman style as happened at Hochschied in the Moselle Region in the second century AD. The Romans constructed more elaborate temples for Celtic divinities. The temple of Sul-Minerva at Bath, as mentioned previously, became the centre of an important cult. The temple of Nodens at Lydney (Gloucestershire), where the worship of a Celtic god became the focus of healing by Roman ingenuity, comprised a cluster of buildings, including a temple, a guesthouse and a long low building divided into cubicles where worshippers or patients could be housed. The treatments could include sleep-induced healing and possibly, according to Celtic belief, healing by dogs licking a person. A bronze figurine of a dog was found on the site.

Once Roman influence dominated, the worship of Celtic deities took place in temples, but these were of a Celtic nature. Most took the form of a tall cella 20–25 square feet (1.86–2.32 square metres), lit by windows in the upper storey, surrounded on four sides by a veranda 8–10 feet

(2.4–3 metres) wide, on the walls of which votive plaques could be placed. The portico had a sloping wooden or tiled roof. The remains of one cella can still be seen at Autun (France). A complex of temples at Trier (Germany), one dedicated to the worship of the syncretised Roman-Celtic god Mars Lenus, served the tribe of the Treveri. Occasionally, there are octagonal temples such as the one at Chew Stoke (Gloucestershire), which had no external veranda but was supported inside by pillars. Most of these temples are surrounded by a temenos or enclosure marking the sacred nature of the site. Inside the temple there might be statues to the deity or a humble altar. As far as is known, worship of the deity need not have been corporate but depended on individuals making a vow and obeisance to the god for protection against the ills which could befall them during the year.

Priests and Druidism

Temples such as these presumably needed priests to supervise rituals and staff to care for upkeep. Little evidence survives of this. Ceremonial regalia include crowns and headdresses found at Cavenham (Suffolk) and Hochwold (Norfolk) and priestly sceptres from Willingham Fen (Cambridgeshire) and Farley Heath (Surrey). Cult vessels such as cauldrons, like those of the Gundestrup Cauldron, indicate ritual practices, but their meaning can only be speculative. At Woodeaton (Oxfordshire), there seems to have been some kind of pilgrimage site around the temple. Judging by the number of votive offerings found in archaeological excavations, traders set up stalls to take advantage of the demands of the worshippers to present these to their gods. The site might also have been that of a local fair or market so that the worship of the gods was suitably attached to projects of a more mundane economic nature.

The priesthood of the Druids remains the most tangible evidence of a Celtic priesthood, but it is salutary to recall T.D. Kendrick's words, written in 1927, that 'many centuries of antiquarian interest and popular renown have invested the word Druidism with an undeserved significance, and it is important to remember that in reality it donates a very ordinary primitive faith, and not one that is remarkable either for its advanced philosophy or an unusual theology'. It is probably that the word 'Druid' provides the fascination.

Knowledge of the Druids is derived almost entirely from classical writers in their references to Gaul and Britain. Irish sagas also mention the Druids. They were regarded as priests, soothsayers and prophets. They predicted omens, prophesised the future and could dictate the course of a battle, as did the Irish Druid who ordered Queen Medb to delay her advance for two weeks to avert disaster in war. Julius Caesar commented that the Druids' main cult centre was in Britain and was transferred from there to Gaul, and that those who wished to study went to Britain to do so. Caesar personally knew two Druids, Divitiacus, who was a chieftain of the Aedui and whose stronghold was at Bibracte (Mount Beuvray, France), and Dumnorix, who was his younger brother. Caesar's knowledge therefore, may have come from first hand. Caesar also said that in the territory of the Carnutes in Gaul (near Chartres), the Druids presided over the worship of Celtic deities and predicted the cycle of the year.

A vivid description comes from Pliny who describes white-robed Druids climbing a sacred oak to cut a mistletoe bough with a golden sickle on the sixth day of the moon. Before the mistletoe was cut, two white bulls were sacrificed below the tree. He also implied that human sacrifice might take place there to propitiate a god. Oak was selected for the sake of that tree, and the Druids would not perform any ceremony without having some oak leaves. Mistletoe, he said, was rarely found on oaks, and when it was, it was treated with great ceremony, because its name was 'cure-all'. Mistletoe in a drink made sterile animals able to bear young and was an antidote to poisons. He added scornfully that such frivolous faith do people give to frivolous objects. Yet the sacred nature of mistletoe was indicated by the fact that traces of the plant were found as a last meal in the stomachs of victims believed to have been sacrificed to the gods.

The Druids also seem to have presided over human sacrifice. Diodorus said that they would stab a man and prophesised the future from his fall, the convulsions of the limbs and the spouting of the blood. Caesar referred to sacrificial burnings in huge wickerwork cages and the Irish Druids burned victims on the feast of Samhain. The purpose of these sacrifices was to appease the gods and to promote the fertility of the earth.

The Romans suppressed the Druidic priesthood for two reasons. They abhorred the practice of human sacrifice, and they were determined that the Druids would not challenge their political power. In the first century AD, Pliny remarked that Tiberius had dispersed the Druids and Suetonius commented that Claudius had entirely abolished the religion of the Druids. Pomponius Mela, writing in the first century AD, implies that they had been put down in Gaul. Yet the Druids seem to have survived. In his *Life of Alexander Severus*, Lampridius says that Alexander's death was predicted by a Druidess, thus implying a female priesthood, so their power might have lingered.

Magic or religion

The term religion when applied to the Celts is not concerned with a single doctrine. The terms 'magic' or 'ritual practices' may seem more appropriate in the period before the Roman Conquest. The practice of divining from the death struggles of human beings or the flights of birds is a belief in magic. The placing of skulls next to carved heads is a form of inducement magic. Rites connected with the growth or crops and the burial of the dead are ritual practices. Yet, if these actions are controlled by a priesthood, and if they were common to most of the Celts, then the term religion can be applied.

The emphasis amongst the early Celts was on vegetation and fertility cults, linked to a feeling of propitiation. Conditions of life were uncertain and it was necessary to ensure the goodwill of the unkown forces to ensure a good harvest or to avert chaos. There would be great fear of famine conditions, and failure of food crops would be disastrous. It would be necessary to propitiate water spirits to ensure a constant supply of water, sky spirits to ensure good weather and deities of the earth to provide fertile soil. Animals and birds also had a part to play. At first, they were part of the great pantheon of nature; later, they were regarded as attributes of the divinity or divine in themselves.

The shape-changing nature of Celtic gods and their lack of one common name for a god of water meant that several Celtic gods could be linked to one Roman god. The Romans also encouraged the Celts to portray their gods in human form, as was the custom in their own religion. Roman sculptors thus merely reproduced Celtic deities in a likeness to Roman gods or in human form with a Celtic attribute – the horns on the head of Cernunnos or the hammer held by Sucellus. Celtic sculptors, trained by classical craftsmen, portrayed what they believed was the nature of Celtic gods. This accounts for the different artistic interpretation in reliefs, sculptures and other objects.

It was the Romans who gave these gods names through the practice of the *interpretatio Romana*. The Romans were extremely tolerant of other religions and did not suppress them unless, like the Druids, they challenged their political power. It is probable also that Roman soldiers and traders, when in strange areas, would take care to propitiate the local divinity to ensure their safety and their welfare. Celtic magical and ritual practices, which may be termed religion, thus survived into the Roman period as an active thriving phenomenon and even beyond it so that the Christian church had to work hard to ensure its own dominance.

Chapter 9
Death and Burial

Evidence for Celtic burial practices can be found in literature and archaeological excavations. In the *Gallic Wars*, Caesar stated that they could be costly and magnificent. Everything that the dead man owned, including his animals, was placed on his funeral pyre. Caesar implies that he had talked to people who were still alive who could remember when slaves and retainers were also burnt on the pyre. If this had been the custom, it was not practised in all Celtic areas. Graves of chieftains and even of important women have been found with grave goods such as their personal effects intact. Sometimes, a grave contained miniature tools and weapons, symbolic of their larger counterparts, which, quite obviously, a grieving friend or relative might have been reluctant to consign to the grave.

The evidence for funeral rites comes from texts and graves relating to the noble and the warrior classes. Richly endowed burials were for those persons with wealth and status. Little is known about inhumation disposal for the dead of the ordinary Celts. They might have been buried haphazardly in a convenient ditch or even dumped in a pit. More likely, the Celts followed the practice of excarnation, where the body was exposed in some specific area where the flesh would rot and the remains could be devoured by wild animals. Even less is known about burials of infants and children, for hardly any evidence has been found of their graves, a rather curious feature as infant mortality must have been frequent. Sometimes there might have been a reason for the absence of grave burials. Aelian, a Greek rhetorician who lived in the first century AD and who wrote a collection of books dealing with human life and history, said that the bodies of people who died from disease in the Vaccaei, a Celtic tribe living in Spain, were burned. They might have known that this was a practical method to stop disease from spreading or they might have thought that the gods cursed such people. Warriors who died in battle were exposed to vultures. This is akin to the practical method of sky burial in Tibet and the Zoroastrian cult of the placing of the dead in the Towers of Silence in Goa, India, where vultures are encouraged to eat the dead bodies.

There is evidence in the Late Iron Age for cremation of the dead. This became the standard practice in south-east England in the first century BC. Cremation burials were found at Aylesford, which gave its name to the tradition. At Aylesford, burials took place in irregular circles, but in other places such as Baldock and Owslebury, they were laid out in square funerary enclosures. One of the largest burial sites was found at King Harry Lane, St Albans (Hertfordshire), where over 455 cremation burials was found dating to the first century AD. Many of these were placed within ditched enclosures with a central burial usually in a larger pit and less important burials placed round it. The excavators referred to these as family groups. In most of the graves, the ashes had been placed within pottery urns; some had the calcined bones placed directly in the pit. Most of the grave goods consisted of brooches; there were a few knives, mirrors and other toilet implements. Later, after the Roman invasion when the town of Verulamium was founded, the Romans disturbed the graves of the Celts by building a road leading to Silchester through the middle of the cemetery. Many Celts must have felt that their ancestors' graves had been desecrated.

The Otherworld

The Celts believed that there was a life after death and a mythology grew around this. This related to the mythical Otherworld, which seemingly was identified with an existence parallel to what had been enjoyed by those of the warrior group. It is not clear whether belief in this existence extended to that of the lower classes. They may have hoped for a better life in the Otherworld, but if this was the case, no evidence is available to relate to this. Irish literature portrays the Otherworld as a place of perpetual feasting and as a worthy home for warriors. This would bear out Pomponius Mela's comments that the Druids urged on the Gauls in battle so that they would not fear death and if killed, as their souls were immortal, they would inevitably be conveyed to the heroic Otherworld. There, they would live out a new life, but when they died in that life they would be reborn into the real world again.

In Irish literature, the Otherworld is referred to in a large number of references. It is Tír na nÓg (the Land of Youth), Tír inna mBea (the Land of the Living), Tír Tairnigiri (the Land of Promise) and Magh Mell (the Plain of Happiness). All these terms indicate a better and happier existence. It was a magical place, sometimes believed to be an island off the west coast, where time did not exist. In the tale of the *Voyages of Bran*, he and his twenty-seven companions reach the Land of Women. Each man was given a wife and bed, and food and drink were constantly provided. They stayed here for what they thought was a year, but in the Otherworld, a hundred years could be but a day. When Bran and his companions returned to the real world, they found that they were old men and no one had heard of Bran. In another version of the story, when Bran the Blessed was wounded, he told his companions to cut off his head, which continued to live after the decapitation. It entertained his men as they journeyed to the Otherworld where it continued to entertain them, as they feasted and made merry for fourscore years, having no concept of the passing of time or what sufferings they had undergone. Finally, one of the men opened a forbidden door. Immediately, the Otherworld vanished and they were back in the land of suffering. Bran instructed them to make their way to London and bury his head there to act as a talisman to prevent plague and disaster. Another version was that the head would scream when disaster was near.

Sometimes there was no way back. In the Connacht tale of Nera, when a man went through the entrance to the Otherworld, which was a hole in a rock, he had to stay there because he had become one of the dead. Other heroes who made their way to the Otherworld could return to tell of their adventures. It had its disadvantages. Oisin, son of Finn mac Cumaill, who went there with Niamh, the daughter of the sea god, Manannán mac Lir, stayed there for 300 years, which in terms of the real world, left him on his return as a helpless, hopeless, blind old man. King Cormac, the son of Art, also went there, taken by a grey-haired warrior, dressed in splendid raiment and carrying a silver branch bearing three golden apples. When these were shaken, men who were wounded or people who were sick would fall into a peaceful sleep. The man, as he told Cormac, came from a land where there was neither age nor decay nor gloom, nor sadness, nor envy nor jealousy nor hatred nor haughtiness. Cormac refused to go at first, but when he went, his adventures were very different from those of Oisin, for he found there much the same life as he had left.

The Otherworld was revealed to the world of reality on one day of the year – that of Samhain, the evening of 31 October, which though celebrated to record the end of summer and the beginning of winter, also marked the time when the living and the dead could mingle freely. If the living entered the dead world they must be sure to return before the dawn of the next day. Equally, those persons who had been wronged might return to haunt the living. So prevalent was this belief that the Christian Church was unable to counter it. Therefore, 31 October became Halloween, which still has remnants of its pagan belief. The next day, 1 November, became All Saints Day, which is reminiscent of its pagan origins in invoking the saints to counter evil spirits. The next day, 2 November, became All Souls Day, the commemoration of the faithful departed and an implied invocation that the dead should be left in peace.

Going into the Otherworld should not be linked with shape changing. This is mentioned often in the Irish tales where people change into animals to avoid disaster or to perform a task. Finn changes into a salmon to avoid a flood. In Wales, Gwion Bach, who acquired wisdom from sucking his fingers when three drops of distillation from a magic cauldron fell on them, is chased by his master. During the chase, he transmutes himself through several changes of animals and birds and even a wheatear, which, not surprisingly is gobbled up by a chicken, until he was transformed into Taliesin. As a sixth-century AD poet, he claimed to be a composer of songs and a Druid as well.

Magic cauldrons

There might be another way to be brought back to life. Magic cauldrons are a constant theme in Celtic literature. In the second branch of the *Mabinogion*, Bendigeidfran gives Matholwch a magic cauldron, whereby anyone who was killed, if cast into it, would by the next morning be restored to his fighting spirit, except that he would not have the power of speech, an obvious reference to the fact that the men had returned from the land of the dead. In Irish literature, the Dagda had a cauldron from which dead men could return to life. This may also be referred to on the Gundestrup Cauldron where instead of the man being sacrificed in the cauldron he was inserted in order to be brought back to life, especially as another plate on the cauldron displays a procession of armed warriors.

Immortality of the soul

There was, however, a variation on belief regarding the Otherworld. Caesar said Druids taught the immortality of the soul which made them indifferent to death and thus was a doctrine they promoted to make warriors fearless in battle. Ammianus Marcellus, using Timagenes, an Alexandrian writing in the first century AD, said that the Druids were men of lofty intellect, absorbed in matters secret and sublime and were united with the followers of the sixth-century BC Greek philosopher Pythagoras in declaring souls to be immortal. Strabo also noted the Druidic preoccupation with moral philosophy and their assertion that the soul is indestructible, and Diodorus Siculus commented on this belief of the souls of men passing from one body to the next. Thus, a death in one world would result in a life in the Otherworld and in turn would result in a rebirth and new life in the real world. So great was this belief that according to Valerius Maximus, an early first-century AD writer, the Gauls lent money to each other to be repayable in the next world. The Pythagorean doctrine, however, indicated that how a soul had behaved in one life determined what should be its status, human, animal or even plant, in the next. The Celts preferred to believe that the soul of a warrior would return as a warrior in a new life.

There is no actual evidence that Pythagoras came into contact with the Celts, indeed nothing survives of Pythagoras' writing. All his ideas have been handed on through the writings of other men. It is also doubtful if the doctrine would have spread so far from Greece. The theory of transmigration of souls was also alien to Greek philosophers. The Celtic doctrine could have developed quite independently from any classical thought. It is most probable that classical writers seized upon one particular point of Druidic teaching, which approximated closely to what they understood.

The head cult

The Celts believed that the head contained the soul, but cutting off the head did not destroy the soul for the soul was immortal and indestructible. Striking off the head was customary in the Irish Celtic tales as the final act in a fight representing the triumph of the hero. When the warriors fight over who shall have the champion's portion at Bricriu's feast, Cu Chulainn declares that whoever fought with him and lost would lose his head. The contest of Cet and Conall for the champion's portion, mentioned previously, shows to what lengths the Irish warriors would go to assert their superiority and also insult a man by using his head as a weapon. The head also acted as a warning. In the tale of *The Cattle Raid of Cooley*, Cu Chulainn slew the two sons of Nera and their charioteers, who were guarding a ford, and decapitated them. He placed the heads on a forked pole in the middle of the ford. Cormac Conlonges was sent to see what had happened and when he got to the ford he saw the four heads dripping blood down the pole into the stream's current and the marks of a single charioteer and a single warrior leading eastwards out of the ford.

Cu Chulainn had no mercy on any who fought with him. In his fight with Ferchú Loigsearch and his followers, twelve men attacked him at once. He cut off their heads, put twelve pillar stones into the ground and placed a head on each one of them. The place where he put Ferchú's head was thereafter called Cinnit Ferchon or the head-place of Ferchú.

In Cu Chulainn's last fight, realising that death was near, he tied himself to a pillar-stone so that he might die standing up. 'It is a shame', remarked Erc, son of Cairbre, 'not to take that man's head in revenge for my father's head, which was taken by him.' Cu Chulainn was finally defeated by Lugaid, who arranged Cu Chulainn's hair over his shoulders, before he cut off his head. As he did this, the sword of Cu Chulainn fell from his hand and cut off Lugaid's right hand. In revenge, Cu Chulainn's right hand was cut off, and his enemies marched away to Tara carrying the right hand and the head. There, says the storyteller, is the 'Sick-bed' of Cu Chulainn's head and right hand. Lugaid himself was slain by Conall who fought with one hand bound behind his back so that Lugaid would have the same opportunity of victory. Lugaid was slain and his head was taken in revenge for Cu Chulainn's head.

Cutting off the head of an enemy might have been done in some cases to prevent a dead warrior from returning to life especially if he had been feared, as was obviously the case with Cu Chulainn. By doing this, the killer probably thought that he controlled the spirit of his enemy. Some burials found in Roman Britain have the head of the person placed by the side or at the feet, possibly also a Celtic practice continuing what was a preventive measure. This did not only apply to heroes. The decapitated person could have been a criminal or someone repulsive to the community. Women whose heads has been found at their feet might have been regarded as witches or having the evil eye, and this practice totally barred their return to haunt the living.

Skulls have often been found in very deep shafts and pits. Casting a body into a pit might have been one method for disposing of dead people, but the fact that only skulls have been found indicates some kind of ritual practice. It has been suggested that one purpose of the shaft was to make a connection with, or a way into the Otherworld. Shafts were dug in the Bronze Age, like one found at Wilsford (Wiltshire) dated to the fourteenth century BC. Pits and shafts have been found throughout Europe but are especially prevalent in Britain and in southern Germany. One shaft found at Findon (Sussex) was 7 feet (2.1 metres) in diameter and 250 feet (76.2 metres) deep. To emphasise its importance, the top had been encased with flints. The pit contained skulls of deer and antlers indicating more a cult connected with stags than a human head cult.

In Gaul and Britain, it would seem that the head could be venerated. The shrines in the temples at Entremont and Roquepertuse where decapitated heads were placed in niches show the respect in which they were held. A study of the Roquepertuse heads determined that they were of males none above forty years of age, which would indicate that they could be warriors in their prime. Stone heads, named by the French as *têtes coupées*, are often placed alongside them or depicted in stone as having an identity of their own. At Entremont, one seated stone figure had a lap destined to receive the severed heads. The many stone heads, some in duplicate like a Janus head, others in triplicate, indicate the same belief of the head being divine or representative of the dead. There are some curious representations of the dead, which are difficult to explain, such as the so-called Monster of Noves.

Birds are a link with the Otherworld and this is probably indicated by the giant bird, probably a goose, above the Roquepertuse shrine and the sculpture of a janiform head in the same temple with the giant beak placed between the two heads. A small bronze object found at Rotherley (Wiltshire) is in the form of a human head engraved into the back of a goose. Birds represent the means by which the dead souls could be taken to the Otherworld, but they are also the harbingers of death. After Cu Chulainn had tied himself to the pillar, the battle goddess, or the Morrigan, and her sisters, in the form of crows, settled on one shoulder of the warrior, indicating his fate.

Human sacrifice

The Celts practiced human sacrifice presumably in the hope of pacifying deities, ensuring the health of a person or the tribe and of achieving a good crop. Strabo said that the Druids struck the victim in the back of the head with a sword and then divined from his death struggles. The Celts would shoot their victims with arrows or impale them in temples. They built huge wicker and straw men, filled them with wild animals, cattle and human beings and made a burnt offering of the whole thing. Caesar also mentioned that some Gallic tribes had huge figures woven out of twigs, which were filled with men and set on fire. He said that, as a nation, the Gauls were an extremely superstitious people who held regular state sacrifices, thinking that the gods preferred the execution of men who robbed or plundered, but when they were short of criminals, they did not hesitate to make up the number with innocent men.

Strabo mentioned one particular rite, which he linked to the cult of Dionysus. He said there was a small island at the mouth of the Loire inhabited by the women of the Samnitae. Each year it was their custom to take off the roof of the temple and re-roof it in the same day. To do this, each woman brought a load of material. If one woman dropped her load, and presumably defiled the material or the temple, the other women would batter her and tear her to pieces, carrying the pieces round the temple and screaming. They did not stop until their fury had abated.

The Celts were not alone in practising human sacrifices. It has occurred in many areas. Tacitus mentioned a German tribe, the Semnones, where at an appointed time, delegates from groups of blood relations would meet in a wood to celebrate with a human sacrifice in grim imitation of their ancestors' barbarous rites. He also recounts the various death penalties meted out. Traitors and deserters were hung from trees; cowards, poor fighters and evildoers are plunged into marshes with a hurdle placed over their heads. This last punishment recalls the circumstances in which some bodies found in Denmark have been put into bogs with branches and twigs placed over them. The fact that the Semnones met in a wood is akin to the Roman poet Lucan's description in his *Pharsalia* of people meeting in a grove in Gaul, although here the rites were more fearful and seemingly taking place more often. He described it as a place of darkness and cold shade where the gods were worshipped with savage rites, the altars were heaped with hideous offerings and every tree was sprinkled with human blood.

Dio Cassius, in his account of Boudica's rebellion, said that the Iceni impaled the women they had captured lengthwise through the body and that they did this especially in the grove of Andate, a name that they gave to Victory. The Druidic groves in Anglesey was destroyed by the Romans not only to break the power of the Druids but also to put an end to the savage rites held there, where Tacitus said, it was part of their religion to drench their altars with the blood of their captives and to consult their gods by means of human sacrifice.

Strabo's comments on the Germans included a description of a group of priestesses who carried out ritual killings of prisoners of war. They would first crown the prisoners, presumably with some kind of wreath, and then lead them to a large bronze vessel. One priestess would mount a step and cut the throat of a prisoner who was held over the vessel to collect the blood. Other priestesses would cut open the body to study the entrails to determine whether their countrymen would be victorious.

The holding of a man over a vessel recalls the scene on one of the inner plates of the Gundestrup Cauldron where a huge figure, dressed in the same body-clinging ribbed garment as those worn by warrior riders, is about to plunge a victim into a large vessel. This man is dressed the same as the other men on the cauldron and so would seem to be one of their company. A dog and a serpent, companions of death, accompany the procession. Another interpretation of the scene is that the vessel is a rejuvenation cauldron that contains the elixir, which would bring a dead man back to life.

The two commentaries on the *Pharsalia* state that sacrifices were made to the Celtic god Teutates by thrusting the victim headfirst into a cauldron of water, to Taranis by burning victims and to Esus by hanging victims from trees or even, if the text is amended, as being torn apart by the tree. A life of St. Marcel, an obscure French saint, ended when, having refused homage to pagan statues or to take part in a ritual banquet to the pagan gods, he was tied to the branches of a tree which when released tore the body apart. The tree itself therefore became the executioner, which would fit in with the text of the commentary that the body was hung in the tree, not from it. Esus had a function as a Celtic war god and was also the god of trees, so the sacrifice was a suitable one. The sacrifices referred to by Lucan relate the victim to the elements of water, air and fire and their burial in earth would complete the circle. Whatever was done in these sacrifices was to appease the gods, ensure the fertility of the ground and gain victory over enemies. It was this practice of human sacrifice that was obnoxious to the Romans, although they themselves could not be considered blameless of bloodletting given the events, which took place in the Coliseum and other amphitheatres. There was also a political motive in their actions for they realised that prohibiting it was one way of curtailing Druidic religious and political authority. The sacrifice of animals to the gods was part of Roman religious practice and this continued through the Roman period.

Grave evidence

More realistic than legend and superstition is the evidence found in graves. The wealth of the goods placed in graves to accompany the burial of Celtic men and women indicate that these goods would provide them with all the comforts they required in the Otherworld. This practice continued throughout both the Hallstatt and La Tène periods and in Celtic graves in the early Roman era. Over 2,000 graves have been excavated at the Hallstatt cemetery, most dating to the seventh and sixth centuries BC. Many of the warriors' graves contained weapons, drinking vessels, bowls and cups; the women's graves contained jewellery. Elsewhere there are finds of splendid graves dating to the Hallstatt period. The Hochdorf chieftain lay not on his wooden four-wheeled waggon, which was encased in iron sheeting, but on a bronze couch obviously imported from the classical south. This was decorated with lively figures of fighting warriors and four-wheeled waggons on each of which a solitary figure brandishes a sword. The eight wheels of the couch took the form of dancing girls inlaid with coral and mounted on wheels placed between their legs. The couch was not placed in the centre of the tomb but on the west side. The west was believed to be the side nearest to the Otherworld. An iron razor and a wooden comb would help him to keep up appearances. Fishhooks and arrows would enable him to pursue his favourite pastimes. Bronze weapons allowed him to fight his enemies. Nine sets of bronze dishes and nine drinking horns ensured that he would have companions to entertain him and it was suggested that these had been used, together with the huge cauldron, now containing the dregs of mead, for his living companions to have joined him in one last drinking carousal before he was committed to the grave.

Other richly endowed graves of Hallstatt warriors are found at Grafenbühl, Hirschlanden and Kleinaspergle in Germany. At

Hirschlanden, a huge stone figure, wearing a pointed helmet and with arms clasped across his chest, probably was placed on top of the burial mound. The nakedness of the figure, having only a sword belt and a torc indicates the way in which classical writers describe the Celts as going into battle. At Hohmichele (Germany), a large barrow had been placed above two wooden pits, one containing a female burial with a waggon, the other a man and woman, buried with waggon and harness. The contents included weapons, pottery, clothing and some drapery. These were dated to the sixth century BC. Other graves have been found but had been plundered by grave robbers so that their wealth can only be guessed. These princely burials continued into the La Tène period as, for example, the one at Rodenbach (Germany) where the male personage had been adorned with gold bracelets and rings, and those at Schwartenbach (Germany) where two graves contained jewellery, dishes, drinking equipment and gold masks.

Women could also be buried in great splendour. The body of princess Vix was placed on the floor of a four-wheeled cart, but the wheels had been dismantled and placed at the side. Presumably, it had been decided that her status in this world would enable her to get the cart put into working order in the next world. She was surrounded by wine and drinking vessels, some imported from Greece, the largest being the huge krater with a capacity of 242 gallons (1,100 litres). She wore a collar of large stones and amber beads, bronze ankle rings and brooches. Round her neck was a huge torc of 17 ounces (480 grams) of gold decorated with delicate patterning of filigree work and beaded threads made from about twenty pieces carefully joined together. A woman buried at Reinheim in the fourth century BC had been placed in an oak-lined tomb with her elaborate jewellery.

In Britain, there are few such elaborate burials. The majority have been found in East Yorkshire where the so-called Arras burials are similar to those found elsewhere in Europe and especially in the Marne and Champagne regions in France. This might be the result of migration into Britain from eastern Gaul, especially as the name of the Yorkshire tribe was the Parisii, the name of the tribe which inhabited north-western Gaul. The pattern of burial is shown by a reconstructed burial in the Reims (France) Museum where the man was laid out between the wheels of his chariot accompanied by his helmet, armour and weapons. Most of the graves in Britain and in Europe have been surrounded by a square ditch, with the spoil placed on top of a barrow. At least

700 graves of this type have been identified in Yorkshire since 1960, dating from the third to the first centuries BC, some having parts of chariots in them. Much of the wood has rotted, leaving only a dark stain from which to calculate the remains of the vehicle. There is one particular difference in the position of the body. The East Yorkshire graves show the skeleton of the body lying in a sideways or a foetal position, which is not found on the continent. This seems to have been a local tradition. A burial of a warrior at Ebberston contained two swords broken into pieces probably according to ritual practice so that the theoretical cutting efficiency of the weapons might go with the man into the Otherworld.

One grave at Wetwang Slack was of a woman, who was clearly of importance and who died in her mid-twenties, probably in the fourth century BC. She was buried with a dismantled cart or chariot, about 5 square feet (4.5 square metres), with a 9 feet (2.74 metres) long pole, which would be placed between two horses or ponies. The cart was decorated with coral from the Mediterranean which may have helped her, as did other chariots in graves, to pass into her journey to the Otherworld. The wheels were strengthened with iron bands. There was harness for two horses as indicated by bronze bits with iron cores and five bronze rein rings. Vanity, however, triumphed over her warrior status for amongst her possessions was a mirror to help her to keep up appearances in the Otherworld.

Inhumation had been the normal practice from the seventh to the first centuries BC. A change to the practice of cremation came in the late second or early first century BC. The change to cremation may have been for a practical reason but, given the Celtic adherence to religion and superstition, could indicate a belief that the soul is freed from the body by the burning flames and therefore could be conveyed by this action to the Otherworld. Some ashes were placed in pots, others were scattered. Those areas, which had come under Roman rule such as Gaul, probably adopted Roman practice. In Britain, the practice was followed in cemeteries dating to the late first century BC and the early first century AD found at Aylesford and Swarling (Kent) and in the Thames Valley. Ashes could be placed in bronze-bound wooden buckets placed in pits, but pottery vessels assumed to be associated with wine or beer drinking might accompany these. A second group of rich burials that was found in Essex and Hertfordshire revealed evidence of the practice of cremation.

Many graves indicate that Roman traders, possibly taking advantage of Caesar's invasions and realising the possibilities of trade, had sold their wares in Britain before the Roman conquest and that the wealthy elite were willing to take these products with them to the Otherworld. Some clung to their Celtic beliefs. In a grave at Baldock (Hertfordshire), a large cauldron contained the ashes of an adult male. The rich vessels which surrounded this cauldron included a Roman wine amphora and two bronze-bound wooden buckets. There was also a joint of pork, symbolic of the champion's portion, and a pair of iron firedogs, possible on which to cook the pork.

The burial chamber at Lexden, probably dated to c.15–10 BC, situated beneath a barrow 100 feet (30 metres) in diameter, contained Roman amphorae, which had once held imported wine. Most of the contents had been ritually broken or cremated on a funeral pyre before being placed in the pit. The nobleman who was interred there had obviously preferred a more sophisticated drink than Celtic beer and may even have adopted other Roman habits. The grave contained pottery and bronze vessels, which may be evidence either that his burial was the scene of a large carousal by his retainers or that he expected to have continued his drinking and feasting bouts in the Otherworld. The grave contained his suit of iron chain mail, which was fastened by bronze buckles and hinges. It also contained a medallion of the Emperor Augustus (27 BC to AD 14). This may have indicated that the nobleman considered himself as equal to Augustus in status or that, burying it with him could guarantee his status in the Otherworld. A grave found at Welwyn Garden City was of a wealthy noble, cremated in a bearskin, who indulged in Roman wine as indicated by the number of amphorae placed there.

An excavation in 1996 at Stanway (Essex) revealed a roundhouse occupied from 200 to 50 BC, situated within an enclosure. Though abandoned about 50 BC, it had acted later as the focus for five enclosures, which were the sites of five burials, all taking place within the time span AD 40–60. All the bodies had been cremated and each one had been placed separately inside a wooden chamber. In one enclosure, the remains of the funeral pyre were found and in two other enclosures, there were platforms on which, it was suggested, bodies were exposed to decay. A collection of broken pottery might have been a feasting place for those undertaking the burials. The burials all contained personal items, but two were exceptional. One seemed to have been the grave of a warrior who had been buried with the usual drinking and eating equipment, an amphora of wine and a red and black dinner service on which food could be placed. A Gaulish flagon decorated with three cranes was probably chosen because the birds were indicative of the soul being carried to the Otherworld. A copper-alloy jug probably contained water to wash his hands before a meal. A shield and a spear indicated his warrior status, but he had the intellectual capacity to enjoy some kind of game for a gaming board and counters had been included. His prized possession, a large bowl of amber glass, probably made in Italy in the first century AD, had been carefully placed in a wooden chest, but this had shattered when the wood decayed and the earth slid onto it.

The other grave contained traces of metalwork recognised as the corners and hinges of a gaming board on which were a set of counters and most surprisingly a set of surgical implements. At one end of the grave were a set of dishes, a bronze saucepan and a strainer bowl. At the other end was another set of medical instruments and eight copper-alloy rings. Four copper-alloy and four iron rods were suggested to have been used for divination purposes. The medical implements and the other objects suggest that the grave contained a person who provided some form of medical treatment, even recommending healthy drinks – dregs in the strainer bowl were analysed as the remnants of a herbal drink. The excavators of this surprising grave noted the combination of Celtic and classical cultures and suggested the possibility that the remains were of a man who had been some kind of private physician to a noble household, even that he might have been a Druidic healer. This small group of people alive in the first century AD would have seen the change from the Celtic world they knew best to a new age dominated by Roman forces. The objects they chose for their burial reflected the old and the new regimes.

Bog burials

Burials also took place in bogs; many examples have been found in Britain, Ireland, Holland, Germany and Denmark and date from the Bronze Age to the Iron Age. In Denmark, where more than 418 bodies have been found, several have been found with their clothing preserved and the clothing is now exhibited in the National Museum in Copenhagen. Some parts of the bodies have also been preserved. In 1950, the body of a man was found in Tollund Fen in Jutland. He was

naked except for a pointed cap made up of eight pieces of leather with
the remaining hair placed against the head. It was held beneath his chin
by a bow and it is with this that the head has been preserved and is now
in the Silkeborg Museum in central Jutland.

Tollund Man portrayed a face so fresh that it is assumed this was
evidence of a recent murder, especially as a noose had been placed round
the neck. Later it was decided that he had been hanged, not strangled.
Once the police were convinced that this was a burial relating to the
second century BC, the body was placed in a box together with the peat,
which surrounded it. This weighed over a ton and in the lifting, one man
died of a heart attack. The ancient gods had presumably claimed a life for
a life. The body was removed to the National Museum in Copenhagen,
where the stomach contents were analysed. These were shown to be
a vegetable gruel made of grains and weeds – barley, linseed, gold of
pleasure and knotweed amongst others. A similar meal was prepared for
an English archaeological television programme in 1954 when Professor
Glyn Daniel and Sir Mortimer Wheeler ate it. They declared it to
be totally unpalatable and had to wash it down with Danish brandy.
If, however, such a concoction was prepared and honey was added
to it, it would ferment and give it an alcoholic content, which might
lead to intoxication enough to drug a man.

Many other burials have been found in bogs in Denmark. Grauballe
man, dated to the Late Iron Age, found in 1952 in Nebelgård Fen, 11
miles (18 kilometres) to the north of Tollund Man, did not show such
peaceful features as those which Tollund Man displayed, for his throat
had been cut with several strokes and the facial features were twisted
with pain. This man had suffered from incipient rheumatoid arthritis
in his spinal column. His teeth were in poor condition with holes in
the roots, which would have caused toothache. The condition of his
hands indicated that he had not been a manual worker and so well
preserved were the fingerprints that the Danish police could deduce
that the somewhat similar loops would occur in about 68 percent
of the present Danish population. His last meal was of a kind of gruel
made up of at least sixty-five different grains. Amongst them were
clover, spelt, buttercup, yarrow, wild camomile and hawksbeard. There
were no traces of summer fruits, so the man obviously met his death
in midwinter and the contents of his meal may indicate a ritual meal
given to him before he was killed, possibly at the time of the midwinter
celebrations, as a human sacrifice to hasten the coming of spring. This

time the whole body was preserved and it is now in the Museum
of Prehistory at Aarhus.

Other male bodies have been found with their clothing preserved,
and examples of clothing are now exhibited in the National Museum
at Copenhagen. Women's bodies and clothing have also been found.
One body, of a woman aged about fifty, found in the nineteenth century
in Juthe Fen, south of the royal seat of Jelling, was, rather fancifully,
claimed to be that of the Norse Queen Gunhild, consort of King Eric
Bloodaxe. Historical sources depict her as being shrewd, witty, clever and
eloquent, but also false, cruel and cunning. She was enticed to come from
Norway to Denmark to marry King Harald, but when she arrived, she
was ill treated by slaves and drowned. The story is fantasy and has been
given credence only because of the fact that the woman was placed in
Gunhild's bog. As the body was, however, pinned down by stakes and
branches, the woman may have been regarded as a local witch and staked
to the ground to prevent the body or the spirit returning to molest or
haunt the living.

One body dating to the first century AD, found at Domland Fen,
Eckernforde, in Schleswig, when peat cutting was taking place, was
of a young girl, aged about fourteen. She had been tightly blindfolded
and her right arm was bent against her chest. Her hair had been shaved
off completely on the left side, probably with a razor; on the right,
about 2 inches (5 centimetres) of hair had been left. This recalls
Tacitus's comment that the Germans shaved the heads of adulterous
women before scourging them out of the community. There was no trace
of any external violence but the body had been pinned down under birch
twigs and a large stone. Later, the naked body of a middle-aged man was
found nearby, held down by forked stakes, sharpened and driven down
into the layer beneath the peat. It is possible that the man and the woman
may have been condemned for adultery and were punished by being
staked down in the bog, but equally, both could have been the victims
of ritual murders.

If several of the bodies found in Denmark and Holland may have
been ritual burials, more definite evidence of a ritual killing was found
in England. In 1983, two peat workers found a woman's skull in a peat
bog at Lindow Moss near Wilmslow (Cheshire). This was taken to the
police, but radiocarbon dating proved the skull was not a modern one.
In a bizarre twist, a man confessed to murdering his wife and burying her
in the peat bog. For this he was convicted of his wife's murder at Chester

Crown Court even though no trace of the body had been found. In 1984, a human foot was discovered and later the upper half of a body. The acidic water in the peat had preserved the body so well that the police, thinking that this might be the body of the missing woman, insisted that the corpse be disinterred in a single day. The body, however, was male and radiocarbon dating proved that it could be dated somewhere between the first century BC and the first century AD.

Elaborate methods were taken to preserve this unique find. The body was first freeze dried and then allowed to slowly dry out. It was extensively examined in the British Museum and a reconstruction was made of a sensitive face with a heavy ginger-brown beard and moustache. The hair and fingernails had been preserved in relatively good condition and the fingernails were neatly polished and trimmed, thus indicating that he was not a man who had been engaged in heavy labour.

Further examination revealed that Lindow Man had died or been killed in his mid-twenties, probably sometime in the first century AD. He was probably about 5 feet 6 inches (168 centimetres) tall and, as he had heavy muscles, weighed about 154 pounds (68 kilograms). His blood group was identified as 'O', the most common group in the British Isles. He was not entirely fit as he had evidence of rheumatism in an ankle (which was found nearby) and osteoarthritis in the lower spine. Whipworm was present in his intestine, which could be the result of eating badly cooked pork. He had been buried naked except for a fox fur band placed round the upper left arm after a very brutal killing. First he was struck twice on the top of the head with a narrow-bladed axe. These blows did not kill him, nor did a vicious blow to his back which broke a rib, so a cord was placed round his neck, a stick inserted in it to twist the cord and he was garrotted so violently that his neck was broken. In a last ritual gesture, his throat was cut before he was placed face downwards in the bog. The triple murder in some way recalls the Celtic obsession with the triad and triplication of deities. The ritual aspect was increased in an analysis of the contents of his stomach. These included finely ground grains of emmer and spelt wheats, which seemed to be parts of charred elements of baked bread or porridge, and also grains of pollen from the mistletoe plant. This was a plant sacred to the Druids, hence the suggestion that this was a Druidic sacrifice, but this might be taking speculation too far.

The charred cereal remains have references to Celtic cake ceremonies. In Perthshire (Scotland) in the eighteenth century, at an ancient ceremony, which was still being recorded as the Beltane feast, a specially baked bannock was broken and handed round. Whoever got the most blackened piece was given the nickname of 'the devoted one', that is he or she was marked for sacrifice, and was then referred to for the rest of the ceremony as 'the dead'. This custom and ritual, preserved in folklore and re-enacted throughout the last 2,000 years, have ensured that Celtic superstitious and religious attitudes relating to the world of the dead have lingered well into modern times.

Chapter 10
The Decline and Revival of the Celtic World

All great civilisations have a finite end and that of the Celtic era was no exception. In one sense, the demise of the Celts had its roots in the lack of unity, which existed between the warlike tribes who fought each other and mostly could not unite against a common enemy. By the fifth century, they were menaced by invasions from northern tribes such as the Vandals and the Huns. In another sense the demise was inevitable given the rise of the more powerful and determined Roman state. Wherever they conquered the Romans established an administration and a culture that dominated their opponents, yet allowed them certain freedoms, for example in religion. Where Roman rule was not established, in the north of Scotland and in Ireland, Celtic ways of life survived until this culture was absorbed into Christianity.

Roman expansion

The most efficient opposition to the Celts came from the Romans. Their disciplined armies used strategy and tactics, which outwitted the more individualistic tactics of the Celts. On the whole, they refused to obey the Celtic tradition of single combat, but when they did, as when Manlius Torquatus accepted a challenge in 367 BC and M. Valerius Corvinus in 348 BC, their Celtic opponents were defeated. The Roman army had a staying power and a persistence that overcame obstacles. Rome had created a military machine, which needed conquest in order to deploy fully its armies. Roman administration was ready to create provinces in conquered territories, which would give employment to high-ranking citizens, and there was always the possibility that fortunes could be made from these conquered or absorbed lands. Provinces were created from conquered areas in Gaul, Spain and Britain and would have been created further north had the German tribes not defeated Roman legions in AD 9.

Roman military persistence in siege tactics had worn down Celtic resistance in Gaul, and had conquered most of Britain, but the Roman administration exercised considerable prudence in knowing when to withdraw. The Roman advance into Scotland was halted after the Battle of Mons Graupius in AD 84. Agricola, the Roman governor of Britain, may have claimed that he had won the battle but the Roman administration knew otherwise. The Emperor Hadrian's travels round the Empire in the AD 120s indicated his strategy of surveying the boundaries of the lands which could be practically held by Rome. The boundaries of the Empire were then fixed. In Scotland, there was an advance during the reign of the Emperor Antoninus Pius to establish a frontier on the Antonine Wall but soon the frontier was moved back to the one indicated by Hadrian's Wall. In Europe, the Empire drew its frontiers along the rivers Rhine and Danube, except for the creation of the province of Dacia. Within these boundaries, the Romans could successfully impose their own form of administration and concentrate on creating loyalty and obedience to a civilised form of existence, which they believed should be part of their empire.

Celtic towns

The Celts had pursued a policy of warfare leading to conquest, as well as enjoying this warfare for its own sake. The greatest expansion of their civilisation came when they invaded Galatia in Asia Minor in the third century BC. From then on, Celtic warrior influence in some areas started to decline. But this was not only because of Celtic subjection to a more powerful state. The Celts north of the Alps in the last century BC had already begun to form towns, which Caesar called *oppida*. *Oppida* were hillforts and were much more than merely fortified enclosures, they proved their value as refuges against marauders. Before the Roman advance most *oppida* had houses laid out along streets and supported their population by trade and industry. Manching's growth was due to its skilful trading methods. It did show its power by building a strong wall of *murus gallicus* type and this may indicate that it still feared Celtic enemies could overrun it. Bibracte, the chief *oppidum* of the Aedui tribe covered 320 acres (135 hectares). These *oppida* were the beginning of an urban way of life for the Celts and indicated that warfare was not their main preoccupation. They could also be communal distribution points, as was Danebury, for that of grain.

Oppida could, however, be symbolic of open resistance to the Romans, so when the inhabitants appeared to be openly hostile,

Rome removed its people from its hillfort and forcibly settled them in a planned settlement. Around 12 BC, the Aedui were established in a second settlement at Augustodunum (Autun), which was laid out as a planned town, where the streets followed the grid pattern and the houses were placed alongside these. This may have been achieved because the inhabitants had preferred their new quarters, but the Romans had no compunction about removing people from any area that they considered to be dangerous. The Celtic tribe of the Durotriges in Britain had bitterly opposed the advance of the Roman armies to the west after AD 43. A stand was made at the hillforts of Hod Hill and Maiden Castle (Dorset). After a Roman attack, the inhabitants of Hod Hill were driven from the hillfort and a Roman fort was established in one corner.

The inhabitants of Maiden Castle had also resisted the Roman advance. The fighting was severe but Maiden Castle was taken, the Romans allowed the people to stay in the hillfort although the gates of the hillfort were dismantled and the ramparts slighted. A Roman fort had been founded nearby to protect the crossing of the river Frome. This soon attracted traders, camp followers and other people to live in, or seek protection in, the *vicus*, a civil settlement attached to a fort. Soon this expanded so much that the people from Maiden Castle were forcibly transported to or induced to move to swell the population of the *vicus* either for protection or companionship or because someone wanted to keep a check on their movements. Gradually, an urban centre grew out of this that became Durnovaria (Dorchester).

Trade

Towns became trading centres, an important factor in their development. Finds in graves indicate that wealthy nobles had made purchases to enhance their status in this life and to ensure a comfortable existence in the Otherworld. There was more to it than evidence of trade with Rome and buying of goods from the classical world. Cicero noted that all Gaul was filled with traders, and the Gauls enlisted Roman help to carry out trade. Caesar commented that Roman merchants from Italy had established trading posts in Gallic *oppida* presumably before the 50s BC when he entered Gaul. The Greeks had already established a trading post at Massalia about 600 BC and this was the signal for other Greeks to begin trading in southern Gaul.

Imports of Roman wine had entered Britain well before the Roman conquest of AD 43. Tin was being exported from Cornwall. Strabo mentioned that Britain exported grain, cattle, gold, silver and hides besides slaves and hunting dogs. These would be taken by boats built in Britain or by the Veneti on the coast of Gaul. Caesar said that the latter had many vessels that they were accustomed to sail to Britain. Strabo said that the four main crossings were to the mouths of the rivers Rhine, Seine, Loire and Garonne. From there goods would presumably be sent upriver in barges or transported overland, some goods to be traded in Gaul, others to be sent further afield, even to Rome. Trade was not only a source of wealth but also a factor of cultural exchange between the two civilisations, which inevitably began to alter the mindset of some Gauls.

For trade to be developed there needed to be a development in language, possibly even some form of patois Celtic-Latin, but given the growing dominance of Rome, Celtic traders would be forced to become more fluent in Latin as well as in the use of a mutual accounting system. Trade might be carried out by barter but there needed to be a more efficient medium of exchange. Gallic coinage developed copying Greek coins, in particular those of Philip of Macedon. Kings and chieftains placed their own names on the coins. Cunobelin in Britain issued coins of handsome design; Vercingetorix in Gaul issued gold coins. Sometimes coins carried representations of Celtic gods. A second-century BC coin had an image of a seated figure in a lotus position which could represent the god Cernunnos; others had heads which might be those of Celtic gods but might also have been representations of chieftains and kings, imitating the coins of the Roman republic.

To win the confidence of the Celts in order to pursue their trading ambitions, traders and merchants would need to know the political affiliations and alliances of the tribes. This information would be passed onto the Roman authorities. Caesar himself said that he asked traders from all areas about the position and presumable the political situation in Britain before he invaded the island in 55 BC. He admits he could get little or nothing from them, but this might have been because they were wary about giving away information that would alienate them from their trading partners. Much earlier, information which had trickled in, about conditions in Gaul, had indicated the weaknesses of the tribes and the hostility that existed between them. This would certainly have reached Caesar before his advance into Gaul and would no doubt have been a factor in his move across the Alps. Similar information may have been assessed before the Roman invasion of the Iberian peninsular, although the Roman attack in that area seems mainly as a response to the advance of Hannibal into Roman territory.

Political situation

There was no doubt that the Celtic political structure paralleled that of the classical world. The Romans had driven out their kings but had elected consuls. Their wealthy elite would have been equivalent to the Celtic nobility. Warriors and soldiers appreciated their own martial prowess, and the Celtic taking of booty and land could certainly be paralleled by the action of Roman troops after battle and the settling of veterans in *colonia* and being given the provision of some agricultural land outside the town. The Gallic tribes had already begun to elect magistrates. The Aedui each year elected a *vergobret*, a chief magistrate who held the power of life and death. A general assembly, composed of 300 nobles, met in the territory of the Nervii. The Druidic priesthood shared many of the same functions as the Roman priesthood, not of course that of human sacrifice, although both followed the practice of animal sacrifice, and divination by studying the entrails of the animals was common to both priesthoods.

Once the Romans had conquered an area, they did not necessarily subdue a tribe. They could follow a policy of establishing a client state, which gave the tribe protection against their enemies. The Helvetii became a client state as early as 83 BC. After the invasion of Britain, the Atrebates and the Brigantes availed themselves of this protection. This could lead to their absorbing a more Roman way of life.

Military conquest

The expansion of Rome into Celtic lands was probably inevitable. There was not only the provocation of Celtic incursions into Italy and the humiliation of the sack of Rome in 390 BC, but also the efficient army the Romans had created, a fighting military machine which had to be kept occupied. A Celtic attack on Etruria in 225 BC was successfully defeated at the Battle of Telamon which led to Roman expansion into Cisalpine

Gaul and the gradual subjugation of the tribes of the Boii and the Insubres. Further Roman expansion was delayed by having to combat the invasions of Hannibal over the Alps in 218 BC, which led to the Second Punic War and the defeat of Hannibal at the Battle of Zama in 202 BC. When Rome finally defeated Carthage, it had profound consequences in that it resulted in Rome becoming dominant in the Mediterranean region and ready to seek power elsewhere. As Hannibal had allied with the Celts when he led his armies from Spain, the Celtiberian peninsula became the next target for Roman expansion, but the Romans were also aware of the political machinations of the Greeks and the threat they assumed would come from the Galatians in Asia Minor.

The Romans invaded Spain in 197 BC, but the Celtiberians resisted with such fury that it took the next sixty years to finally subdue them. Brutality existed on both sides, but it was the siege of Numantia in 133 and the final taking of the town and hillfort that broke the back of the resistance. The Roman General Scipio Aemilianus had to use over 60,000 troops to besiege the hillfort before the town was destroyed and the inhabitants enslaved. Even so, fighting continued until the Emperor Augustus led a Roman army in 26 BC to achieve a final subjugation of the tribes. A concerted effort to Romanise the province succeeded and the Iberian peninsula became one of the most prosperous parts of the empire contributing a great deal to the Roman economy.

Celtic tribes had settled in Galatia in the third century BC. The Romans tolerated their presence there, regarding them as a useful ally against the Greeks, until 88 BC when the balance of power was upset by Mithridates, king of Pontus, attacking Roman allies in Asia Minor. These included the Galatians. Mithridates invited sixty Galatian chiefs to meet him at Pergamon, whereupon he attacked them and only three escaped. He also massacred their families. This immediately made the Galatians ally firmly with Rome and they helped Pompey defeat Mithridates in 66 BC and in 64 BC they accepted Pompey's reorganisation of their government into three tribes, each governed by a tetrarch. One, Deiotarus of Tolistobogii, eventually became the dominant leader, and the Romans accepted him. His son, Deiotarus II, succeeded him, but soon Galatia was absorbed into the empire although it retained its separate status until AD 74, when it was incorporated into the Roman province of Cappadocia. Some Celtic elements survived, seemingly the Celtic language. St. Jerome, who settled near Bethlehem in AD 386, commented that the Galatians around Ancyra spoke a language that was almost the same as that he had heard with the Treverii, who lived on the river Moselle.

As already indicated, classical influence had begun in Gaul through trading relations and in the increasing similarity of the political and social institutions. The Romans had absorbed Gallia Transalpina as a Roman province, but relations there were uneasy. Roman governors administered provinces as their private fiefdoms. One governor, Quintus Servillius Caepio, had infuriated the Celts by looting the Gallic shrine of the Tolosates at Tolosa (Toulouse) of gold and silver, stated to be about 50 tons.

The military move into Gaul was the result of the political manoeuvring and ambition of Julius Caesar. Caesar had become Pontifex Maximus in 63 BC and Praetor in 62 BC. Probably no other Roman at that time exercised such political astuteness, administrative resourcefulness, military prowess and a genius for combining all these with a gift of oratory that would inspire a devoted following. Believing that he was destined for the highest offices, his ambition was boundless and was allied with a ruthlessness, which would achieve his ends. After he had been made consul he became governor of Transalpine Gaul in 59 BC, mainly to obtain money to pay off his creditors. He quickly extended his remit to the administration of Gallia Transalpina, Gallia Cisalpina and Illyricum.

He seized his opportunity in 58 BC when Orgetorix of the Celtic Helvetii tribe in Switzerland decided to expand his territory westwards. Caesar had no mandate to move into their territory, but taking this strategic advantage, he moved north, shattered their army and sent the Helvetii, together with their other tribal allies, back to their lands, although he admits that as his soldiers had taken their possessions and destroyed their territory, they had nothing to live on.

From then on, Caesar exploited every opportunity to extend his mandate, even to the extent of invading Britain in 55 and 54 BC and attacking the Germanic tribes. He made alliances with or accepted the surrender of other tribes. The Gauls made one last stand under Vercingetorix, but this confederation was defeated. Caesar justified his reduction of the Gallic tribes and his reasons for this in the *Gallic Wars*. He ends his book by saying that he had attempted, during the last years of his command, to making the Gallic tribes loyal to Rome and to ensure that they had no pretext for revolt, nor any opportunity for profiting by it. He did this, he stated, by imposing no fresh taxes on the tribes and by giving rich presents to powerful tribal members. By these means, he adds, somewhat cynically, it was easy to induce a people, exhausted by so many defeats to live in peace.

Plutarch records that over a million men died in the Gallic wars and another million were enslaved. By now, the Gauls were only too willing to accept Roman help to rebuild shattered towns and settlements. Gaul profited from this. Caesar also profited from this during his campaigns. The profit he gained from looting allowed him to build an army devoted to him and attract political allies, which enabled him to defy the Senate and cross the Rubicon. It was only his assassination in 44 BC that stopped his overwhelming ambition. The Romans, however, were now firmly established in Gaul and it was probably inevitable that Augustus should use the Roman military might to annexe the Alpine provinces, defeat the Celts on the Danube and move the frontier of the empire to that river.

Romanisation

Augustus was not only a military strategist, but he was also a shrewd politician. Not all Celtic areas were subdued, especially in Britain, but for those that were, he pursued a policy of Romanisation. All people within the boundaries of the empire were to become civilised in the Roman sense of the word, i.e. to live in towns where possible, and to absorb Roman culture. The Celts were encouraged to adopt Roman political administration and private quarrels and wars were discouraged, if necessary by the fighting military machine.

One obvious policy to enforce Romanisation was to influence the young. In *Agricola*, his account of the life of the Roman general and his father-in-law, Tacitus detailed, somewhat cynically, Agricola's methods to encourage this policy. In Britain, obviously in accordance with Roman practice, Agricola trained the sons of chieftains, the next generation of leaders, in the liberal arts. He installed a preference for the Latin language. The toga was 'everywhere to be seen. And so the Britons were gradually led to the amenities, which made life enjoyable – arcades, baths and sumptuous banquets. They spoke of such novelties as "civilization", when really these were part of their enslavement.'

Tacitus might have sneered, but he was a Roman who was in a position to enjoy these amenities as part of his normal life. To the Celts these were not novelties but agreeable improvements to a hitherto austere, even

hard, lifestyle. In the early years of the empire, there was a certainty
that life would improve. Roman baths and fresh water brought
to towns by leets and aqueducts, such as the splendid Pont du Gard,
which conveyed water into Nemausus (Nimes) from where it could
be distributed throughout the town, showed the advantages of Roman
rule. Roman clientship was not so far removed from being a retainer
of a Celtic warrior and if there was regret about the abandonment
of a life of fighting, feasting and excitement, this could be replaced
passively by watching fights in the amphitheatre and actively by joining
gladiatorial ranks or enlisting in the army.

Many enlisted in the army as can be seen in the names of the *auxilia*
regiments which recruited men from Gaul, Spain and other parts of the
Celtic regions. These included Gauls, Britons, Batavians, Tungrians and
those in specialist regiments such as slingers from the Balearic Islands,
many obviously recruited from tribal areas and serving with fellow
comrades. Men would be recruited certain they would find some
elements of their former lives in the company of like-minded men.
Auxiliary service was prized because, provided a man was honourably
discharged, he was granted Roman citizenship. Celtic nobles could
raise their own regiments, as did Julius Indus, from the Trier district,
who raised a mounted unit, the *Ala Indiana*.

In administration, Celtic cooperation was assured by the
establishment of civitas capitals surrounded by tracts of land once
owned by members of the same tribe. Cooperation was probably
aided by bribery of local aristocracy to ensure the compliance of their
followers. Access to civil administration could ensure career opportunity
and the encouragement of appreciation of civic amenities.

The Celtic way of life would certainly continue in the wilder areas
of the countryside, especially in Spain and Britain, but the introduction
of new crops influenced many enterprising farmers. Vine growing in
Celtic areas most suitable to vines – Provence, Burgundy, the Rhineland
and the Moselle, Spain and parts of Britain – led to the establishment
of a wine industry. Celtic farming techniques had already exploited
the heavier soils and Celtic farmers were aware of the use of Roman
implements to make the best use of their land. The introduction of Roman
villa estates provided opportunities for agricultural improvements
and a surplus of cash crops, which would supplement an income. The
Romans also exploited marginal land. A growth in population meant
that more food needed to be produced. The population of Britain had

been estimated to have risen from over a million to three to four million and the population of Gaul expanded from eight to twelve million during the Roman period.

Villas and farms supplied urban markets. This development was aided by the growth of towns. The development of roads enabled produce to be taken to market. These improvements did not mean that all the population became wealthy or that everyone took an opportunity to improve their standard of living. Many clung to their Celtic ways, especially those living on small, isolated farms. Evidence of settlements in the Northumberland region and the Scottish lowlands in Britain indicate a peasantry living in subsistence conditions.

Religion

The Romans were tolerant in worship of other deities and this was probably part of the policy in reconciling the Celts to Rome. The Romans promoted the religion of their own deities and this was evident in their erection of classical temples dedicated to the gods of the Roman pantheon. Emperor worship was encouraged as necessary to bind citizens of the empire to the political power. The Temple of Augustus and Livia at Vienne (France) with a raised podium and Corinthian columns stands as an expression of this belief. So does the Temple of Claudius in Britain; although burnt down in the rebellion of AD 60, it was quickly rebuilt to remind the Britons of their loyalty to the emperor.

Celtic gods continued to be worshipped, but as many had the same function as the Roman deities, they became syncretised or absorbed into each other. Epithets added to the Celtic deities also allowed for similar functions. Thus, Mars, the Roman god of war, became linked through the *interpretatio Romana* to Cocidius and Belatucadrus, the warrior gods of the Celts. Some Celtic gods had such individual personalities that they continued to exist in their own right. Epona and Cernunnos continued to be worshipped without syncretisation, although, in the case of Cernunnos, he might have been given a Roman consort. A wariness of the powers of Celtic deities may also account for the continuation of their worship.

The Celtic priesthood was allowed to survive and to look after individual temples and shrines. The Druids were proscribed because of their political influence and also their encouragement of human sacrifice. Animal sacrifices were acceptable because these were part of Roman religion. Divination by studying animal entrails was also common to both religions.

Resistance against Rome

Not all Celtic areas were defeated or allied to Rome. After the Battle of Mons Graupius the Roman administration decided not to advance further into Scotland and later established the frontier line on the Antonine Wall. Northern Britain was never truly pacified, and three or four legions together with numerous auxiliary regiments were permanently stationed in Britain. In parts of Britain, there were tribal units which were willing to become client states or to adapt to Roman rule. In the northern areas, isolated units and loosely organised groups were not willing to do this. Rome did not have the manpower to hold down the wilder parts of Britain.

Rome was even less willing to undertake the conquest of Ireland. During his governorship in Britain, Agricola met an Irish prince who had been driven from his homeland. It is possible he got some information from him because he thought that Ireland could be conquered by a legion and a few auxiliaries and that the conquest would pay for itself if Roman armies were visible everywhere so that liberty (presumably that of the Celtic tribes) was banished from Roman sight. Tacitus thought that Ireland could be a valuable link between the provinces of Britain and Spain. Both Tacitus and Agricola knew little or nothing about conditions in Ireland. It would have been impossible to subjugate that country with so small a force. The Roman poet Juvenal, writing in the second century AD, expressed wishful thinking when he said that arms had been taken beyond the shores of Ireland. The Irish kings and their warriors were more adept at chariot warfare, and it is probable that this high-spirited and warlike nation would have welcomed fights with such a worthy opponent. The subjugation of Ireland might have become a war of attrition tying down more Roman troops than could be spared. There was some contact between Rome and Ireland in the first four centuries AD as indicated by finds of Roman coins, brooches, pottery and other artefacts but this can only be evidence of trade.

There was an equal problem with the German tribes, and the defeat of the Roman general Varus, with three legions in the Teutonic forests, in AD 9 put an end to further conquest northwards. Even when the frontiers were established on the Rhine and the Danube, troops had to be permanently stationed manning the frontiers of the Empire.

By AD 120, the Roman Empire had ceased to expand, apart from the creation of the province of Dacia, and Hadrian had made it quite clear where the boundary of the empire was established.

Christianity

What did change Ireland and elsewhere was the coming of Christianity. The historical Irish were feared in the west as seafarers and raiders with a reputation for savagery. Some founded settlements in Wales and Cornwall. Ireland seems to have followed its own preferred Celtic warrior lifestyle until the fifth century AD. This can be deduced through its myths and legends and it is somewhat difficult to determine fact from fiction. Preservation of these legends is due to the monastic orders recording them often from the tales being handed down orally. The three great cycles, the Mythological Cycle, the Ulster Cycle, with its hero Cu Chulainn, and the Finn MacCuil or Ossianic Cycle, have been preserved, seemingly almost intact. These tales and legends recall a believable universe peopled by heroes, deities and mythical beings. A debt of gratitude must be made to the storytellers who handed down these tales, and the monks who recorded them to ensure the survival of a heroic Celtic tradition.

Historical fact begins with the fifth century. It was the arrival of Celtic missionaries from Britain and Gaul that began the conversion of the Irish to Christianity. This was aided first by the arrival of Palladius who was sent by Pope Celestine I in AD 431 to establish a bishopric, possibly in the Leinster and Meath areas, and then by the arrival of St. Patrick somewhere between AD 432 and 455. Patrick established a bishopric at Armagh near to the site of Emain Macha. As well as respecting this Celtic stronghold, he was careful to preserve the social patterns of the Irish tribes and incorporate their beliefs with Christian ones, thus ensuring continuity of tradition. Monastic centres were established which began to dominate the former Celtic country.

Christianity was careful to avoid conflict. It was easier to merge a Celtic deity with a Christian saint. This was not a re-interpretation of the *interpretatio Romana*. There was no attempt to provide a double name. The goddess Anu became St. Ann; the Celtic goddess Brigit became St. Bridget. The Druidic tradition was suppressed. Monasteries and shrines were established in or on Celtic sacred places. The transition from paganism to Christianity appears to have been successful.

Scholars from all over Europe came to Ireland to study in Irish monasteries and returned to their own lands taking with them traditions of art and learning. The Celtic church produced an art form, which adopted the pagan Celtic designs and symbolism into its own individual art. This was a hybrid art combining Celtic, Pictish and later Anglo-Saxon designs with techniques such as Roman enamelling and milleflore glasswork and the twisted serpentine forms ending in human heads. These arts of metalwork, illuminated manuscripts and sculpture, flourished until the invasion of the Vikings in the ninth century. The Vikings first attacked the east coast of Britain in AD 789. By AD 793 they were attacking Lindisfarne, and two years later they landed on the coast of Ireland. Dublin was established as a Viking city in AD 852, the first of a series of towns, yet the Christian Celtic tradition was strong enough to assimilate these invaders.

Before the invasions, scholars and missionaries went to Europe to Christianise the pagan Celts. The English king, Egbert, sent St. Willibroad to convert the Friesians; he founded the monastery at Echternach in AD 698. St. Gal, who lived and died as a hermit, had a monastery dedicated to him in Switzerland at St Gallen, c. AD 719. St. Columbanus, sent to Gaul to convert the Gaulish tribes, eventually founded a monastery at Bobbio in northern Italy in AD 615. This dissemination of Christian tradition ensured that the Celtic monks developed a reputation for piety. As well as that, they ensured that their ornamental designs based on Celtic patterning were used to illuminate manuscripts and decorative art works. This is particularly apparent in the elaborate initial capital letters displayed in the Gospels and is brilliantly displayed in the Irish *Book of Kells*, produced in the monastery at Kells, c. AD 800, and in the *Lindisfarne Gospels*, c. AD 700. Many of these manuscripts survived the ravages of the Norsemen and demonstrate the continuation of the Celtic tradition.

Suppression of Celtic traditions

A form of Celtic lifestyle continued in the Highland regions of Scotland well into the eighteenth century. Scotland retained its independence

as a separate country until the seventeenth century when James VI
succeeded to the English throne as James I in 1603. In 1707, an Act of
Union united England and Scotland. Rebellions in 1715 and 1745 ended
with the defeat of the Stuart claimant Prince Charles Edward Stuart
at the Battle of Culloden in 1746. Proscriptions against the Highland
clans led to the banning of tartans, the elimination of private warfare and
severely curtailed clan inheritance. The fighting spirit of the Highland
clans was directed into the Highland regiments, such as the Black Watch
and the Gordon Highlanders, which were founded to become part of the
British army. The former clan spirit was kept alive by regiments raised
as semi-private armies, like the Fourth Duke of Atholl did in 1777
by creating the 77th Regiment of Food, later to become the Atholl
Highlanders.

The Jacobite rebels were transported to the Americas where they
established clan and Celtic revivals, especially in Canada. The most
devastating exodus came with the Highland clearances after 1800 when
huge areas of the Scottish Highlands were cleared of settlers to allow
a more profitable economy of sheep rearing and deer stalking. Thousands
of people left for Canada and the Americas, or migrated to the towns
to swell the population of Edinburgh and Glasgow.

In Ireland, the suppression of Celtic traditions began with Norman
forces under Richard de Clare, earl of Pembroke, nicknamed Strongbow,
arriving in Ireland in 1169 on the invitation of Diamait Mac Murchada,
king of Leinster, to regain his kingdom from which he had been exiled.
The Normans quickly began to establish castles and to make the Irish
their serfs. The English king, Henry II, alarmed at this Norman
dominance of his barons landed with his army at Waterford in 1171
and gradually the English crown began to control the Norman forces.
Even so, a series of events including the Black Death in 1348 weakened
both the Normans and the English, until English-controlled territory
was confined to the area around Dublin. The Irish under the powerful
earl of Kildare dominated much of Ireland.

In the sixteenth century, Henry VIII decided to curtail the earl's power.
He proclaimed himself king of Ireland in 1541 and set about reclaiming
the territory. For the next two centuries, a series of military campaigns
managed to bring Ireland under English control and carry out a policy of
plantation. Thousands of English and Scottish settlers came to Ireland to
take over the lands of the Gaelic speaking Irish. This was particularly the
case under James I when he established the Plantation of Ulster in 1607.

The Irish, who were predominantly Catholic, became increasingly hostile to their Protestant neighbours. In 1649, Oliver Cromwell, who had become Lord Protector of England on the execution of Charles I, landed in Ireland and until 1653 subjected Ireland to a bloody campaign intent on wiping out Irish resistance. In doing this, he drove the Celtic elements of Ireland underground. Later, the Protestant William III completed English domination after winning the Battle of the Boyne in 1690 against the Catholic forces of the deposed James II. Union with England did not come until 1801, when the Kingdom of Ireland was merged with the Kingdom of Great Britain (a union of England, Scotland and Wales).

Attempts were made to revive Irish nationalism and its Celtic roots during the nineteenth century, both politically and by rebellion, but to no avail. A large exodus of the population in the 1840s was due to the failure of the Irish potato crop. Blight struck the main subsistence crop so that huge numbers of the population died. Many of the survivors decided to emigrate. At that time, the United States had an open policy of admission so that thousands became citizens of the New World. Others settled in areas of Scotland such as Lanark to work in the mills. By the twentieth century, it was estimated that at least five million people had died or had emigrated out of a population of eight million leaving a lasting hatred of English rule in Ireland and a determination to revive Celtic cultural traditions.

In Wales, nothing so dramatic happened. The collapse of the Roman province of Britannia led to a succession of invasions by the Angles, Saxons and Jutes which led to the Britons being pushed further to the west and into Wales. Numerous short-lived British kingdoms rose and fell. Part of Wales was occupied by the Scotti, a tribe from Ireland. Eventually, a series of Welsh kingdoms arose with each owning allegiance to a high king. Threatened by Norse raids, the Welsh sought help from the English, but it was not until the eleventh century that the English began to attack what remained of Celtic values. The Normans began to establish positions there, but the ferocity of the Welsh resistance confined them to establishing a border territory along the Welsh Marches. In the 1270s, however, Edward I invaded Wales and destroyed the principality of Gwynedd, killing the last Welsh prince of Wales and installing his son, the future Edward II, as Prince of Wales, a tradition which survives today in the investiture of the eldest son of the monarch to that position. Wales was politically united with England in 1536–1545 by acts passed by the English parliament during the reign of Henry VIII.

Elsewhere Brittany, an intensely Celtic area, had received refugees and mercenaries from Britain in the fifth century. They did not subdue the Gallic population but allied with it, although bringing with them their own form of language akin to modern Cornish. These people attempted to ward off attacks by the Franks and Danes and succeeded until the Vikings invaded the area. Later, it became part of the Carolingian Empire. Eventually, it became the Duchy of Brittany, but lost its independence when it was forcibly united with France in 1532. The Celtic Asturias region in Spain was finally incorporated into the Kingdom of Spain during the reign of Ferdinand and Isabella in the late fifteenth century.

The Celtic revival

The Celtic revival movement began in the nineteenth century, when a strong appeal to a Celtic past emerged. It took two forms: a literary movement and a political movement. A spirit of rebellion had been kept alive by the bardic tradition of myths, legends and folklore, which had continued throughout the centuries. It encompassed what has become known as 'The Celtic Fringe': Ireland, Scotland, Wales, Brittany and Cornwall. This was linked to a revival of the traditional languages, some of which, such as Irish and Gaelic, had never died out.

In France, as already been indicated, nationalists began to promote their descent from the Gauls and this was aided by Napoleon III's promotion of the excavations at Alesia. The struggles of Vercingetorix against the Romans were identified with the battles of the French against the Germans, and Vercingetorix became the symbol of resistance, both then and in subsequent wars. Further excavation of Celtic sites, and a determination to continue French Celtic heritage, led to French schoolchildren learning about this through their history books and later in the adventures of Asterix, the comic but wickedly accurate cartoon books by Goscinny and Uderzo. Even the Swiss, by adopting the name Confederation Helvetica for the republic, instituted a reminder of the Celtic tribe of the Helvetii.

The emphasis had been placed, not necessarily on race, but on culture and this intensified in the nineteenth and twentieth centuries. It has given a sense of being a member of a distinctive group, even having a national identity. This, in some areas resulted in political violence, as when the Breton regionalists revolted in May 1968 with the slogan,

Bretagne-Colonie and in the constant problems in the Basque region of Spain. A more cultural tradition has been promoted in music, dance and folklore as for example in northern Spain.

In Cornwall, the emphasis has been on language. The revival was begun in 1904 with the work of Henry James and Robert Morton Nance. This gathered momentum so that in 1924 The Federation of Old Cornwall Societies was founded. Politics became involved with the founding of Gorseth Kernow in 1928 and the political party, the Mebyon Kernow in 1951. Although there have been demands for some form of Cornish representation, if not independence, it seems somewhat half-hearted given the number of people who have moved to live in Cornwall to escape urban life and the fact that Cornwall is one of the most popular holiday destinations.

In Wales and Ireland, the Celtic revival was more serious. In Wales, in the nineteenth century, there was a strong reaction to the imposing of urban values on the Welsh countryside. North Wales was developing towns, which played host to the hoards of people who came, many by train, to spend their annual week-long holiday there. Rhyl and Llandudno, for example, became more English seaside resorts than Welsh towns.

The strong resentment against this English leisure and cultural domination became linked to a Welsh Celtic cultural revival, which had begun in the eighteenth century. The Rev. Henry Rowlands, a vicar in Anglesey, became fascinated by the suppression of the Druids in that island and devised an elaborate descent of the Druids from Noah. Others quickly seized on his ideas. In 1819, Edward Williams, who preferred to call himself Iolo Morganwy, persuaded the organisers of the Carmarthen Eisteddfod to incorporate a procession of Druids into the procedure. These men dressed themselves in what they considered to be Druidic white robes, and so successful was their performance, that the Druidic controlling presence at an Eisteddfod has continued to this day. Since 1880, the Eisteddfod has been held in August with the climax being the Druids crowning a Welsh poet as its bard. In spite of protests, mockery and criticism, the ceremony has survived.

Druids have also appealed elsewhere. Druidic Lodges have been founded, including the British Order of Druids. Winston Churchill, long before he reached the High Offices of State was installed in the Albion Lodge of the Ancient Order of Druids at Blenheim Palace in 1908, obviously submitting in order to gather more votes in a forthcoming by-election. The desire to incorporate Druids in other media resulted in the composer Vincenzo Bellini giving them a central role in his opera *Norma* composed in 1831, an opera now a firm feature in the operatic repertoire. In 1850, Holman Hunt painted *A Converted British Family Sheltering a Christian Priest from the Persecution of the Druids* (now in the Ashmolean Museum, Oxford). Although this did not win the acclaim he had expected, it indicated the interest that was felt in a Celtic past. Modern Druids have insisted on their continuation with the past even to the extent of being allowed to celebrate the coming of the midsummer solstice at Stonehenge, although there is no evidence that the Druids were ever associated with Stonehenge.

In Ireland, the Celtic revival took three forms: artistic, literary and political. The first, the artistic, had always been under the surface. Now, interest was revived in such masterpieces as the *Book of Kells*, the Tara Brooch and the Ardagh Chalice. Celtic patterns were used in the design of jewellery, in stained glass and other artistic works. These intricate designs achieved a momentum of their own so that artists felt they were rediscovering their past.

The second, the literary, was linked to the interest in the Irish Celtic tales of heroes and gods in the nineteenth century, which had never been suppressed. Possibly, Charlotte Brooke's *Reliques of Irish Poetry* (1789) and Douglas Hyde's book, *A Literary History of Ireland* (1899) sparked an interest, but rather ironically it was the Scottish eighteenth-century poet, James Macpherson, who wrote a series of poems about Finn, and the Anglo-Irish gentry, such as Lady Gregory, W.B. Yeats and Oliver St. John Gogarty, who promoted interest in Celtic culture. The movement aimed at reviving Irish folklore, legends and traditions, but translating Gaelic into English added a new dimension. In 1893, a Gaelic League was formed to revive the Irish language, which had been pushed almost to extinction, being spoken only in isolated rural areas, but in doing so it had to revive Irish culture. This developed into a vigorous literary force leading to a discovery of much of Ireland's past history. This revival led to literary masterpieces written in the Irish cultural tradition, such as the poetry of W.B. Yeats who referred to the Knock area in Sligo, traditionally the tomb of the Celtic Queen Medb. Many of the mountains referred to in the Celtic Irish texts are mentioned in his early poems, such as *The Wanderings of Oisin* (1889). Most of the intensely dramatic plays of J.M. Singe and Sean O'Casey were put on at the Abbey Theatre in Dublin that became the focus of the Irish literary renaissance.

The third strand of the Celtic revival, the political interest, was revitalised by this literary movement. There had always been an undercurrent of resentment and rebellion against English rule in Ireland. The desire to have an Irish identity was now stimulated by the publication of Irish myths, legends and traditions, the creation of new works dwelling on Ireland's past and in the rhythm and music of Irish Gaelic. Even so, the struggle for Ireland to become a nation took a long time. England was reluctant to cede any political power to Ireland. The British Prime Minister William Gladstone was eventually converted to the idea of Home Rule for Ireland in 1886, but the political struggles continued for the rest of the century. The Third Home Rule Act in 1914 would have established self-government in Ireland, but the outbreak of the First World War led to its suspension. The result was political violence between 1916 and 1921.

The Easter Rising of 1916 in Dublin proclaiming the 'Republic of Ireland' was put down with such violence that the result was a swing in support for Celtic Ireland. Further violence, a guerrilla war in fact, known as the 'Troubles' led to the British agreeing to the foundation of the Irish Free State in 1921 in southern Ireland. The politicians in Dublin had expected the whole island to become one country but this did not take account of religious and political differences. In spite of its Celtic past, the six mainly Protestant counties in the north of Ireland, mostly part of ancient Ulster, hostile to the Catholic southern counties and loyal to Britain, rejected the idea of unification with the rest of Ireland. In 1921, Ireland was partitioned and the six counties became a separate state with the name Northern Ireland, owning allegiance to the British Crown. In 1937, the Constitution of Ireland replaced the Irish Free State with a new state called Eire or, in the English language, Ireland. Once the total independence of the southern part of Ireland from all remaining roles of the British monarch was agreed upon in 1948, the achievement of a Celtic nation was complete.

This Irish Celtic heritage is perhaps personified by a statue placed in the General Post Office in Dublin, the scene of the resistance to the British forces in 1916. Cu Chulainn stands bound to a post with the Morrigan in the form of a crow perched on his shoulder. The statue commemorates the heroism of the greatest Irish Celtic warrior and his determination either to resist death or to succumb to it by standing upright against the forces of evil.

Timeline

c.1200	Celts began to advance across Europe from their original homelands in central Europe
c.750	Adoption of iron working by the Hallstatt Celts
c.600–475	Hallstatt culture
c.600	Establishment of Greek colony at Massalia (Marseilles)
c.540–520	Burial of Hochdorf chieftain
c.500	Trading routes opened between Mediterranean regions and northern Europe
	Earliest mention of the Celts by the Greek scholar, Hecataeus of Miletus
c. Fifth century	Beginning of La Tène culture Celts began to move into the Iberian Peninsular
c.480	Burial of 'Princess of Vix'
c.400	Celts began to invade northern Italy
396	The Insubres established themselves in the Etruscan city of Melpum
390	Defeat of the Romans at the Battles of the Allia and the Sack of Rome by the Gauls
380	Celtic raid on Illyria
369	Celts hired themselves out as mercenaries to the Greeks
367	Titus Manlius defeated a Celt in single combat and acquired the cognomen 'Torquatus'
348	The tribune M. Valerius defeated a Celtic chieftain in single combat and was given the cognomen 'Corvinus'
335	Celts met Alexander the Great on the Danube for the sake of establishing friendship and loyalty

334	Romans signed peace treaty with the Celts
332	Treaty of Senones with Rome
323	Alexander the Great defeated the Persian army. The Celts sent a second deputation to him in Babylon
	Death of Alexander
c.320	Suggested date for visit of the Greek explorer Pytheas of Massalia to Britain
c.300	Celts began to settle in the Ukraine region
298	Celts invaded Thrace. Defeated at Mount Haemus
297	Celts and Samnites allied and defeated the Romans at Camertium
295	Celts defeated Romans at Battle of Sentinum
284	Romans defeated by the Celts at Arretium
283	The Boii were defeated by the Romans at Lake Vadimonis
281	Celts under Bolgios invaded Greece. They defeated and decapitated King Ptolemy Ceraunus of Macedon
280	Celtic forces quarrelled and divided. An army under Leotarios and Leonorios moved towards Asia Minor and eventually established a Galatian state. Another Celtic group under Brennus and Achichorius went south, but was defeated by the Greeks at the Pass of Thermopylae. Brennus sent part of the army to fight the Aetolians. Sack of Callium
279	Brennus crossed the mountains by a separate route and marched south. The Celts reached Delphi, but retreated before attacking the shrine. Death of Brennus
278	Establishment of Celtic settlement in Thrace
	Nicomedes of Bithynia invited three Celtic tribes to ally with him in warfare. The Celts entered his service as mercenaries

277	King Antigonos Gonatas of Macedonia defeated Celts at Lysimachia ending any threat to Greece
275	Celts under Leotarios defeated at Seleucia by Antiochus I, but began to settle in Asia Minor
c.270	Celts were recruited as mercenaries by the Egyptian pharaoh, Ptolemy I
240	Celts defeated by Attalus of Pergamon and persuaded to settle in lands allotted to them in Asia Minor
225	The Gaesatae and the Gauls invaded Etruria. Defeat of Celts by Romans at the Battle of Telemon
224	Roman attack on the Boii
222	Roman attack on the Insubres. Battle of Clastidium
218	Hannibal crossed the Alps to invade Rome supported by Celtic warriors
202	Battle of Zama
200	Celtic settlement in Thrace was crushed
c.200	Beginning of building of brochs in Scotland
197	Romans attacked the Celtiberians. The conflict in Spain continued until 179
191	Battle of Bologna
190s	Final subjugation of the Boii and the Insubres
190	Galatians allied with Antiochus III of Selucia against the Romans but were defeated at the Battle of Magnesia
179–178	Tiberius Gracchus destroyed over 300 Celtiberian settlements
133	Romans defeated the Celtiberians and captured Numantia
c.124	Romans invaded Gaul and established Gallia Narbonensis

124–123	Siege and destruction of Entremont
122	Romans attacked the Gallic tribe of the Allobroges
	Romans made common cause with the Celtic tribe of the Aedui
121	The Avernian King Bituitus sent ambassadors to negotiate with the Romans. When his advances were rejected, he attacked the Romans and was defeated allowing the Romans to advance along the Rhone valley
	Gallia Narbonensis became a Roman province
118	Establishment of Roman colonia at Narbo (Narbonne) and founding of the province of Gallia Transalpina
106	Shrine of Tolosa (Toulouse) looted by Romans
88	Revolt of Mithridates VI of Pontus against Rome and his invasion of Greece
86	The Roman general Sulla captured Athens and forced Mithridates to retreat
74	Mithridates resumed war against Rome
66	Final defeat of Mithridates by Pompey
64	Reorganisation of administration in Galatia which was created as a client kingdom by Pompey. New provinces of Bithynia, Cilicia and Syria established
59	Caesar became Consul
58	Caesar marched into Gaul to turn back the westward invasion of the Helvetii into the territory of the Arverni
57	Caesar attacked the Belgae
55	First invasion of Britain by Caesar
54	Second invasion of Britain by Caesar
53–52	Revolt of Gauls against Caesar

52	Siege of Alesia and defeat of Gaulish revolt led by Vercingetorix
50	Commius fled to Britain taking many of the Atrebates with him
49	Caesar returned from Gaul to Italy, crossed the Rubicon and declared Gaul was pacified
44	Assassination of Caesar
42	Cisalpine Gaul absorbed into Rome
27	Octavian, the designated heir of Caesar, declared the restoration of the Republic and assumed the name of Augustus
	Division of Gallia Comata into three parts: Gallia Belgica, Gallia Lugdunensis and Gallia Aquitania. Gallia Transalpina was renamed Gallia Narbonensis
26–19	Campaigns of Augustus in Spain
25	Galatia became a Roman province
21	Revolt in Gaul was defeated
19–15	Roman advanced against Celts on the upper Danube and crushed resistance
19	Celtiberian resistance in north-west Spain was finally defeated by Rome
12	Dedication of Altar of Rome and Augustus at Lyon
AD	
43	Claudius dispatched Aulus Plautius to invade Britain
	Caratacus resisted Romans, defeated and fled to Wales
47	Cartimandua became client queen of the Romans
50	Last stand of Caratacus in Wales
51	Caratacus fled to Brigantia and was betrayed by Cartimandua

60	Attack on Druidic stronghold in Anglesey by Suetonius Paulinus
60–61	Revolt of Boudica
69	Rebellion by Brigantian tribe over Cartimandua's divorce of Venutius was put down by Rome
70	Reputed death of Queen Medb
74	Galatia was incorporated into Cappadocia
78–86	Agricola was governor of Britain
80	Roman frontier region was divided into Upper and Lower Germany. Consolidation of Rhine-Danube frontier
80s	Emperor Domitian invaded Dacia and created a client state
84	Agricola defeated Caledonian tribes at Battle of Mons Graupius but withdrew from Scotland
101–106	Campaigns of Trajan in Dacia and creation of Roman province
117–138	Reign of Emperor Hadrian. Establishment of frontiers of Roman empire
120–122	Building of Hadrian's Wall in England
142	Establishment of Antonine Wall in Scotland
212	Roman citizenship was granted to all free citizens of the Roman empire
358	Frankish tribes invaded Gaul and began to settle there
367	Picts, Scots and Saxons began to attack Britain
406–407	Invasion of Vandals, Sueves and Alamanni into the Roman empire. Collapse of Roman rule in Britain and Spain. Vandals moved into Spain
c.410	Suggested end of Roman administration in Britain
415	Birth of St. Patrick

431	Capture of St. Patrick by pirates
	Palladius sent by Pope Celestine I to Ireland to act as bishop to the Irish
455	Possible date of return of St. Patrick to Ireland to convert the pagan Irish to Christianity
560s	Beginning of spread of Celtic monastic influence throughout Europe
753	Vikings attacked Lindisfarne
795	Viking raids on Iona and in Ireland
852	Vikings established a settlement in Ireland which became the city of Dublin

List of Illustrations

1. Aerial view of Hod Hill hillfort, Dorset, indicating the Roman fort constructed within the hillfort after the Celts had been evicted. Cambridge University Collection of Air Photographs, Unit for Landscape Modelling.

2. Aerial view of Maiden Castle hillfort, Dorset, showing the formidable defences. Cambridge University Collection of Air Photographs, Unit for Landscape Modelling.

3. Statue of Vercingetorix, Alesia.

4. Statue of Boadicea (Boudica) on the Embankment at Westminster Bridge, London, created in 1902 by Thomas Thornycroft (1815–1885). She is accompanied by two females, possibly her daughters. Thornycroft depicted the chariot with scythes on the wheels. Joan P. Alcock.

5. Reconstructed round house, Little Butser, Hampshire. Joan P. Alcock.

6. Reconstructed turf hut at The Dutch National Heritage Open Air Museum, Arnhem, Holland. This would have been similar to a Celtic hut. Joan P. Alcock.

7. A spear and a reconstructed wooden shield. Rheinishes Landesmuseum, Trier. Joan P. Alcock.

8. Anthropoid hilts of Iron Age swords from the Marne region. Joan P. Alcock.

9. Reconstructed model of a chariot. Margaret Roxan.

10. Statue called the Dying Gaul. A Roman marble copy of a third-century BC Hellenistic bronze original made to celebrate the victory of Attalus of Pergamon over the Galatians. Capitoline Museum, Rome. Joan P. Alcock.

11. Detail of head of Dying Gaul showing the torc. Joan P. Alcock.

12. Statue of Gaul stabbing himself after killing his wife. Roman copy from the Pergamon statues. Palazzo Altemps, National Museum, Rome. Joan P. Alcock.

13. Statue of a captured Gaul. Vatican Museums. Joan P. Alcock.

14. Rotary quern. Chedworth Museum. Joan P. Alcock.

15. Relief showing a reaping machine in the Institute Archéologique du Luxembourg, Arlon, Belgium. Joan P. Alcock.

16. Model of woman wearing a torc, bracelets and a brooch. The British Museum. Joan P. Alcock.

17. Gold plate from Mold, Wales, at The British Museum. Joan P. Alcock.

18. Village sign at Snettisham, Norfolk, showing a torc. Over 200 torcs were found in the area between 1948 and 1992. Joan P. Alcock.

19. Gundestrup Cauldron. John Lee. The National Museum of Denmark, Copenhagen.

20. Relief of Genii Cucullati, Housesteads. Joan P. Alcock.

21. Relief of Mother Goddesses in hierarchical pose, Corinium Museum, Cirencester. Joan P. Alcock.

22. Relief of Mother Goddesses in relaxed pose, Corinium Museum, Cirencester. Joan P. Alcock.

23. Relief of Esus, Rheinishes Landesmuseum, Trier. Joan P. Alcock.

24. Seated figure of Cernunnos on Gundestrup Cauldron holding a serpent and a torc, and surrounded by animals. The National Museum of Denmark, Copenhagen. John Lee.

25. So-called Temple of Janus, Autun, France. This is a surviving cella of a Romano-Celtic temple. Joan P. Alcock.

26. Model of Celtic temple. Joan P. Alcock.

27. Reconstructed door frame from the shrine at Requepertuse, Bouches-du-Rhône, France, showing the niches in the pillars ready to display decapitated heads and the bird placed above, ready to fly, which will carry the souls of the departed to the underworld. Joan P. Alcock.

28. The 'Tarasque de Noves', Lapidarium du Musée Calvet, Avignon, Bouches-du-Rhône, France. Joan P. Alcock.

29. Chariot Burial. Archaeological Museum, Abbey de Saint Remy, Reims, France. Joan P. Alcock.

30. Celtic tomb burial at Welwyn Garden City. The Trustees of the British Museum.

31. Reconstructed head of Lindow Man, in wax. The Trustees of the British Museum.

32. Head of Tollund Man at The Silkeborg Museum, Denmark. Lennart Larsen. The National Museum of Denmark.

Selected Bibliography

Primary sources

Cross, T.P., and C.H. Slover. 1996. *Ancient Irish Tales*. New York: Barnes and Noble.
Ganz, J. 1981. *Early Irish Myths and Sagas*. Harmsworth: Penguin.
Ireland, S. 1986. *Roman Britain: A Sourcebook*. Beckenham, England: Croom Helm.
Jackson, K.H. 1971. *A Celtic Miscellany*. Harmondsworth, England: Penguin Books.
Jones, G., and T. Jones. 1974. *The Mabinogion*, trans. Manchester: The Philips Press.
Kinsella, T. 1970. *The Tain*, trans. Oxford: Oxford University Press.

Secondary sources

Alcock, Joan P. 1962. 'Celtic Religion in Roman Britain', unpublished MA thesis. University of London.
Alcock, Joan P. 2006. *Food in the Ancient World*. Westport CT: Greenwood Press.
Allen, D.F. 1980. *The Coins of the Ancient Celts*. Edinburgh: Edinburgh University Press.
Arribas, A. 1964. *The Iberians*. London: Thames and Hudson.
Audouze, F., and O. Buchsenschutz. 1992. *Towns, Villages and Countryside of Celtic Europe*. London: Batsford.
Biel, J. 1985. *Der Keltenfürst von Hochdorf*. Stuttgart: Konrad Theiss.
Brogan, O. 1953. *Roman Gaul*. London: Bell.
Brothwell, D. 1986. *The Bogman and the Archaeology of People*. London: British Museum Publications.
Bruneaux, J.L. 1987. *The Celtic Gauls: Gods, Rites and Sanctuaries*. London: Seaby.
Chadwick, H. 1966. *The Druids*. London: Pelican Books.
Chapman, M. 1992. *The Celts: The Construction of a Myth*. New York: St Martin's Press.
Chilver, G.E.F. 1941. *Cisalpine Gaul: A Social and Economic History from 49 BC to the Death of Trajan*. Oxford: Clarendon Press.
Collis, J.R., ed. 1977. *The Iron Age in Britain: A Review*. Sheffield: Sheffield University Press.
Collis, J.R. 1994. *The European Iron Age*. London: Batsford.
Crummy, P., S. Benfield, N. Crummy, V. Rigby and D. Shimmin. 2007. *Stanway: An Elite Burial Site at Camulodunum*. London: The Roman Society.
Cunliffe, B. 1979. *The Celtic World*. London: Bodley Head.
Cunliffe, B. 1991. *Iron Age Communities in Britain*. London: Routledge.
Cunliffe, B. 1993. *Danebury: Anatomy of an Iron Age Hillfort*. London: Batsford for English Heritage.
Cunliffe, B. 1995. *Iron Age Britain*. London: Batsford for English Heritage.
Cunliffe, B. 1997. *The Ancient Celts*. Oxford: Oxford University Press.
Curchin, L.A. 1991. *Roman Spain: Conquest and Assimilation*. London: Routledge.
Dillon, M., and N. Chadwick. 1967. *The Celtic Realms*. London: Weidenfeld and Nicolson.
Drinkwater, J. 1983. *Roman Gaul*. London: Croom Helm.
Duval, P.-M. 1976. *Les Dieux de la Gaule*. Paris: Petite Bibliothèque.
Duval, P.-M. 1977. *Les Celts*. Paris: L'Universdes Formes, Gallimard.
Duval, P.-M., and C.F.C. Hawkes, eds. 1978. *Celtic Art in Ancient Europe*. London: Seminar Press
Edwins, U. 1952. 'The Early Colonisation of Cisalpine Gaul'. *Papers of the British School at Rome* 20 (New Series 7).
Ellis, P. Berresford. 1984. *A Brief History of the Druids*. London: Constable.
Ellis, P. Berresford. 1998a. *A Brief History of the Celts*. London: Constable.
Ellis, P. Berresford. 1998b. *Celt and Roman*. London: Constable.
Eluère, C. 1993. *The Celts: First Masters of Europe*. Translated by D. Briggs. London: Thames and Hudson.

Fell, R.A.L. 1967. *Etruria and Rome*. Cambridge: Cambridge University Press.

Filip, J. 1977. *Celtic Civilisation and Its Heritage*. Wellingborough-Prague: Collet's-Academia.

Finley, I. 1973. *Celtic Art: An Introduction*. London: Faber and Faber.

Glob, P.V. 1969. *The Bog People: Iron Age Man Preserved*. London: Faber and Faber.

Green, M. 1986. *The Gods of the Celts*. Stroud: Alan Sutton.

Harbison, P. 1993. *Pre-Christian Ireland: From the First Settlers to the Early Celts*. London: Thames and Hudson.

Harding, D.W. 1974. *The Iron Age in Lowland Britain*. London: Routledge and Kegan Paul.

Hatt, J.-J. 1970. *Celts and Gallo Romans*. Translated by J. Hogarth. London: Barrie and Jenkins.

Haywood, J. 2001. *The Historical Atlas of the Celtic World*. London: Thames and Hudson.

Hedeager, L. 1992. *Iron-Age Societies: From Tribe to State in Northern Europe, 500 BC to AD 700*. Oxford: Blackwell.

Helm, G. 1978. *The Celts*. London: Weidenfeld and Nicolson.

Herity, M., and G. Eogan. 1977. *Ireland in Prehistory*. London: Routledge and Kegan Paul.

Hubert, H. 1984. *The Greatness and Decline of the Celts*, new edn (originally published 1934). London: Constable.

Hubert, H. 2002. *The Rise of the Celts*. Translated from the French by M.R. Dobie (originally published 1934). New York: Dover Publications.

Jackson, K.H. 1964. *The Oldest Irish Tradition: A Window on the Iron Age*. Cambridge: Cambridge University Press.

Jackson, K.H. 1970. *A Celtic Miscellany*. Harmondsworth: Penguin Books.

Jacobsthal, P. 1944; repr. 1969. *Early Celtic Art*. Oxford: Oxford University Press.

James, S. 1991. *The Atlantic Celts: Ancient People or Modern Invention*. London: British Museum Press.

James, S. 1993. *Exploring the World of the Celts*. London: Thames and Hudson.

Joffroy, R. 1954. *Le Trésor de Vix (Cote d'Or)*. Paris: Presses Universitaires de France.

Kendrick, T.D. 1927. *The Druids: A Study in Keltic Prehistory*. London: Methuen and Co.

King, A. 1990. *Roman Gaul and Germany*. London: British Museum Publications.

Kruta, V., and W. Forman. 1995. *The Celts of the West*. London: Orbis Publishing.

Kruta, V., O. Frey, B. Raftery and M. Szabo, eds. 1991. *The Celts*. London and New York: Thames and Hudson.

Laing, L. 1979. *Celtic Britain*. London: Routledge and Kegan Paul.

Laing, L., and J. Laing. 1992. *Art of the Celts*. London: Thames and Hudson.

MacCana, P. 1970. *Celtic Mythology*. London: Hamlyn.

Mackillop, J.A. 1998. *Dictionary of Celtic Mythology*. Oxford: Oxford University Press.

Megaw, J.V.S. 1970. *Art of the European Iron Age*. New York: Harper and Row.

Megaw, R., and J.V.S. Megaw. 1989. *Celtic Art: From Its Beginning to the Book of Kells*. London: Thames and Hudson.

Nash, D. 1987. *Coinage in the Celtic World*. London: Seaby.

O'Kelly, M. 1989. *Early Ireland*. Cambridge: Cambridge University Press.

O'Rahilly, T.F. 1946. *Early Irish History and Mythology*. Dublin: Institute for Advanced Studies.

Olmsted, G.S. 1979. *The Gundestrup Cauldron*. Brussels: Latomus.

Pascal, C.B. 1964. *The Cults of Cisalpine Gaul*, vol. LXXV. Brussels: Collections Latomus, Revue d'Études Latines.

Piggott, S. 1968. *The Druids*. London: Thames and Hudson.

Pleiner, R. 1993. *The Celtic Sword*. Oxford: Clarendon Press.

Pobe, M., and J. Roubier. 1960. *The Art of Roman Gaul*. London: The Gallery Press.

Powell, T.G.E. 1966. *Prehistoric Art*. London: Thames and Hudson.

Powell, T.G.E. 1980. *The Celts*, new edn. London: Thames and Hudson.

Raftery, B. 1994. *Pagan Celtic Ireland: The Enigma of the Irish Iron Age*. London: Thames and Hudson.

Raftery, J., ed. 1964. *The Celts*. Cork: The Mercier Press.

Rankin, H.D. 1987. *Celts and the Classical World*. London: Croom Helm.

Rees, A., and B. Rees. 1961. *Celtic Heritage: Ancient Tradition in Ireland and Wales*. London: Thames and Hudson.

Reynolds, P.J. 1979. *Iron-Age Farm. The Butser Experiment*. London: British Museum Press.

Reynolds, P.J. 1987. *Ancient Farming*. Princes Risborough, England: Shire Publications.

Ritchie, W., and J. Ritchie. 1985. *Celtic Warriors*. Princes Risborough, England: Shire Publications.

Ross, A. 1967. *Pagan Celtic Britain: Studies in Iconography and Tradition*. London: Routledge and Kegan Paul.

Ross, A. 1970. *The Pagan Celts*. London: Batsford.

Sheehy, J. 1980. *The Rediscovery of Ireland's Past: The Celtic Revival 1830–1930*. London: Thames and Hudson.

Sjoestedt, M.-L. 1949. *Gods and Heroes of the Celts*. Translated by M. Dillon. London: Methuen.

Stead, I.M. 1985. *Celtic Art*. London: British Museum Publications.

Stead, I.M. 1986. *Iron Age Cemeteries in East Yorkshire*. London: British Museum Publications.

Stead, I.M., J.B. Bourke and Don Brothwell. 1986. *Lindow Man: The Body in the Bog*. London: British Museum Publications.

Stead, I.M., and V. Rigby. 1989. *Verulamium: The King Harry Lane Site*. London: English Heritage in association with British Museum Press.

Szabó, M. 1971. *The Celtic Heritage in Hungary*. Translated by Aston. T. Budapest: Corvina.

de Vries, J. 1963. *La Religion des Celtes*. Paris: Payot.

Webster, G. 1986. *The British Celts and Their Gods under Rome*. London: Batsford.

Wightman, E. 1970. *Trier and the Treveri*. London: Hart-Davies.

Wightman, E. 1985. *Gallia Belgica*. London: Batsford.

Withers, C.W.J. 1988. *Gaelic Scotland: The Transformation of a Culture Region*. London: Routledge.

About the Author

Joan P. Alcock is an archaeologist and historian and also an Honorary Visiting Fellow of South Bank University. She is the author of several books on local history and archaeology including *Food in Roman Britain* (2001), *Life in Roman Britain* (2003) and *Food in the Ancient World* (2006) and has had papers on Food History published in the Proceedings of the Oxford Symposium on Food and Cookery. She is a Fellow of the Society of Antiquaries of London.

Index